W9-DJO-336

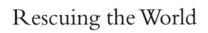

Rescuing the World

Rescuing the World

The Life and Times
of Leo Cherne

ANDREW F. SMITH

Foreword by Henry A. Kissinger

State University of New York Press

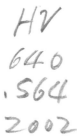

Published by
State University of New York Press, Albany

Printed in the United States of America

For information, address State University of New York Press,
90 State Street, Suite 700, Albany, NY 12207

Production by Judith Block
Marketing by Michael Campochiaro

Library of Congress Cataloging-in-Publication Data

Smith, Andrew F., 1946-
    Rescuing the world: the life and times of Leo Cherne / Andrew F.
  Smith; foreword by Henry A. Kissinger.
        p. cm.
    Includes bibliographical references and index.
    ISBN 0-7914-5379-0 (alk. paper) -- ISBN 0-7914-5380-4 (pbk. :
  alk. paper)
      1. Refugees--Services for. 2. International Rescue Committee--
  History. 3. Cherne, Leo, 1912-   4. Human rights workers--
  Biography. 5. Human services personnel--biography.   I. Title.

HV640 .S64 2002
362.87'526'092--dc21
[B]   2001049419

This is dedicated to the hard-working and devoted staffs of refugee organizations, particularly that of the International Rescue Committee; and to Leo Cherne's friends who helped with this book, especially Lionel Olmer, John Richardson, Liv Ullmann and Marie Gomez.

And this is dedicated to the Kling Family, Alexander and Vera, Russians torn from their native land by World War II, and their two daughters, Alla, born in Austria, and Tatianna, born in Germany, who learned English in the New York Public Schools and became teachers of children of refugees in the same system. My favorite displaced person, Tatiana Kling, my wife, has enriched my life with love, affection, joy, support and inspiration. Without her constant encouragement, this book would not have been written.

Contents

Foreword

In the Jewish religion, it is said that at any one point in time, God preserves the world because there exist ten just men who, without claiming themselves that they are just, give Him a motive for leaving the world intact. Leo Cherne was surely one of those ten just men.

I met Leo in the 1950s before I was Henry Kissinger, when I was still writing short books. He had read one of them and invited me to visit him at the Research Institute of America in New York. He thought that what I had written about foreign policy was important and I should devote myself to it. He gave me a copy of the bust of Abraham Lincoln, which he had sculpted, and he asked, of course, nothing for himself except my best performance.

To me he was a mythic figure, because he had been at the Hungarian border the year before I met him. And having been a refugee myself before there was an IRC, I knew how much it meant to have individuals who looked after refugees, not as an act of charity, but as an act of inner necessity. And Leo, in those days, was dedicated, above all, to the care of the downtrodden. He opposed Communism, not on the grounds of a foreign policy strategy, but as a contribution to the liberation of the human spirit— as a necessity for the liberation of the human spirit.

Every once in a while he would give me a call and give me some assignment which he thought needed to be done in the field of the humane impact of foreign policy, or express some concern he deeply felt. And he became an important fixture of my life.

It was one of these curious phenomena that I, as time went on, became involved in so many struggles and in so many concerns on the more sheer political side that I felt I could always come and take Leo for granted, because he would know when I needed to hear from him. And indeed he did.

I served in government in a very tragic period of the American spirit, when American perfectionism turned on itself and conceived the idea that we had to be humiliated before we could be worthy of conducting foreign affairs. Leo never made this assumption. Leo always believed, as I believe, that America has a duty to stand for freedom and to make sure that the weak can be secure and the just can be free.

In the tragic period when the helicopters lifted off the roofs in Vietnam in 1975, we thought, above all, of the hundreds of thousands that were being left behind. It was a slight solace to know that there was Leo, who would worry about them and make sure that whoever could be saved would be saved.

When I was secretary of state, my friend Liv Ullmann honored me at one point by saying that she had been asked to do something for the International Rescue Committee and she wanted to know whether it was a CIA agency. Of course if there was any person who could not have told her the truth, it was I. But I knew she was going to be in the care of Leo, and he removed any doubts about what the IRC was about. And what the issues of our period were about.

I admired Leo's intensity, his passion, his faith, his unselfishness, his nobility, and the purity of his soul. To be active in the political arena; to be head of the President's Foreign Intelligence Advisory Board, where I had the privilege of working with him; to know the tactics but never to be submerged by them; never to raise any question about his motives; never to be engulfed in the discussions of the short term, so characteristic of our political life. And to do this for over half a century is a record that has ennobled all of us who had the privilege of knowing him.

At one point, Liv told me I had to call Leo, that he wasn't very well. And so I did. But he didn't want to speak about his problems. He didn't want to hear my commiseration. He talked about what moved him. The causes in which he believed. And he honored me by thinking I might play a small role in supporting them.

Surely there is one less just man in the world today, and none of us can claim his mantle. But perhaps if all of us try a little harder, maybe we'll help fulfill his mission which will continue as long as there are free people and suffering humanity.

Henry A. Kissinger

Introduction

> I have thought of writing an odd kind of biography. Even now I don't have much patience for a biography which involves a sequence of events; I'm much more interested in a combination of the active and the introspective.
>
> —Leo Cherne, 1961.[1]

I first met Leo Cherne in May 1998. I had heard about him for years, but our paths had not crossed. This meeting had been arranged by John Richardson, a mutual friend, who had confided that Cherne had wanted for years to write his autobiography and needed advice. I was dubious about what advice, if any, I could offer, but I jumped at the chance of meeting Leo Cherne, whose reputation was filled with paradox. He was considered variously as a Renaissance man, a dynamic orator, a lightweight gadfly, a behind-the-scenes power broker, a thoughtful advisor to nine presidents, a flamboyant economic futurist, a playboy closely connected with the nation's rich and famous, a high-level fundraiser for humanitarian causes, a master spy in the employ of an American intelligence service, a highly successful businessman, and a powerful conservative Cold Warrior.

When I first met him, the eighty-six year old Cherne was physically immobile, had difficulty seeing and hearing, and was suffering from a host of medical complications; I'm sure he was in pain. Yet, his eyes danced and his smile flashed when he remembered a particular event or a person. He was clearly upset with his deteriorating physical condition and occasional memory lapses, but courage and confidence exuded from him.

One meeting led to another. On the surface, his life presented a mystifying facade filled with improbability. He had been born into a secular Jewish family of newly arrived immigrants from Russia, yet he rose quickly to the pinnacle of economic and political power in WASP America. He was educated as a lawyer, but left the practice of law to launch a business venture in the midst of the Depression. With his business thriving, Cherne devoted considerable time and talent to humanitarian causes, particularly the rescuing of political refugees. Although not a trained economist, he enthralled America's business elite by prognosticating economic trends annually for fifty years. In his spare time, Cherne became a self-trained sculptor, and his works graced the Cabinet Room at the White House, the Smithsonian Institution, and numerous museums around the world.

Cherne received no pay for his humanitarian work and little compensation for his public service, although he was rewarded with hundreds of honorary degrees and awards from around the world, including the Federal Republic of Germany's Commander's Cross, France's Legion of Honor, and the Director's Medal from the Central Intelligence Agency. Cherne was proudest of the Presidential Medal of Freedom bestowed upon him by President Ronald Reagan, who proclaimed that although Cherne was never elected to public office, he had more influence on American foreign policy than did most elected officials.

Cherne was clearly an intelligent, creative, talented man who exuded public confidence and charisma. He was a consummate networker with the uncanny ability to identify and cultivate talented people before they became prominent; such were William Casey, Daniel Patrick Moynihan, Claiborne Pell, and Henry A. Kissinger. Cherne also befriended a diverse set of prominent political and cultural leaders from William Buckley, Nelson Rockefeller, and Bayard Rustin to Eleanor Roosevelt, Joan Baez, and Marilyn Monroe. And Cherne served as an advisor to every president, with one exception, from Franklin Roosevelt to George Bush. But Cherne did not cultivate the present and future high-and-mighty just to hobnob or bask in their public glory: he was committed to rescuing political refugees. To this end, he preferred working behind the scenes using the old-boy network; but if quiet diplomacy did not succeed, Cherne was not averse to proclaiming loudly his concerns in front of the camera. He was good at both approaches; this twin threat made Cherne a powerful man.

When I finally broached the subject of his autobiography, Cherne was uncharacteristically vague. He admitted trying to write it on several occasions, but he failed to complete even a chapter. I wondered why. He mumbled something about being a shy person, not wanting to take credit for his successes. I shared this explanation with Cherne's friends and they promptly dismissed it. Throughout his life, Cherne had no problem taking credit for things he had accomplished, his friends claimed, and no one believed that Cherne suddenly turned bashful in his old age.

There had to be a better explanation why Cherne had not completed his autobiography. I could not attribute his reticence to a lack of writing skills: he was an accomplished wordsmith, with a clear and forceful writing style, who had published best-selling books and had written numerous articles for popular magazines and technical journals. As he had kept extensive records about the important events of his life and had easy access to them, it was not lack of documentation. Neither was it a lack of time: Cherne's early and middle life were filled with activity, but during his last decade, he could easily have written his autobiography. In the end I concluded that the apparently gregarious, outgoing Leo Cherne simply could not write a book about himself because it was unseemly for him to do so.

Cherne did not shy away from the prospect of someone else writing about him, however, and he just assumed I would do it. He was right: after the first few meetings, I was hooked. His life was a good story—a story I wanted to tell. What piqued my interest was not only that he had influenced so many important people and been involved in so many significant events that had shaped the twentieth century, from Hitler's rise to power in the 1930s to the fall of the Soviet Empire in the 1990s. Neither was it merely Cherne's amazing chutzpah in responding to those events and people. Whether one agrees or disagrees with his political positions on various issues, his public life demonstrates that one committed person with courage can make a worldwide political and humanitarian difference. His is a message that we need to hear as neo-isolationism resurfaces in new guises and as even deeply committed Americans give up hope of resolving difficult and apparently intractable global problems.

With the exception of the first chapter, which explores Cherne's early life and establishes behaviors that emerged. Later, chapters examine ways in which Cherne combined the insider's network with the outsider's ability to go public. This book is not intended as a "how to" recipe book that others may use to affect the world. It simply chronicles the creative ways in which one person influenced the significant events of his times. His life demonstrates that citizens can alter worldwide events.

A Note on Sources

Throughout our meetings, Cherne patiently responded to my questions, as if he had all the time in the world. He was not opposed to exploring the more controversial parts of his life and was willing to discuss almost anything. There were two exceptions. The first related to his private life. He would neither confirm nor deny stories others told relating to his private life. As I had decided to focus the biography on his public life, this was not a major handicap. The second exception related to his involvement with the President's Foreign

Intelligence Advisory Board (PFIAB) and the Intelligence Oversight Board (IOB). With regard to his specific activities in PFIAB and IOB, Cherne had taken an oath "not to reveal classified information acquired through their service on the Board." He revealed no such information in my discussions with him; neither would he comment on material collected by Freedom of Information Act that he believed related to classified PFIAB documents.[2]

However, I investigated in depth his relationships with American intelligence agencies. After extensive discussions, interviews, and a careful examination of his papers, I uncovered no evidence that he ever worked for any intelligence organization except for those relationships noted in his public record regarding his membership on the PFIAB and IOB. I located no evidence suggesting that he, or any of the humanitarian organizations with which he was connected, knowingly sought or accepted funds from the Central Intelligence Agency or any other intelligence organization.

A rich, voluminous quantity of material on Leo Cherne has survived. By my count Cherne wrote three major books, dozens of professional reports, introductions, or chapters in books, more than four hundred published articles, and thousands of letters. His testimony in Congressional hearings is extensive, as is the coverage of his press conferences. During just the twenty-six–year period from 1944 to 1970, Cherne appeared on 283 radio and television programs and gave 836 known speeches; many scripts have survived, as have many audio and visual tapes. In addition, articles about Cherne or references to him appeared in thousands of magazines, newspapers, and books. Within his papers, the most helpful sources were these: Cherne's 143-page autobiography written in 1943, and almost solely concerned with his early work with the Research Institute; his 578-page Oral History, compiled from July 14, 1960 to December 23, 1961 by Jerrold Auerbach, then of Columbia University; and his various autobiographical notes written in the 1980s and early 1990s. Also helpful were copies of taped interviews with Dale van Atta in 1984 and 1985, used as the basis for his *Reader's Digest* article; and my own interviews in 1998.[3]

Much of the material resides in his archive at the Special Collections and Archives of Boston University's Mugar Memorial Library. *Rescuing the World* focuses on Leo Cherne's public life and is not intended as a comprehensive biography. I encourage others to delve into his life and archive.

Acknowledgments

This book could not have been written without the support of Leo Cherne. It was not just his fascinating story or his willingness to open his archives. It was his infectious enthusiasm that kept this work on task during the crucial early months. When Leo died in January 1999, this support and assistance was continued by Lionel Olmer, former undersecretary of commerce and currently partner at Paul Weiss Rifkind Wharton & Garrison, Washington, DC, and one of Cherne's closest friends for the last twenty-five years of Cherne's life. Without his encouragement and help, this book could not have been completed. Likewise, John Richardson, former assistant secretary for educational and cultural affairs at the State Department and friend of both the author and Leo Cherne, made the initial contact and provided constant help and assistance with this work. Both Olmer and Richardson read and reread the various versions of the manuscript and responded to thousands of questions.

Many thanks go to Marie Gomez, Cherne's executive assistant at the Research Institute of America and the International Rescue Committee, who conducted research, kept up the encouragement, and constantly assisted the author with locating sources and scheduling interviews; Henry Denker, writer, New York, who was Cherne's dearest friend; Dale van Atta, writer, who kindly forwarded transcripts of his 1984 and 1985 interviews with and about Leo Cherne; and Adri de Groot, who forwarded his 1992 taped interviews with Leo Cherne. I particularly want to thank Leo Cherne's brother, Jack Cherne, who answered many questions about his brother's early life and forwarded photographs for inclusion in this book. In addition, I gratefully acknowledge all those who agreed to be interviewed: Henry A. Kissinger, former secretary of state, currently president of Kissinger Associates; Vera Blinken, member of IRC's board; James Butler, former executive, Research Institute of America; Andreas Castellano, former official at the United Nations; David Cohen, former director for operations, Central Intelligence Agency; Ira Cooperman, Cherne family relative; Fred Demech, formerly of the President's Foreign Intelligence Board and currently director, Intelligence and Systems Information, Systems Operation, TRW; Peter Drucker, president, Peter Drucker Foundation; Henry Goldstein, president, Oram Associates; Gilbert Jonas, former staff member of the Research Institute of America, and currently president, Gilbert Jonas Associates; Valerie Lanyi, professor of rehabilitation medicine, New York University Medical Center; Shepard Lowman, former deputy assistant secretary of state and current vice president for policy, Refugees International; Lionel Rosenblatt, president, Refugees International; Karen Salzmann, wife of Richard Salzmann, late president of the IRC; Jay Schulberg, vice chairman, Bozel, WW Inc.; Liv Ullmann, actress and vice chairman international, International Rescue Committee; Winston Lord, former U.S. ambassador to China and assistant secretary of state, currently co-chairman, International Rescue Committee;

Leonard Sussman, former executive director of Freedom House and long-time friend of Cherne; John C. Whitehead, former deputy secretary of state and Cherne's successor for eight years as Chairman of IRC, currently president of AEA Investors; William J. vanden Heuvel, former U.S. Representative, United Nations European Office, Geneva, and currently vice president, Allen & Co.; Claiborne Pell, former chairman of the Senate Foreign Relations Committee; Marge Levenstein, wife of Aaron Levenstein, one of Cherne's closest friends; Mort Feinberg, former employee of the Research Institute of America; Daniel Patrick Moynihan, U.S. Senator and lifelong Cherne friend; Mary Ellen Burgess, Cherne's former secretary at the Research Institute of America; Warren Meeker, former president, Research Institute of America; Marcel Faust, former director of the IRC office in Vienna, Austria; Jerry Steibel, former associate at the Research Institute of America; Nancy Starr, volunteer, International Rescue Committee; Rose Kraut, Cherne's assistant at the Research Institute of America during the late 1930s and early 1940s; James Strickler, former dean of the Dartmouth Medical School and currently co-chairman, International Rescue Committee; and many others.

I particularly thank the current and former staff of the International Rescue Committee who kindly answered my frequent questions, searched for documents, and reviewed early drafts of this book. These include Alton Kastner, Robert DeVecchi, and Carel Sternberg. I also want to thank the many librarians who located material for this book, including Howard Gotlieb, Special Collections and Archives, Mugar Memorial Library, Boston University; Library of Congress; New York Public Library; St. Louis University; Seeley Mudd Library, Princeton University; Gerald R. Ford Library, Ann Arbor; Special Collections and Archives, Indiana University/Purdue University at Indianapolis; and University Archives at New York University. I also want to thank several people who reviewed all or portions of the manuscripts and offered editorial comments. In addition to those already mentioned, I thank Tanya Kling, Michael Beiser, Bonnie Slotnick and Karla Paul for their comments and suggestions.

While all suggestions and critical comments were appreciated, this work reflects only my opinions and judgments, and I am solely accountable for all interpretations and errors that may appear.

Chapter 1

Setting the Stage

[In 1928,] a devastating hurricane ripped through the Caribbean, leaving Puerto Rico and its people in desperate need of food, water, and health supplies. The survival of thousands was in grave doubt. We students at Morris High School were suddenly summoned to the auditorium for an unscheduled assembly. Principal Bogart opened the proceedings, but not with the usual prayer or a reading from the Bible. Instead, he introduced a student who had been the instigator of this unusual assembly. Onto that stage burst a skinny, dark complexioned student, with a shock of unruly black hair, not unlike many other students at Morris High School in those days. But one thing about him was different. His eyes. Even from the ninth row I was struck by his eyes. The intensity in his voice matched the look in his eyes. And after he described the devastation left in the wake of that hurricane, he asked—no, he demanded—help of any kind, in any amount, whatever we students could spare. And more, he insisted, tomorrow bring food, in cans and containers. Food! That afternoon, the money began to pour in. Quarters, dimes, nickels, even pennies, our lunch money. The next morning bags and boxes appeared in the corridors. By day's end they were filled with cans of food. I made my contribution and then consigned the matter to history. I did not know on that day that I was witnessing the beginning of a lifetime of dedication to victims of all forms of suffering, whether inflicted by nature or by man, which ofttimes is the most devastating.

—Henry Denker, February 3, 1999

Prologue

America is a land populated by successive waves of diverse peoples. Some migrated in prehistoric times; some arrived in chains and slavery; others came as indentured servants and prisoners; but most emigrated because they chose to enjoy religious freedom, escape from somewhere or someone, or seek their fortunes in a new world.

Early European immigrants mainly came from the United Kingdom and Ireland, with a smattering from other Western and Northern European countries. In the 1880s this immigration pattern changed as peoples from Southern and Eastern Europe flooded into the United States. The pace of immigration exploded in 1900: nine million people arrived in American cities.

When H. G. Wells visited America in 1905, he described the mix of these newcomers as a "long procession of simple-looking, hopeful, sunburnt country folk from Russia, from the Carpathians, from Southern Italy and Turkey and Syria." He saw confusion and little coherence in an America filling with these immigrants speaking different languages, practicing different religions and possessing different cultural heritages. Wells lamented the likelihood that these immigrants would ever become real Americans. Most did not speak English, and Wells predicted they were not likely to learn it in America. It was most probable, claimed Wells, that these immigrants and their children would end up working in factories, dividing the United States into two nations: one, a rich aristocracy descended from Western European immigrants; and the other, a dark-haired, darker-eyed, uneducated working class from Central and Eastern Europe.[1]

Five years after Wells's visit, it looked as if his prediction were sure to come true. New York had more Italians than Rome, more Jews than Warsaw, more Irish than Dublin. Immigrants from all over Eastern and Central Europe poured into America. A large number of these were Jews from Eastern Europe. This latter group was not welcomed by mainstream America or by the 450,000 Jews who had previously migrated from Germany. The *American Hebrew* asked: "What can we do with these wild Asiatics!" The United Jewish Charities in New York encouraged some Jewish immigrants from Russia to return home and tried to talk others out of emigrating in the first place. Pushed out by pogroms, however, Jews streamed out of Russia and Eastern Europe; whole villages and families emigrated en masse to America.[2]

The Jews who arrived during the first years of the twentieth century were commonly portrayed as wild, unkempt anarchists. A bill introduced into Congress sought to exclude Jews by imposing a language test that excluded Yiddish and Hebrew. The Jewish community united to defeat the bill. This victory energized a resurgent Jewish community to form or expand relief agencies for the refugees. Many such organizations served all immigrants, not just those who were Jewish. And Jews moved into active leadership roles in America. Some led America's most effective and radical labor unions, while others published Yiddish and other periodicals, which endlessly debated socialism, anarchism, and Zionism.

Despite Wells's prognostication, Jewish immigrants quickly learned English, demonstrated a passion for education unmatched by other immigrant groups, and became firmly grounded in American patriotism. Wells might have extrapolated this outcome from his visit to a Jewish school on New York's Lower East Side, where he observed immigrant children waving American flags and singing in English, "God bless our native land."[3]

Early Life

Among the mass of Jewish immigrants from Eastern Europe was one Max Chernetsky, who had lived the first two decades of his life near Kishinev, a city in Bessarabia, then a part of Russia, but now in the nation of Moldova.[4] He was a compositor by trade and was a member of the social democratic underground. He frequently printed underground anti-Czarist tracts, which circulated freely in Kishinev. In retaliation for anti-Czarist activities, Russian officials instigated a pogrom, resulting in the massacre of many Jews in the city during April 1903. Almost all the remaining Jews in Kishinev left Russia. Max Chernetsky's family migrated to New York's Lower East Side, while he himself went to England, where he acquired a working knowledge of the English language. His first employment was in a canning factory. When he discovered an amputated finger in a food-filled can, he decided to pursue printing as an occupation. Around 1905, he traveled to Canada, and a few months later entered the United States through Ellis Island.[5]

In New York, Max Chernetsky took up printing, the only trade for which he was skilled. To better his prospects, he attended night school, where he met Dora Bailin. She had been born in the ghetto of Disna, a small town then in Russia—today, Belarus. Her parents had arranged a marriage for her in Russia. Rather than go through with the unwanted wedding, she left Russia in about 1906, joining her brother in New York. She landed a job as a garment worker, but she too was interested in bettering herself, so she attended night school.[6] Max and Dora fell madly in love but chose not to marry. For them it was not a question of strong mutual commitment or deeply held affection: those were undeniably present. But as socialists and agnostics, they did not believe that any religion or government agency should officiate over their personal commitments to each other.[7]

Around 1910, Max Chernetsky and Dora Bailin merged their lives and their economic fortunes when they purchased a small business on East 138th Street in the Bronx and lived in a railroad flat above the store. Here, they framed pictures and sold lithographs, prints, engravings, and plaster of paris busts of Bach, Brahms, and Berlioz.[8] At the time, the area was predominantly Irish, and the Chernetsky's store was in the shadow of Saint Jerome's Catholic Church. As there was not much of a market either for picture framing or art reproductions, Dora and Max struggled to make ends meet. Both worked from dawn to late into the night, trying to keep the business afloat while they explored more financially rewarding directions.

Into this world, Leopold Chernetsky was born on September 8, 1912. Leo's Aunt Lena moved in with the family and filled in for his working parents. Because Max Chernetsky was an agnostic, he was separated from the Orthodox Jewish members of his family who lived on Delancey Street on New York's Lower East Side. Max's father, Leo's grandfather, taught Hebrew, and what Leo learned about Judaism in his early years, he learned from his grandfather. When Leo was nine, his brother Jack was born.[9] Neither received their Bar Mitzvah nor did they frequent the synagogue in their early years.

Leo entered PS 9 in 1917. Elementary school was a traumatic experience for him. Specifically, he had problems with grammar and with the English language in general. He was left-handed, and teachers forced him to use his right hand. Forty years later he still remembered the pain of the teacher's ruler hitting his knuckles. In addition, he was not athletically inclined or particularly friendly with the other students.[10] His parents, however, drummed into him the importance of education, an education that they had been denied. While Leo was never a scholar and indeed rebelled against formal schooling, he did become socialized by the educational experience and became an avid reader.[11]

During this time, the Chernetskys converted their shop to a stationery store that also sold candy and school supplies. They were the first franchised dealers for Hallmark Greeting Cards in the area. The Chernetskys then became the first franchised dealer in the Bronx for the Eastman Kodak Company and sold film, cameras, and supplies to photographic studios. By the end of World War I, the demand for photographic equipment and supplies had skyrocketed. They acquired a car, permitting Max to pick up and deliver supplies to customers throughout the Bronx. The business moved to larger quarters, and a printing press was installed in the back of the new store. This press printed private and commercial stationery for a variety of small businesses in the South Bronx, advertising brochures, personalized Christmas cards, and other odd jobs.[12] As a result of selling photographic equipment and supplies, Max became interested in photography as an art form and subsequently won awards for his photos, including first place in the amateur division of an international contest in Paris.[13]

Despite their improved financial circumstances in capitalist America, the Chernetskys retained their radical political interests. Dora proved to be an intellectual who loved the works of Friedrich Nietzsche, Arthur Schopenhauer, and Sigmund Freud. Max and Dora quickly became a part of New York's intellectual milieu, fusing unequal parts of socialism, agnosticism, nihilism, and idealism. They were ardent supporters of Eugene V. Debs, the Socialist. Max was also a member of the Workmen's Circle, a Jewish fraternal and insurance society, which brought together others with similar social democratic political perspectives.

Friends frequently dropped by their home for serious discussion. Small talk was not possible for these intense young people. As Leo later summarized: "They worked hard, they hoped hard, they dreamed hard, they argued hard." Relaxation for them only postponed their intellectual exploration.[14] Cherne began reading books and taking part in these discussions, which offered him the opportunity to converse about important topics of the day. What was more significant, his parents permitted him to disagree with them, thus encouraging independent thinking.[15]

Within a few blocks of the Chernetsky's store, many ethnic, religious, racial, and immigrant groups mingled. When Leo was old enough, he explored the neighborhood on foot, and often hitched rides on the trolley or trains to visit other boroughs and neighborhoods of New York. In this way he met all kinds of people, including immigrants from all over the world. Leo frequently joined his father in making deliveries; and the family made occasional longer trips to the Catskills, Kingston, Poughkeepsie, and Rhinebeck. Those journeys were possible only when a national or Jewish holiday attached to a Sunday made it possible to close the store for two days. Even though his parents were not religious, they nevertheless closed their store on Jewish holy days to avoid upsetting religious neighbors and partially to demonstrate their respect for their own Jewish heritage. These holy-day trips upset Leo's grandparents, who were very religious. His grandmother was not only horrified at the thought of her son driving a car on Rosh Hashanah or Yom Kippur, but equally certain that God would literally inflict physical retribution for these lapses. On one occasion, the family did have an auto accident on Yom Kippur, confirming the grandparents' direst imprecations. On another Jewish holy day, the car would not start due to a dead battery. Leo was embarrassed as the family carted their luggage home, encountering on their way their more devout neighbors heading for the synagogue.[16]

Two developments during this period of Leo's life were defining ones. The first was his membership in a gang. He had never been particularly sociable with kids his own age. A local gang was the first group that accepted him, which was all the more surprising as he was the only member of the gang who was of Jewish heritage. Gang members played games in the street, gathered on rooftops, evaded the police, sneaked into movies, loitered around stoops or in front of the candy store, rallied to defend their territory against marauding attacks from other gangs, or sallied forth into another gang's turf. For the most part, the activities of this gang were nonviolent, but at times fists, elbows, and an occasional knife were employed. Leo often came home with bruises; occasionally his parents retrieved him from the police station.[17]

The second development opened up a very different world, when his parents acquired an annual subscription in the Family Circle of the Metropolitan Opera House. The Chernetsky parents loved music. Since they could not afford to close their store, one parent would go at a time. Sometimes they would take a friend; often they took Leo.[18] In junior high school, Leo's music teacher suggested that he audition for the Metropolitan Opera Children's Chorus. In each session, the chorus rehearsed two or three hours, three times a week. For the three years that Cherne sang in the chorus, he enjoyed extraordinary experiences backstage at the Metropolitan, where he met the opera stars of the day.[19] During three succeeding years, he sang in *Carmen, La Gioconda, Jewel of the Madonna, Mephistopheles,* and he wangled occasional opportunities for parts in operas ranging from *Der Freischütz* to *La Boheme.*[20] The children were taught to sing phonetically and Cherne never understood a word he sang, but he maintained a love for music and especially opera throughout his life.

Leo entered Morris High School in 1926. As the school was overcrowded, he ended up at the Hunt's Point Annex, four miles away from the main campus. He participated in the drama club, performed in plays, and joined a debate club. At the Annex, he rehearsed for and acted in Shakespeare's *The Taming of the Shrew.*[21] He was next scheduled to play Willie Baxter in Booth Tarkington's play, *Seventeen.* Unfortunately, he acquired a mastoid infection that required surgery. Before the play opened, he was discharged from school. However, when the student playing Willie Baxter took ill, Leo came back just to perform the role, although he was in excruciating pain. The school records report that he saved the play. Despite his own illness, it was his "enthusiasm that made the play the astonishing success it was," according to a contemporary observer.[22]

Until his fourteenth birthday, Leo spent summers in Jewish camps in the Catskills, such as the Workmen's Circle Camp.[23] Through the Workmen's Circle, his family became friends with Henry Aron, a respected member of the Republican Party in the Bronx. Aron was a customs inspector, a patronage job. Just before Leo's fifteenth birthday, Aron landed him a job as an ordinary seaman on the Ward Line, which sailed for the Caribbean. To prepare for the trip, Leo grew a little moustache and spent time in the sun to get a darker complexion; he wanted to look like a hoodlum in hopes the crew would not pick on him as a newcomer. But his new tough appearance did not help him. Although he was seasick the first day, he was nevertheless thrown onto the floor and was forced to work from five in the morning until eight at night. The crew stole his camera, knife, and money. When the ship docked, Leo was assigned backbreaking manual labor carrying loads of sugar and bananas on and off the ship. Had he been able to easily jump ship during the first few days, he would have done so. His stubbornness and courage were simply not enough. He later reported that he was glad that the first trip lasted two weeks. Had it been any shorter, he would never have sailed again. However, he survived the appalling conditions and mastered his fears. By the time the ship docked in New York, he was ready to sign on for another voyage. In all Leo completed four trips to the Caribbean in 1927 and additional trips the following summer.[24] By his final trip, he was a veteran sailor treated with respect by the crews he sailed with, despite his youth.[25]

When Leo entered the fall semester of his junior year at Morris High School, the big topic of discussion was a hurricane that had devastated Puerto Rico. At a meeting of the school's Service League, of which he was a member, Leo announced the formation of a "Hurricane Committee." At the time, few Puerto Ricans lived in the Bronx and Cherne knew none. His parents had not been particularly interested in events in Puerto Rico. Newspapers' reportage was intense, but newspapers had covered many previous natural disasters, to which neither Leo nor other students paid much attention. However, this disaster was different. Leo had been in the Caribbean a few weeks before, and the ship had sailed through the edge of a hurricane. As the self-appointed head of the "Hurricane Committee," he requested an assembly of the entire student body to solicit aid for Puerto Rico. The principal consented, and Leo volunteered to make an impassioned plea. Henry Denker, a student attending the assembly, reported that there had never been anything like it at Morris High School: money poured in that afternoon, and the following morning, food cans filled bags and boxes in the halls.[26]

As Leo later commented about his speech, he had a need to "seek the public platform," and the hurricane provided the opportunity to gain public recognition. His involvement in the Puerto Rican hurricane relief provided a model that served him well in future years: quick intervention in seizing the public platform, altruistic motives, positive responses of others, and record-breaking results. Another immediate outcome of his hurricane speech was that Leo was elected president of the student body, the first time in the history of Morris High School that a junior won that post. The following year he was reelected, another unprecedented event. He asserted that the prime qualification for success was "nerve," which he defined as "overpowering self-confidence."[27] This too provided a model for his future approach to life.

In August 1929, Leo's father legally changed their family name from Chernetsky to Cherne.[28] In his senior year, the newly named Leo Cherne was selected editor of the high school newspaper, the *Morris Piper.* Henry Denker, a student who had witnessed Cherne's Puerto Rican speech, became the paper's columnist and humorist. The two worked together under the strict supervision of an English teacher named Julius Drachman. Outwitting Drachman's edicts united Cherne and Denker as co-conspirators. The two bonded, and that friendship lasted a lifetime.[29]

Cherne was involved in other extracurricular activities during his high school years. He was actively interested in the events and issues of the day. One hotly debated issue during the 1920s concerned two Italian-born anarchists, Nicola Sacco and Bartolomeo Vanzetti. In April 1920, they had been arrested for the murder of a paymaster and guard in Massachusetts. At the time of their arrest, both men were armed. During the previous year, Congress had passed a law permitting the expulsion of immigrants who were anarchists. When they were apprehended, Sacco and Vanzetti, fearing deportation to Italy, gave false statements to the police. Despite contradictory evidence, both were found guilty of murder in July 1921 and sentenced to death. The Massachusetts Supreme Court upheld their convictions. After their execution in August 1927, mass demonstrations erupted, raging against this presumed injustice. One mass rally was held in Madison Square Garden in New York.

Denker and Cherne believed the Sacco-Vanzetti verdict was a miscarriage of justice, and they longed to demonstrate their support by attending the rally. Neither Cherne nor Denker could afford the entrance fee. Cherne went to his father's printing press and printed a very official-looking letterhead for a fictitious newspaper, *The Westchester Daily Sentinel.* On the letterhead, Denker typed a message: "To Whom It May Concern, This is to inform you that staff reporters Leo Cherne and Henry Denker have been assigned by the *Sentinel* to cover the Sacco-Vanzetti rally in Madison Square Garden. We insist they be treated accordingly." Boldly, they approached the press gate of Madison Square Garden and presented their bogus credentials. After thorough scrutiny by uniformed guards, they were escorted to the press section in the very first row.[30]

From the age of sixteen to twenty-one, Cherne was a member of Aleph Zadik Aleph (AZA), a youth organization of B'nai B'rith. After he joined, he pulled Denker and other friends into the AZA chapter. With their support, he was elected chapter president. Through the AZA, he participated in oratorical and debate contests. This gave him his first real experience of travel in the United States. He took part in oratorical contests in Jersey City, Hartford, St. Louis, Milwaukee, and Springfield, Massachusetts. His early themes promoted peace and railed against munitions makers, who, according to the wisdom of the time, had caused World War I. Cherne was required to leave AZA at the age of twenty-one, so he graduated into the Junior Order of B'nai B'rith. There he continued to participate in oratorical contests, becoming the "international oratorical champion."[31]

Cherne's favorite speech was "The Four Horsemen of the Apocalypse" about William Randolph Hearst, Father Charles Coughlin, Huey Long, and Hugh Johnson. With Hitler's increasing power in Germany, Cherne added the Führer's name to his enemies list. On April 3, 1932, Cherne tried to organize a citywide mass meeting sponsored by the AZA to deal with "this new international problem which has recently arisen, and which is best denoted by the name of its chief exemplar—Hitlerism." Cherne's purpose was "to combat this venomous spread of fascism."[32] At this time in isolationist America, these stands were courageous, and not everyone appreciated Cherne's fiery speeches. Particularly offensive to some was his inclusion of Hugh Johnson, then the head of the National Recovery Act (NRA), as one of Cherne's apocalyptic horsemen. Cherne saw disturbing similarities between Roosevelt's NRA and public-works programs in Hitler's Germany and Mussolini's Italy.

Cherne was advised by Judge Albert Cohen, a family friend, to tone down his remarks. Some Jewish leaders believed that Jews should maintain a low profile and avoid provoking anti-Semitism. Aggressive assaults on anti-Semites might well serve as an excuse for attacking Jews. When Cherne continued to speak out forcefully, he was censured by his B'nai B'rith lodge. Through this experience, he learned to handle censure from others, particularly when he was convinced that he was right and his critics wrong.[33]

New York University

While at Morris High School, Cherne gave little consideration as to what to do after graduation. Cherne's grades were not distinguished, but he had excelled in extracurricular activities. He had won the Harvard Prize, an award given by Harvard University to outstanding high school students. The newspaper article about the award reported that he had overcome a speech impediment in elementary school to star in dramas and public speaking. This award opened up the possibility that Cherne could attend Harvard, but he cavalierly dismissed it. For a while, he considered attending Duke University in North Carolina. In the end, he remained in New York. Ineligible to enter New York's City College because his grades were not good enough (or so he later claimed), Cherne and Henry Denker enrolled in New York University (NYU), which at the time accepted almost anyone with the financial wherewithal to pay the tuition.[34]

At NYU Cherne decided to major in journalism. He had been the editor of the Morris High School student newspaper and he enjoyed writing. During the fall of Leo's freshman year at NYU, Elias Jacobs launched the *South Bronx News* to compete with the *Bronx Home News* with its circulation of 100,000 in the Bronx and Harlem. Jacobs was interested in selling advertising to local merchants and banks. Cherne saw the first few issues and approached Jacobs with the proposition that he convert the *South Bronx News* into a newspaper catering to the South Bronx, Harlem, and Northwest Queens. Jacobs agreed and named Cherne editor. Cherne wrote the content and Jacobs acquired advertisements from merchants to cover costs. Cherne expanded the newspaper and renamed it the *Tri-Boro News,* advocating the construction of a single bridge to connect three boroughs of New York: the Bronx, Queens, and Manhattan. Cherne called this then–hypothetical bridge the "Lewis Morris Bridge." Morris (whom Cherne's high school had been named after) was the only signer of the Declaration of Independence from the Bronx.

As two out of three of the newspaper's circulation areas were slums, it is surprising that the *Tri-Boro News* achieved a circulation of 30,000. When the Depression hit the Bronx full force in 1933, advertisers dried up and the newspaper folded. But the idea of connecting the three boroughs was a good one. The bridge was constructed in 1936; however, it was named the more descriptive "Tri-Borough Bridge."[35]

Cherne's first year at New York University was actually spent in an annex at the Metropolitan Life Insurance Building. He had no serious academic orientation, and he found the courses unstimulating with two exceptions. One was an English class, in which he was required to write a paper. At the time, Prohibition was still the law of the land, and Cherne noted that newspapers were filled with stories about deaths on the Bowery as a result of the illegal sale of "smoke," a mixture of wood alcohol and water, which had a smoky appearance. It sold for fifteen cents a bottle—sometimes just a dime. Every morning ambulances would arrive on the Bowery and cart away the bodies. Some victims needed medical treatment, but many died from alcohol poisoning. Cherne convinced Lillian Herlends, his English teacher, to give him credit to live for a month on the Bowery and write up the experience, provided that a newspaper agreed to publish his stories. The editors he approached at *The Daily Mirror* bought the idea.[36]

Cherne lived on the Bowery disguised as a bum frequenting speakeasies. He reported daily the addresses of the places that sold smoke, which *The Daily Mirror* dutifully published. The police read the stories and raided the speakeasies identified in Cherne's articles. This had two results: the speakeasies threw comatose bodies into the alleys behind their establishments rather than out the front door, where they would have been visible; and every proprietor on the Bowery began looking for the informer. At first Cherne had been able to order smoke and spill it out without drinking it, but as things heated up, he had to drink what he ordered. He remained on the Bowery for ten days, living in flophouses. One morning, he awoke to find himself piled with the others in the back of a speakeasy. He'd had enough. *The Daily Mirror* was happy with the results and his teacher gave him an A+.[37]

The other class that Cherne enjoyed was a sociology course on organized recreation. In this course, students were required to examine and report on recreational entertainments. As a result of this class, he found himself watching movies for eight to twelve hours per day. (Due to his writeup of this experience, the Department of Sociology nominated him to the National Board of Review of Motion Pictures, on which he served for two years.) Cherne also frequented pool halls as part of his study. His parents had purchased a pool table for him when he was sixteen, and now Cherne honed his skills and became a pool shark. He devoted special efforts to his study of dance halls, often staying out until they closed at 2:00 A.M. Persuaded that his assignment required him to learn more about the women who charged a dime a dance, he dated several of them. In his paper for the sociology course, he offered a frank explanation of what two dollars worth of tickets could buy, much to the dismay of the instructor.[38]

Cherne continued his interest in journalism: he became the editor of the NYU student newspaper and he again tried his hand at publishing, this time with *The Putnam Times*, catering to the citizens of Danbury, Connecticut, and Brewster and Pawling, New York. His parents had property in Putnam County which Cherne visited regularly during this time. *The Putnam*

Times engaged in muckraking for several social causes, but it too soon folded. Undaunted, Cherne continued to prepare for a career in journalism. By the end of his sophomore year at NYU, the *New York World* collapsed. Cherne was advised that it would take ten years for the newspaper profession to absorb the reporters then on the market.[39] He needed another career path.

Cherne cavalierly decided to take up the study of law. Moved by Gene Fowler's *The Great Mouthpiece*, he saw his future in arguing high-profile cases such as the Sacco-Vanzetti case.[40] However, at the time, there was not a great demand for lawyers. The Depression was in full swing; many lawyers were under- or unemployed. Neither businesses nor government agencies were hiring many lawyers; hence, the need for new lawyers was extremely limited.[41] The main reason for Cherne's choice of law was again due to the influence of his best friend, Henry Denker. At that time, it was possible to enter law school after taking a two year pre-law course of study in college. Denker had completed such a program and, at the end of his sophomore year, he applied to the New York Law School (which, despite the similarities in names, had no connection with New York University).

Unlike Denker, Cherne had been taking courses preparing him for a career in journalism. Cherne decided to take all the required courses for the pre-law track during the summer following his sophomore year. Years later he candidly admitted how this feat was accomplished: he had approached his long-term girl friend, Julia Lopez, who was an excellent student at Hunter College. He asked her to sit in for him on two required courses—mathematics and French. She agreed. Simultaneously, Cherne took the compulsory pre-law courses, and thus, all requirements for the two-year pre-law course of study were completed during the one summer of 1931.[42]

New York Law School

New York Law School had the least-demanding entrance requirements and it had the reputation of being the easiest law school around.[43] Having completed requirements during the summer, Cherne entered New York Law School in October 1931. The school had about one hundred students and was housed at the Twenty-third Street YMCA, an ancient building with open caged elevators.[44] Cherne attended class five nights a week for three years, studying contracts, torts, criminal law, trial practice, and a host of other legal subjects, but he was bored with them and spent considerable time playing table tennis and hustling for money in the YMCA's basement poolroom.

With the Depression in full swing, the school suffered financial problems. When it was announced that the school would close after Cherne's class graduated, lax enforcement of regulations and a morose atmosphere prevailed. However, the students became very close friends and engaged in frequent debates during the breaks between classes. The election of Franklin D. Roosevelt as president and the launching of the New Deal in 1933 electrified America and the students hotly discussed the public issues of the day. With the exception of the NRA, Cherne generally supported the programs of the New Deal, but never with the blind adulation expressed by others. He idealized law and envisioned that it could provide a source of relevant answers to the problems facing America. Looking back, Cherne saw these extracurricular discussions as his most valuable experience at law school.[45]

Cherne and Denker befriended another student named Aaron Levenstein, a militant socialist. Cherne later claimed to have neither attended many classes nor purchased any law books after his first year. Yet he graduated in 1934 first in the class. Actually, Aaron Levenstein had achieved the highest grade average, but Levenstein had transferred from the day session to the night session and the prize was awarded only to a student who had been consistently in either session.[46]

Practicing Law

Soon after Cherne entered law school, he began work as a law clerk in the law firm of Blau, Perlman and Polokov for the handsome salary of five dollars per week. He gained this position with the help of Henry Aron, the Republican boss of the Bronx. Aron knew the three partners in this law firm, who were also Republicans: Judge Blau; Nathan D. Perlman, who became a judge; and Moses Polokov, who had been an assistant federal prosecutor. While in the Department of Justice, Polokov enforced Prohibition, fought income tax evasion, and prosecuted the nation's top gangsters. As soon as he left federal service, he defended the same criminals he had jailed earlier, including Dutch "Baby Face" Schultz and Lucky Luciano. Perlman had a long association with labor movements, particularly the American Federation of Labor. The firm was also one of the most active in bankruptcy practice, a lucrative sure bet during the Depression.[47] Cherne's role as a law clerk included serving as a messenger boy. He was paid $1.50 for each summons he served—then, as now, an unpleasant undertaking; but it was extra money, so he served as many as possible.[48]

After graduation in June 1934, Cherne, Denker, and Levenstein crammed for the New York Bar examinations. It was expected that only about 30 percent of those taking the exams would pass, but it was possible to retake the exam a total of three times. Their intense preparation paid off.[49] All three passed the exams the first time.

When the results were announced, Cherne was hired as a lawyer at Blau, Perlman and Polokov. He was paid $350 per month, a good beginning salary at the height of the Depression. He first handled bankruptcies and became particularly good at writing briefs. Later, Cherne became involved in criminal cases, especially that of Lucky Luciano, who was one of New York City's best known, most successful, highly organized, ruthless gangsters. Luciano specialized in numbers rackets, smuggling, gun running, and dope peddling. Thomas E. Dewey, the ambitious district attorney, had targeted Luciano, who was indicted on charges of engaging in prostitution. Dewey's case rested on the testimony of two madams, some prostitutes, and a lawyer who had been persuaded to cooperate with the district attorney. Cherne had no doubt that Luciano was guilty of many crimes, but was convinced that the gangster was not guilty of the charge of prostitution, mainly because Cherne believed that there was not enough money in it to attract Luciano.[50]

To ensure Luciano's conviction, the prosecution had sequestered witnesses in Westchester, making it difficult for the defense to interview them, and the prosecution had promised boat trips to witnesses. The prosecution also permitted one incarcerated witness to leave the prison two days a week to visit a prostitute, or so reported Cherne. Cherne had no doubt that the citizens of New York were better off without Luciano on the streets, but he was deeply offended by Dewey's tactics, which resulted in Luciano's conviction. The prosecution's efforts shattered Cherne's idealistic view of the law. Cherne was also bored with the mundane routine legal practice and yearned for more action. He fell into a state of depression, and for the first and only time in his life, started drinking heavily.[51] He needed a new direction for his life.

Epilogue

• Aaron Levenstein and Leo Cherne remained friends and professional colleagues for much of their lives. Levenstein subsequently wrote histories of two organizations—Freedom House and the International Rescue Committee—with which Cherne was closely connected.[52]

- Henry Denker and Leo Cherne also remained friends for life. Denker spent a short time in the legal profession before he launched a career in writing. He went on to write thirty-four books and six plays. For ten years, he wrote and produced the radio program "The Greatest Story Ever Told." Despite their hectic schedules, Denker attended many of Cherne's speeches and all of his famous ones at the Sales Executive Club; Cherne in turn attended every one of Denker's opening nights, whether in New York or Washington.[53]

- Each of the ships that Cherne served on during the summers of 1927 and 1928 subsequently sank in storms or collisions.

- When Thomas Dewey ran for president in 1948 on the Republican ticket against Harry Truman, Cherne supported Truman.

Chapter 2

Researching America

The Research Institute of America, a thriving business run by a young lawyer from the Bronx named Leo M. Cherne and a young Bible sales-man from Emporia, Kansas named Carl Hovgard, is built around the sim-ple proposition that Calvin Coolidge will never return. The Institute advises businessmen on how to survive in spite of the Niagara Falls of government regulations constantly descending on them.

—George R. Leighton, 1940[1]

Prologue

A few weeks after the Luciano verdict in late 1935, Charles Siegel, a law clerk at Blau, Perlman and Polokov, brought to Cherne's atten-tion an advertisement in the *New York Law Journal* seeking a lawyer familiar with Social Security laws to work on unemployment insurance leg-islation. It offered $25 per week, much less than Cherne was making at the time. As a lark, Cherne applied. He met with his prospective employer, Hugo Black (unrelated to the Supreme Court Justice of the same name), who had undertaken to write a book on unemployment insurance taxes. As a demonstration of ability, Black requested that Cherne describe and ex-plain Washington's unemployment insurance law. Cherne immediately se-cured a copy of the Federal Social Security Act and worked feverishly to prepare a clear, definitive analysis of that statute. He completed his analysis two days before the deadline and submitted it to Black, only to be informed that his assigned task was the State of Washington's unemployment insur-ance act, not the federal legislation emanating from Washington, DC. Cherne asked if he could still be considered if he resubmitted the correct analysis before the deadline arrived. Black consented. Cherne worked for forty-eight hours straight and produced an in-depth analysis for the Unem-ployment Compensation Act of Washington State.[2]

Several days later Cherne received a postcard turning him down for the job. By this time, he had mentally left his law firm and he really wanted the new job. Rather than meekly taking the turndown, Cherne headed straight to Black's office. Black stated that Cherne's analysis was better than that of the applicant he had hired, but frankly admitted that he was worried that Cherne knew more about the topic than he did. Over the next hour, Cherne argued that he really knew very little about the subject and Black clearly knew much more. Black was moved by Cherne's groveling, but he had already hired another lawyer. Cherne offered to work for lower pay for thirty days to prove his worth. If it didn't work out, Cherne would leave. Black agreed. Cherne's first day on the new job was January 6, 1936.[3]

Cherne learned several things during those thirty days. Black knew almost nothing about the topic on which he had contracted to write the book. Black had placed the ad in the *New York Law Journal* with the expectation that it would generate a large pool of applicants, which it did. From the pool, Black had selected the best qualified candidates and assigned each to analyze a different state's unemployment insurance system. With little effort, he had a rough draft of the book prepared by applicants. All Black really wanted in the job candidate was a person with the ability to take what the prospective unsuccessful applicants had already written and convert it into a book. Cherne soon discovered that he was extremely competent at this task, especially when compared with Black and the other young lawyer Black had hired. After thirty days, Black fired the other lawyer and turned the entire project over to Cherne.[4]

But Hugo Black did not divulge who had hired him. Black had presented himself as an expert on the insurance laws and had convinced the unidentified client that he had written the New York unemployment insurance law, which he had not. When the person who had hired Black for the job began asking questions that Black could not answer, Black reluctantly turned him over to Cherne. Three months after Cherne was hired, he finally met the client, Carl Hovgard.

Hovgard was a Midwesterner whose parents had emigrated from Denmark. He was proud of the fact that his great-great-uncle was the existentialist philosopher Søren Kierkegaard. He was also proud of the fact that he had never read any of Kierkegaard's works. A graduate of the College of Emporia in Kansas, Hovgard was more interested in practical matters. In the midst of the Depression, he helped build the Mills Wolf Advertising Agency in Tulsa, Oklahoma. He excelled in direct mail marketing techniques and he quickly became a partner in the firm. The business thrived, but Hovgard had few opportunities in Tulsa to test his new approach to advertising. With a nest egg of $4,000, Hovgard moved to New York, possessed by the dream that he could make millions by applying the techniques nationally. He was a believer in the view that image mattered in the advertising business, so he opened a plush office in the newly completed Chrysler Building. Unfortunately, he mailed his first promotion just days before Roosevelt closed the banks. The flyers ended up in the trash and the company failed. Hovgard went to work at Prentice Hall.[5]

At Prentice Hall, Hovgard learned the publishing business. He still believed that his direct marketing techniques, combined with the right business publication, could turn a solid financial profit. His boss, R. P. Ettinger, disagreed and fired him in September 1935. Hovgard decided to take this opportunity to test his idea through another business venture. He formed a partnership with Ed Whittlesey, a former journalism teacher from the College of Emporia, then taking postgraduate courses at Columbia University. The newly named Whitgard Services started up in a twelve-foot-square room in the modest surroundings of the Chanin Building across from Grand Central Station on January 1, 1936. Their capital totaled $700, which they acquired in part by selling Whittlesey's car. The book that Hovgard visualized was called *Minimizing Payroll Taxes*. Black was contracted to write it. Hovgard mailed out an advertisement, generating sales of 10,000 copies at ten dollars apiece. Hovgard then used the money to pay Black to write the book, the printer to publish it, and a distributor to mail it out.[6]

This phenomenal success is comprehensible only in the context of surrounding national events. Businessmen around the country were overwhelmed by the flood of legislation the New Deal was producing in Washington. Most were unprepared, poorly informed, and inadequately served by their lawyers. Some business associations insisted that the new legislation was unconstitutional and encouraged their members to ignore it. Businessmen and business associations were completely unprepared for Supreme Court rulings in favor of many New Deal laws. There could have been no better situation for a new business devoted solely to helping other businesses comply with this new legislation. Hovgard believed that there was an expanding and continuing need for similar services and products.[7]

From their first meeting, Hovgard was attracted to Cherne. Hovgard quickly discerned that Cherne was the brains behind Black. In addition, Cherne knew about publishing. While Cherne was finishing the book, Hovgard hired and trained salesmen to sell the publication on a commission basis. Hovgard asked Cherne to address these salesmen, which Cherne was delighted to do, and his presentation was a success.[8] Hovgard wanted

Cherne to work on his next project, a two-volume looseleaf book called *Payroll Tax Saving Service*. When Hovgard bypassed Black to work directly with Cherne, relationships became confused. Hovgard proposed that Cherne work for Whitgard Services. Whittlesey opposed this. He believed that their only long-term chance for success depended on keeping expenses to a minimum; he was not prepared for the risks inherent in rapid expansion. Hovgard bought him out and Cherne became editor-in-chief.[9] *Payroll Tax Saving Service* proved just as successful as their previous publication

The Tax Research Institute of America

By the end of 1936, Cherne and Hovgard had concluded that a new corporation was needed to publish studies and provide services in all areas in which government affected business. They moved into new offices in the Salmon Tower on Forty-second Street, and the Tax Research Institute of America (TRIA) was born. In this endeavor, Hovgard was the majority stockholder, but Cherne acquired shares. Their next project was a *Social Security Coordinator*. Cherne designed the publication with specific information on concrete cases. This work too proved successful.[10]

The Tax Research Institute of America did not simply reprint the laws or just inform businessmen how the law might affect them. Its purpose was to pass on professional intelligence to businessmen about legislation. In January 1937, the Institute launched the *Business and Legislative Report*, a weekly report to business executives covering government's impact on business, economic change, legislative possibilities, and potential legal issues. Subscribers became members in the TRIA. Cherne edited the newsletter, which, along with its information about developing legislation and the status of bills in Congress connected with business, also offered advice to businessmen on how to respond to the new laws. This advice was promptly attacked from the left. In May 1937 *The Progressive,* published by the La Follette family in Madison, Wisconsin, attacked the newsletter in a front page article titled "Tory Bosses Told How to 'Avoid' Laws." Cherne promptly retorted with a letter itemizing the inaccuracies in the news article, but *The Progressive* refused to print his rebuttal.[11]

The *Business and Legislative Report* projected the likelihood of particular bills passing Congress. As the issue of constitutionality was of prime importance to most businessmen, Cherne began making projections as to the potential fate of laws directly concerned with business.[12] In making these projections he tried to be as objective as possible, and several of his predictions were unpopular. During the General Motors sit-down strike in 1937, for instance, he forecast that General Motors would settle with the Congress of Industrial Organizations (CIO): "The CIO is here to stay—prepare for a CIO victory." This prediction was not popular among the anti-union subscribers to the *Business and Legislative Report*, and a thousand subscribers quit over this "ridiculous" forecast. Two weeks later, General Motors settled. Cherne later stated that had the strike continued for several more weeks, the Institute would have been ruined due to the loss of members.[13]

Another unpopular prediction concerned the National Labor Relations Act (NLRA), which had been passed by Congress after the Supreme Court declared the National Recovery Act unconstitutional. There was nothing more unpopular with the Institute's members than the NLRA, which included the Wagner Act requiring compulsory collective bargaining. Most major business associations, such as the National Association of Manufacturers and the United States Chamber of Commerce, advised their members that the Wagner Act was unconstitutional. Cherne predicted that the U.S. Supreme Court would uphold it by a vote of five to four. In the weeks after Cherne made his prediction and before the Supreme Court made its decision, the newsletter again lost many subscribers. Again, had the Supreme Court put off the decision until the following term, Cherne believed that the Institute would not have survived the storm. Seven weeks after Cherne made his prediction, the Supreme Court upheld the act, thus vindicating Cherne and saving the Institute. Despite his correct prediction, however, the Institute did not regain all the members it had lost.[14]

Cherne's Supreme Court predictions were based on a series of factors, including political and social considerations as well as the knowledge of the individual Justices' personalities. Cherne collected extensive files on each Justice. He acquired some information in Washington, "a small town where everyone talked," as he described it. The Institute staff were good listeners. They were also good analysts, who evaluated sources of information: reliable, self-serving, inventive, or simply gossipy. Finally, there was an unquantifiable component of instinct or informed intuition.[15] Others concluded that the Institute knew so much because it was really an arm of the New Deal. This image was fortified when the Institute later hired senior New Deal officials.[16] Cherne did nothing to squelch these rumors: the Institute's prestige increased because others believed its leaders were Washington insiders.

Cherne's batting average was so high that he developed a national reputation. He was called upon to testify in Congress about Senator Vandenberg's proposal on incentive tax and profit sharing in 1939, and his name began to surface in magazine articles. In January 1940, he spoke at the New York Sales Executive Club, warning of a time of mounting danger. He told the executives that war was coming and that the United States would be involved. The executives needed to expect rationing and systemic priorities. After the German attack on Poland in September 1939 and before the German blitzkrieg on Norway in April 1940, there were few hostilities in Europe, and most observers labeled this the "phoney war." In this the U.S. was not involved, and many Americans wanted to avoid hostilities in the future. To the audience, Cherne's predictions of war were just empty rhetoric. However, the writer George Leighton, witnessing Cherne's performance, was intrigued by Cherne's dire predictions and wrote an article for the *New Yorker,* titled "Cassandra, Inc." Luckily for Cherne, it was published in October 1940, after the collapse of France and while the outcome of the Battle of Britain was still in doubt. Cherne's reputation soared.[17]

Cherne's predictions and Hovgard's marketing talents had combined to make the Institute a fantastic success. Cherne was named Executive Secretary, and the company was renamed the Research Institute of America. By the time their annual budget had reached $442,000, the company needed larger quarters. They found the Johns-Manville Building, an ornate twenty-five story structure. Johns-Manville had moved out and the upper floors were empty. The top floor had a large Gothic chamber with a high ceiling, oak-paneled walls, leaded-glass windows, and an ornate fireplace. It was just what Hovgard and Cherne wanted. In return for their renting what the owner considered a white elephant, the owner agreed to identify the structure as the "Research Institute Building." During the following year, the Research Institute doubled its annual budget. By 1938 the Institute employed a staff of 150 people. By 1940, the Institute grossed $1.4 million.[18]

The Institute's membership increased from seven thousand to nine thousand members. As the Institute expanded, the staff worked fourteen to fifteen hours per day, and more staff were hired. Among the new employees Cherne hired were Henry Denker, Rose Baum, and Charles Siegel, the law clerk at Blau, Perlman and Polokov. Cherne placed advertisements in the *New York Law Review* seeking talented lawyers for fifteen to twenty-five dollars per week. One person responding to the ads was William Casey, a recently graduated honor student from Saint John's Law School in Brooklyn. At his interview, when Casey spoke, he mumbled. As the Institute was short-handed, Casey was hired, but performed his first assignment poorly.

His writing was clumsy and unclear. Cherne trained Casey, who quickly learned to write fast and crisply and soon took over the tax section of the Institute. Cherne was particularly impressed with Casey's gift for synthesis and his instinct for the intent of laws. He could strike at the heart of the law, simplify it, and identify the minimum actions that employers were required to take to comply with it. He soon outworked other Institute employees and his salary increased to thirty dollars per week.[19]

The Institute's expansion and visibility also brought scrutiny. The most disapproving were lawyers and their associations, including the American Bar Association. Several legal associations believed that the Institute's willingness to offer legal advice for businesses violated the law. Their real concern, proclaimed Cherne, was that businessmen were reading the Institute's newsletters and not buying the lawyers' services. The Institute argued that freedom of the press permitted them to offer advice. When one case went to court, Cherne hired the best civil rights lawyer he knew—Aaron Levenstein, his old friend from the New York Law School. When Levenstein left law school, he had become the education director of the AFL's International Handbag and Pocketbook Workers Union. After some hesitation Levenstein, a Socialist, accepted the case. He was not sure that he wanted the management of a private enterprise to benefit from his work. However, he strongly supported freedom of the press and speech, and he believed that lawyers' associations were attempting to muzzle the Institute. Together Cherne and Levenstein prepared a brief that destroyed the case against the Institute.[20]

Cherne's life was not all work in those days. In 1936, Cherne married Julia Lopez, whom he had met when he was sixteen and then dated for eight years. Lopez was the grandniece of Samuel Gompers, founder of the AFL.[21] Four years after their marriage, the Chernes became parents with the birth of their daughter Gail Stephanie, their only child. Cherne's annual salary was reported in the millions. He laughed at such speculation and reported that his salary was really $25,000 per year, still an astronomical sum for 1940. This salary permitted the Chernes to locate a spacious apartment on Central Park West, where they lived for the next twenty-six years.[22]

By 1940 Cherne had gained considerable visibility. In one publication, he was described as looking like the actor Ronald Colman: "dark, slender and very handsome, a high-powered young executive with a dashing presence."[23] Five years later he was described as "The Wonder Boy" who was "a slender chap of medium height, with curly black hair and piercing brown eyes."[24] Another personal characteristic was that he smoked like a fiend, a habit he retained for most of his life.

Mobilizing for War

Beginning in mid–1938, Cherne began commuting to Washington. As he anticipated war in Europe, Cherne explored the War Department and one day he wandered into the Planning Branch, where he met Colonel William H. Sadler. Sadler mentioned that the Planning Branch was preparing plans for industrial mobilization in case the United States became involved in war. The statutory authority for devising the plans had been an outgrowth of the efforts of Bernard Baruch, a financier, who had been appointed by President Wilson as a member of the Advisory Commission of the Council for National Defense and later was chairman of the War Industrials Board. Baruch had played a major role in America's industrial mobilization during World War I, an experience that convinced him that the United States was completely unprepared for the war and that the country should never again be in that position. After World War I, he forcefully urged Congress to enact a National Defense Act, which was finally voted into law in 1921. This required the War Department to develop an industrial mobilization plan. Over the next sixteen years, War Department officials assembled a motley collection of industrial reports and economic forecasts. At first, as war was not imminent, few attempts were made to develop a coherent plan out of this diverse collection of documents. During the 1930s, this changed. Major efforts were launched to ameliorate the problem. Mobilization plans were developed in 1931, 1933, and 1936. Baruch reviewed these plans and declared them inadequate when he testified before a Senate committee. He urged that a new plan be devised. Congress refused to appropriate additional money to develop new plans. Baruch and Cherne discussed these plans; and Baruch may have encouraged Cherne to visit Sadler in the first instance.[25]

When the British and French signed the Munich Pact in 1938 giving Germany part of Czechoslovakia, many American military leaders believed that a European war was now inevitable and that such a war might involve the United States.[26] Sadler had now been ordered to develop a new plan that Cherne had heard about. Sadler read the Institute's reports and was impressed with Cherne. Sadler tutored Cherne on industrial mobilization and introduced him to other members of the Planning Branch. Major Lewis B. Hershey, for instance, was responsible for developing a plan to meet the military's manpower needs in case of war. Hershey later implemented the Selective Service system after Congress approved it in 1940. Cherne also met Louis Johnson, the assistant secretary of the War Department. After conversations with Cherne, Johnson suggested that the Research Institute work with the War Department to inform business leaders of their responsibilities for military production in case of the advent of war.[27]

Cherne, Casey, and other Research Institute staff traveled to Washington and examined the mass of confidential material collected by the Planning Branch. After four days, the group returned to New York. Using a Dictaphone and four transcribers, in six days Cherne wrote a report titled *Adjusting Your Business to War*. Louis Johnson wrote the foreword. It was a straightforward, concise, dispassionate analysis of what would happen to American business if the United States went to war. Ten thousand copies were printed and these were distributed only to Institute members. When published in fall 1938, it made no ripple and many did not bother to read it, as they did not believe that war was even a remote possibility.[28]

The War Department, however, was pleased; and the Institute established itself as a legitimate player in industrial mobilization. Johnson asked for the assistance of Institute staff in preparing the mobilization plan then in progress. Cherne agreed and spent half of each week in Washington for the next six months. Other Institute staff assisted in this process. In late 1938 Cherne was invited to meet with Munitions Building staff and to lecture at the Army Industrial College, which trained Army officers for responsibilities in economic mobilization. The Institute also assisted in drawing up the curricula for industrial mobilization studies at Georgetown University's School of Foreign Service, City College of New York, and Harvard University. Cherne was made an honorary member of Georgetown's faculty and eventually became a member of Georgetown's Institute for World Policy.[29]

As the Army had no appropriation for planning economic mobilization, the Institute was not compensated for staff time or expenses. However, Cherne and Hovgard believed that their unpaid effort was worth it. The Institute was building good connections with governmental agencies, and these relationships would pay off if paid off the United States went to war. Hovgard and Cherne decided to exploit their opening by establishing a Washington office for the Institute. William Casey, an anti-Roosevelt Republican but a strong international interventionist, was sent to direct the office. Casey built up a staff of experts who soon worked closely with the Office of Price Administration (OPA) and many other federal agencies.[30]

When Germany seized the remainder of Czechoslovakia in March 1939, there was a general belief among military leaders that a European war was imminent. Cherne immediately went to Washington, where he was included in meetings of the Planning Branch. He also met a widening circle of officers within the War and Navy Departments. Due to many changes in the mobilization plan, Cherne concluded that *Adjusting Your Business to War*

needed updating. The new edition of *Adjusting Your Business to War* was published in the spring of 1939.[31] The revision included Johnson's original introduction but was expanded to twice the size of the first edition, for it was
based on the 3,000-page Industrial Mobilization Plan.

Unlike the first edition, the second one received a great deal of attention—most of it negative. *Adjusting Your Business to War* alerted labor unions
to the existence of the Industrial Mobilization Plan, which, they believed,
if put into effect, would eliminate the progress that they had made during
the presidency of Franklin Roosevelt. To express their anxiety, a delegation
of labor leaders met with Secretary of Labor Frances Perkins. They so
alarmed her that she rushed over to the White House to demand an audience with the president. She then expressed to Roosevelt her hostility to
the entire concept of an Industrial Mobilization Plan. Persuaded that it
threatened to be the introduction of a corporate state, Perkins insisted that
the entire plan was without merit and if implemented, would create a semi-
fascist control over labor. Roosevelt assured her that he had never authorized the Industrial Mobilization Plan.[32]

Secretary of War Harry H. Woodring, Louis Johnson's boss, was an isolationist, and was also opposed to any planning for the possibility of war.
Johnson and Woodring had had repeated disagreements over this and other
issues related to preparing for a possible war. Woodring called Roosevelt's attention to *Adjusting Your Business to War* during a cabinet meeting. The *Annals
of the American Academy of Political and Social Science,* in a scathing review,
called *Adjusting Your Business to War* "a blueprint for Fascism" which ne-
glected to tell how "this Leviathan, once established, could ever be immobi-
lized." The "America First" movement, led by Charles Lindbergh, opposed
any effort to prepare the nation for war. Simultaneously, Norman Thomas,
the Socialist candidate for President, was a pacifist and therefore was also
against American rearmament.[33]

A reporter noticed that Louis Johnson had written the foreword and
asked President Roosevelt if Johnson's piece meant that the administration
endorsed the work. Roosevelt said he had not read it, but alleged that 90
percent of such books were written by people who knew nothing about
the subject. Johnson had no right to write the preface, announced Roosevelt. Roosevelt's reaction was newsworthy and several newspapers mentioned Cherne's work. Senator Bennett Champ Clark of Missouri saw the
news accounts and tried to acquire a copy. Senator Clark then attacked the
book, and Cherne, on the Senate floor on October 23, 1939. Clark did
give Cherne a backhanded compliment, however, when he said, "Mr.
Cherne's book may be taken as the Bible and Testament of what is intended

under the Army mobilization plan." Other isolationists joined the attack. When Cherne spoke about the book at a meeting in New England, a member of the audience stood up and asked those present to censure the group's board of directors for inviting Cherne to speak.[34] Within a matter of days, the entire Industrial Mobilization Plan was junked.[35]

The controversy did bring increased sales of the Institute's book. Within a few short months, *Adjusting Your Business to War* had sold 17,000 copies, which in those days made it a best-seller. And as a consequence of Clark's attack, Cherne was now identified as a leader of the intervention- ists.[36] Cherne was stunned by these rebuffs; nevertheless, he believed that war was inevitable and planning for war was prudent in any case. He launched a lecture tour. Cherne's presentations were lucid and orderly. His favorite speech was "M-Day" (Mobilization Day). Its theme was: "Control by prior- ities will be the keystone of any control over industries exercised by the gov- ernment in a war period." He reported that it would then "become necessary to divert labor, capital, and raw materials from industrial operations of a character nonessential to the purposes of the war to activities which are essential."[37] Based on his speech, *Harper's Magazine* asked him to write an ar- ticle on M-Day. When the article was published, the editors of Simon and Shuster asked him to expand and revise the article into a question-and- answer form: the lavish pamphlet was published with the title *M-Day and What it Means to You*. Of this popularized version, the Springfield *Republican* said: "Cherne has really written what, in another time, might be regarded as anti-war propaganda."[38]

The Institute capitalized on this new visibility by publishing a loose- leaf book called *War Coordinator*, selling for $55.[39] The *War Coordinator* made its debut on October 15, 1939. By the time this work was published, Ger- many had attacked Poland and the war in Europe had begun. The possibil- ity that America might become involved in war had increased dramatically, and this work served as a blueprint for business leaders to plan for convert- ing a consumer economy into war production. Cherne sent free copies to 500 Army and Navy officers.[40] Cherne also wrote a 58-page pamphlet on mobilization and sent it out gratis to leaders in the War Department, the Navy Department, and the newly created National Defense Advisory Com- mission concerned with Industrial Mobilization.[41]

Cherne, Casey, and other Institute staff hit the road to conduct major conferences on M-Day in large cities all over the country. They attracted thousands of new members for the Institute, which by 1941, had over 20,000 members and a staff of 350. Cherne continued as editor-in-chief, but his reg- ular absences made it difficult to fulfill his usual jobs. Aaron Levenstein, who had won the case against the American Bar Association, agreed to help edit publications.[42] Cherne's next step was to go on radio with a series of programs on M-Day. This led to his own show, called "Impact!" focusing on national and international developments during the week. This increased visibility brought still more business to the Institute.[43]

Not all the publicity that Cherne and the Institute gained was positive. The *Saturday Evening Post* published a less-than-flattering article about the Institute titled "The Rover Boys, 1941." It avowed that the Institute proved that "youngsters of sufficient brass and wit can still flourish in the big city, not only in spite of a major depression but because of it." This article was not particularly favorable to the Institute and Cherne claimed that only threats of a lawsuit encouraged the *Saturday Evening Post* editors to remove false statements. One mocking comment in the article was: "Cherne is hammering away with renewed vigor at a theme dating from 1938: watch the Far East! There America's real war will start." This article with the mocking statement was published on October 11, 1941, less than two months before the United States became involved in war in the Far East.[44]

The Institute had been making such projections for the previous two years. During the summer of 1939, the Institute's *Report* predicted that war in Europe would begin before the end of the year. On August 30, the *Report* stated that war was inevitable and that it was just hours away from beginning. Three days later, Germany invaded Poland and World War II commenced.[45] In January 1940, the Institute's *Business & Legislative Report* advised its members that the military danger point for the United States was in Asia, not in Europe. In April 1941 the *Report* urged members to keep their "eyes on the Far East." While the Japanese and American diplomatic leaders met in Washington for peace discussions, the *Report* warned again about the high probability of war between the United States and Japan in the Pacific. This warning was published on December 6, 1941, one day before the Japanese attacked Pearl Harbor.[46]

Fighting World War II

Even before the United States was attacked, Cherne's efforts in Washington had paid off. In April 1941, the War Department asked the Institute to conduct a study of the German economy. At the time, the United States knew nothing about the German industrial mobilization. Cherne was asked to form a group of scholars "to piece together the anatomy of German industrial mobilization." To help carry out this assignment, Cherne recruited refugees, such as Julius Hirsh, who had played a key role shaping price controls in Germany during their great inflation after World War I. Hirsh and others possessed a body of knowledge that no American had regarding the intricacies and problems of managing inflation. He had escaped Germany and fled to Denmark. When the German armies overran Denmark, Hirsh escaped to Sweden. From Sweden, he traveled to Finland, the Soviet Union, Japan, and finally landed in the United States. Hirsh and other knowledgeable refugees helped complete the study to the satisfaction of the military.[47]

After the United States entered the war, Cherne assisted the government in other critical studies. The Board of Economic Warfare, for instance, asked him to prepare a report on the problems anticipated in the reoccupation of the Solomon and other Pacific islands captured by the Japanese.[48]

In addition to its government work, the Institute advised businessmen as to the constant flood of bewildering wartime regulations. Because Cherne had worked with many federal departments for almost two years, the Institute was looked upon as the expert on federal legislation when America entered the war. From their analysis, the Institute mailed a steady stream of bulletins and newsletters summarizing and explaining these regulations. This required a larger staff. In a time of acute shortage of talented staff, Cherne assembled and trained a new cadre, capable of making government "gobbledygook" understandable to bewildered businessmen.[49] Cherne repackaged their material and in six weeks polished off *Your Business Goes to War,* which was published by Houghton Mifflin in 1942.[50]

Cherne, Hovgard, and Casey were concerned about being drafted. But they were also convinced that if they left the Institute, it would crumble. Cherne and Hovgard took advantage of deferments as essential personnel necessary for the war effort. Casey joined the Navy and was commissioned an officer on June 15, 1943. He was assigned to General William J. Donovan who had directed the London-based Office of Strategic Services (OSS), the forerunner of the Central Intelligence Agency.[51]

Leon Henderson, formerly at the Office of Price Administration, was hired to fill Casey's position as head of the Institute's Washington office.[52] Another important staff addition was Irving Stone, the pen name of Irving Tannenbaum. His first book, a biography about Vincent van Gogh, was rejected by seventeen publishers before it was released in 1934 as *Lust for Life.* It was an immediate best seller. His second work, *Clarence Darrow for the Defense,* was just as successful. Cherne had known Stone since the late 1930s. In 1939 Cherne first visited Hollywood and he stayed at Stone's home in

Encino, just over the hill from Hollywood. Stone had problems with the Screen Writers Guild, which he believed was controlled by Communists. As he could not write screenplays without approval from the Guild, he left Hollywood and moved to New York to take up another line of work. He became fascinated with the Research Institute and served as an editor for a year and wrote a small book on the history of the Research Institute. Stone did not have the necessary background in law and government, and so after a year he left to pursue other opportunities.[53]

Before most Americans believed that the end of the war was in sight, Cherne wrote his second best-selling book, *The Rest of Your Life*, focusing on the conversion from war production to a peacetime economy. Irving Stone, when on the Institute staff, had introduced Cherne to the editors at Doubleday Doran, then the largest publisher in the world. Doubleday Doran published the book, which received wide circulation, selling more than 230,000 copies within one year of its publication date. Wendell Willkie, the Republican candidate for president in 1940, called Cherne's book "an extremely provocative analysis." Another reviewer found it "an amazingly complete inventory of the raw material from which the new world will be built." The *New York Post* called Cherne a "prophet with honor in his own day."[54]

Throughout the war, Cherne contributed articles to newspapers and magazines, including the *Saturday Evening Post, Atlantic Monthly, Liberty,* and *Collier's.*[55] In addition, Cherne prepared a column for the Office of War Information, which was circulated internationally. His radio program "Impact!" was broadcast three times per week on WOR and an estimated three million people listened in. The program focused on the wartime developments and regulations, and on economic issues affecting America. After the war, Cherne continued these broadcasts and often made guest appearances on other programs, such as "The Home Show," moderated by Hugh Downs. Cherne also frequently debated with prominent political leaders such as Everett Dirksen, Robert Taft, Harold Stassen and Norman Cousins.[56]

Epilogue

- Cherne and Stone remained friends until Stone's death in 1989. After Stone left the Research Institute, he wrote seven more best-selling books, including *The Agony and the Ecstasy* about Michelangelo and the *Passions of the Mind* about Sigmund Freud.

- Cherne continued to lecture at the Industrial College of the Armed Forces for thirty-eight years and was made an honorary member of their faculty.

- William Casey, whom Cherne had hired in his first job in 1938, years later became President of the Export-Import Bank, the Undersecretary of State for Economic Affairs, Chairman of the Securities and Exchange Commission, and Director of the Central Intelligence Agency.

- In 1960, the Research Institute celebrated its twentieth-fifth anniversary by giving out medals to prominent Americans. Among those Cherne and Hovgard chose to receive the medallion were: Bernard Baruch, "the great mind behind industrial mobilization;" Frances Perkins, who had opposed the Industrial Mobilization Plan in 1939; Louis Hershey, who developed the plan for military mobilization in case of war; Leon Henderson, who was the first director of the Office of Price Administration and subsequently a Research Institute employee; and General Lucius Clay, who was responsible for defense materiel during World War II and had been closely connected with Cherne during the late 1940s and the 1950s.[57]

- Cherne called the defeat of Hitler "the most honorable obsession of my life."[58]

Chapter 3

Rescuing the Postwar World

Control points have been set up [by the Communists] at 61 streets crossing the border. Another 28 streets are completely shut off. You can see workmen building barricades to seal the Western part of Berlin from the surrounding countryside. Homes and stores are being evacuated to establish 'a zone of death' around Berlin like that which now bars escape along the entire West German border. Temporary shelters have been improvised. When I arrived, Berlin had 72 camps. When I left one week later there were 82. One camp had been improvised on three hours' notice to shelter 500 persons; when I was there it held 4,200.

—Leo Cherne, cable from West Berlin, 1953

Prologue

By February 1945, the defeat of Germany was imminent. The three major Allied leaders—Roosevelt, Churchill, and Stalin—met in Yalta to shape postwar Europe. With the unconditional surrender of Germany in May 1945, the victors carried out their agreement to divide the country into four zones of occupation administered by the British in the north, the French in the west, the Soviets in the east, and the Americans in the south. Germany's capital, Berlin, was deep inside the Soviet zone and was also divided into four sectors.

At the war's end Europe lay in ruins. The United Kingdom, though it had not been invaded, was financially prostrate and many of its cities had been destroyed by the German blitz. On the continent, from France to the Ukraine and from Italy to Norway, cities lay in ruins, economies were destroyed, and homeless and hopeless refugees clogged damaged roads.

Uniting Nations

Many people hoped that the allies would continue to work together to ensure world peace after World War II. These hopes rested on the creation of an international organization with the ability to resolve conflicts before they arose and to end them when they unexpectedly broke out. The term *United Nations*, devised by President Roosevelt, was first used in the "Declaration by United Nations" issued January 1, 1942 by representatives of twenty-six nations, committing them to continue fighting together against the Axis Powers until victory was achieved. In August 1944, representatives of the United States, the Soviet Union, and the United Kingdom met at Dumbarton Oaks in Washington, DC, and agreed to create an international organization to preserve peace. This agreement, confirmed at Yalta, led to an international conference in San Francisco held from April 25 to June 26, 1945, during which the United Nations Charter was drawn up by the representatives of fifty countries amid high hopes all around the world.

One group supporting the creation of the United Nations was the Americans United for World Organization (AUWO). The group believed that the failure of the League of Nations after World War I was partly due to the refusal of the United States to join. The AUWO strongly supported American participation in a new international organization after World War II. Cherne joined AUWO's board in 1943. This had three important consequences. The first was that Cherne strongly supported the 1944 Bretton Woods conference, which created the International Monetary Fund. On behalf of the AUWO, Cherne wrote a monograph about the significance of the conference, which he believed was the cornerstone for world peace. The second consequence was that Cherne met Norman Cousins, another AUWO board member and an influential activist who became the editor of the *Saturday Review*. Their lives were entwined—often stormily—for the following quarter century. The final consequence was that Cherne came into contact with others interested in world federalism. Cherne eventually joined the negotiating team as a representative of the AUWO to form an alliance of like-minded groups resulting in the formation of United World Federalists.[1]

In late April 1945, Cherne covered the U.N. conference as radio station WOR correspondent, and as a representative of AUWO. He attended sessions, consulted with technical experts, and interviewed delegates. Cherne went to San Francisco a strong internationalist, advocating for a world organization with the military power to enforce peace and prevent war. This policy was not adopted. Cherne wrote in one article ("Failure at

Frisco") that the United Nations simply reinforced the old national sovereignties; it would not prevent war: "Neither the individual governments, nor their delegates in San Francisco, nor the people in the countries they represent are yet willing to take the real first step that will actually begin to eliminate war. No one nation is yet willing to give up its sovereign powers as a nation—to live under a higher law." He proclaimed: "When the police have to ask permission of the guilty to act, you have no police. When peace depends on the willingness of any one nation to keep it, war has not been ended."[2]

Rebuilding Germany

Perhaps the greatest single postwar concern was what to do with Germany. The Russians demanded reparations from the Germans, who had caused severe destruction and an estimated twenty million deaths in the Soviet Union. The Soviets trucked away machines and whole factories from their zone of occupation; they also kidnapped thousands of craftsmen and scientists and carted them off to the Soviet Union. In the United States, a similar policy was debated. Henry Morgenthau, Jr., the Secretary of the Treasury under Presidents Roosevelt and Truman, developed a plan to dismember Germany, destroy its industrial base, and create an agricultural and pastoral nation ensuring that it would never again be able to wage war. Some factories in the Western zones of occupation were dismantled, and at the insistence of Moscow, industrial plants were shipped to the Soviet Union or to the Soviet zone of occupation in Germany. Debate soared within the Truman administration whether to continue this policy. In part, the debate centered around the political intentions of the Soviet Union.

Those opposed to the Morgenthau plan, among them Cherne's friend Leon Henderson, submitted an alternate plan calling for reconstruction of postwar Germany. This plan was based on the central concept that Germany was important to the economic recovery of Europe. It provided for joint allied control of defeated Germany, preservation of a large part of German industry, a "minimum standard of living" for the German people, and no dismemberment of Germany.[3] With Roosevelt's death, Henderson's plan was set aside, but it was revived in September 1945. Cherne was approached by David K. Niles, President Truman's administrative assistant, who supported Henderson. Niles was a Jewish immigrant who had been active in creating what later became the International Rescue Committee, where Cherne probably first met him.[4] Niles had subsequently become one of

President Roosevelt's trusted personal aides and was one of the few Roosevelt aides retained by President Truman. Niles asked Leo Cherne to unofficially visit Germany to size up the real situation and make policy recommendations. As the mission was unofficial, Cherne could not go as a representative of the White House. Cherne wanted to go as a military correspondent, and Niles brokered a meeting in New York with Jacob Landau, the managing director of the Overseas News Agency. Landau consented to credential Cherne as a reporter provided that Cherne actually write articles for the Overseas Network.[5] Before his departure, Cherne gathered dozens of letters of introduction, mainly from refugees in the United States, addressed to key leaders in Germany, France, the United Kingdom, and Belgium.

Cherne left for Europe on a military transport on October 30, 1945.[6] Excluding travel, he covered his own expenses and walked so much that he had to buy military boots to make it through the mud. He met and interviewed ranking officials, including General Lucius Clay, the military administrator of the American zone of occupation in Germany. Cherne had first met him during the war, when Clay was the Army's Director of Materiel.[7] Cherne raised money for War Bonds, and Clay helped.[8] When they met in Germany, Clay invited Cherne to attend meetings of the Allied Control Council and Cherne saw first-hand how ineffective it was.[9] From Germany, Cherne traveled to Paris and then to the United Kingdom, leaving to return to the United States on December 4, 1945.

Cherne filed stories for the Overseas News Agency and participated in radio broadcasts in which he described his experiences and thoughts about the postwar world.[10] He also wrote up several special reports on his observations in France, the United Kingdom, Germany, and Europe in general.[11] What Cherne found alarmed him. He saw the United Kingdom and France deep in economic distress, unable to begin the reconstruction needed to rebuild after the devastation of war. He was more disturbed by conditions in Germany. He concluded that the destruction of the German economy would lead to disaster. The intent of the Morgenthau plan, Cherne later reported, was based on a "fantasy" and its implementation was "very counterproductive" to American interests. He was alarmed by the Soviet Union: he deeply doubted their professed good intentions.[12] Cherne forwarded these reports to Niles, Henderson, and perhaps to Truman, and contributed in a small way to the rapidly growing support to change American policies positively toward Germany and negatively toward the Soviet Union.[13]

To revive Europe economically, the United States launched the Marshall Plan. While the offer for aid was extended to the Soviet Union and the

Soviet-occupied countries in Eastern Europe, their governments declined to participate in the program.

Emperoring with MacArthur

While in Europe, Cherne met Douglas MacArthur II, who may have been partly responsible for Cherne's next international mission. Four months after Cherne returned from Europe, he was on his way to Japan to assist General Douglas MacArthur. MacArthur had fought in World War I and become the U.S. Army chief of staff in 1930, then had become the head of the army in the Philippines, at that time a U.S. commonwealth. When Japan attacked in December 1941, MacArthur defended the Philippines. President Roosevelt, concerned that defeat was imminent, ordered MacArthur to escape to Australia. There MacArthur organized the thrust against Japanese military forces in the Southwestern Pacific, eventually liberating the Philippines in late 1944. His popularity in America soared. When MacArthur accepted the surrender of the Japanese leaders in September 1945, he was one of America's most beloved military heroes.

Rather than return home to a hero's welcome, MacArthur remained in Japan, where he became the supreme allied commander. One of his goals was to restructure the Japanese economy to destroy the power of the *Zaibatsu*, Japan's leading industrial groups. The Zaibatsu, in turn, were controlled by about ninety families who monopolized Japan's wealth. MacArthur wanted to redistribute this wealth and stimulate growth of the middle class. He believed that democracy would not take root in Japan unless there was a strong and vibrant middle class, which at the time was almost nonexistent.

On April 1, 1946, Major General O. P. Echols, director of the Civil Affairs Division in the War Department, sent Cherne an official letter offering him the position of taxation specialist with the goal of preparing a Japanese tax law for presentation to the Diet in May. According to Echols, this was "one of the most important and difficult functions of the control and administration of occupied Japan." Echols understood that Cherne had "commitments which cannot be overlooked," but hoped that Cherne might see his "way clear to accept an appointment of such national importance."[14]

At the time, Cherne's impressions of MacArthur were not positive. Cherne recalled that it was MacArthur who led the Army in dispersing the Bonus Marchers in Washington in the 1930s. His image of MacArthur was that of a jingoistic patriot. To Cherne, he epitomized the maxim, "Patriotism is the last refuge of the scoundrel." So Cherne consulted others on the advisability of accepting the offer to work with MacArthur. Roger Baldwin, one of the founders of the American Civil Liberties Union, strongly advised Cherne to go to Japan. Baldwin had met MacArthur and "thought he had seen God." MacArthur, said Baldwin, was devoted to civil liberties.[15] Cherne agreed to perform the work and made sure newspapers were informed of his departure and his important new responsibilities.[16]

En route to Japan, Cherne stopped off in Hollywood to give a speech to the World Federalists, led by Clarence Streit, who believed that the only alternative to recurring war was an international body strong enough to control the sovereignty of independent nation-states.[17] At this meeting were Daryl Zanuck, Douglas Fairbanks, Will Rogers, Hedda Hopper, and Edward G. Robinson. They had come to hear Harold Urey—one of the creators of the atomic bomb and the 1933 Nobel Prize winner in chemistry. Cherne's address outshone Urey's and Cherne received an ovation that continued until he rose to say more. At this meeting Cherne established relationships with important Hollywood leaders, whom he would later exploit.[18]

From Los Angeles, Cherne flew to San Francisco and was scheduled to leave immediately for Japan, but his orders had been improperly issued, so he was unable to leave until April 13. He arrived in Tokyo two days later and immediately was ushered into a session with MacArthur, who preferred to meet people when they were exhausted from the travel. MacArthur, recalled Cherne, "was very intent on the democratization of Japan. He was very clear in his mind about what the impediments to that would be."[19] MacArthur charged Cherne with formulating tax and other incentive legislation to confiscate the wealth of the Zaibatsu and encourage the growth of a viable middle class. He asked Cherne to "recommend the means by which Japan could be encouraged toward the rebirth of its economy in ways which would not only be successful, but which would re-enforce a democratic society."[20]

Since Cherne was not an expert on taxation, he had asked Charles Siegel, the head of the Research Institute of America's tax department, to join him in Japan to deal with this very complicated subject.[21] Cherne was also ignorant of Japanese tax law and other aspects of Japanese life, so he selected Japanese staffers to assist him. He evaluated a number of résumés of distinguished men who had been cleared of any significant involvement in the war effort. From these, Cherne interviewed several candidates, finally selecting several associates, including Hayato Ikeda from the Japanese Tax Bureau and Kiichi Miyazawa from the Finance Ministry.

Cherne was suspicious of what had prompted MacArthur to select him in the first place. Within the first week, MacArthur raised the issue of American politics, asking Cherne what MacArthur's chances were for nomination to the U.S. presidency in 1948. Cherne reported that MacArthur would be welcomed as an extraordinary hero if he returned to the United States, but that MacArthur did not have a viable political base. MacArthur insisted that his base of support was the conservative wing of the Republican party and never absorbed Cherne's conviction that his chances were very slim. Despite Cherne's response, MacArthur plowed ahead with his plans to seek the Republican Party's nomination for president.[22]

Another topic of conversation startled Cherne. MacArthur stated: "I've been identified, perhaps more than any other American, with defense as the safest assurance of peace, preparedness as the only reliable weapon against the threat of war. I now believe there is only one antidote to war: world government." The atom bomb had convinced MacArthur that there must be no more war. MacArthur believed that it was absolutely essential to charter a world federal government with power to prevent war. The revelation that MacArthur was a closet world federalist astonished Cherne, who radically revised his preconceptions about MacArthur.[23]

By any standard, MacArthur was an extraordinary figure. To many Japanese, MacArthur served as their visible emperor. He played the role well: Japanese crowds mobbed the sidewalk to watch him enter his place of work at precisely the same time every day. Likewise, he always left at the same time to ensure that he would be noticed by the Japanese. In meetings with Cherne, MacArthur always stood and paced while his visitor was required to sit. Cherne believed that this was a control technique used by MacArthur to have the other person constantly looking up at him. Cherne also thought that it was significant that MacArthur had only one sculpture in his office—that of Alexander the Great.

Regardless of MacArthur's eccentricities, Cherne was enormously impressed with his intellect. When Cherne presented his tax plan, he expressed his willingness to explain the plan to MacArthur, as it contained highly technical and complicated content. Rather than listen to Cherne's explanation, MacArthur asked him to leave the plan and return the following day. Cherne came back prepared to review the 120-page plan, but as he recalled years later, there was not a thing in the plan that he had to explain. MacArthur had mastered its contents on his own.

MacArthur presented two objections to Cherne's plan. Cherne had recommended reopening the Japanese stock exchange. According to Cherne, MacArthur was adamant that as long as he was the supreme commander, he would not reinstate the exchange, which was "an instrument for gambling. It serves no useful economic function." Cherne explained to MacArthur that the reopening of the stock market was a critical component of his plan to confiscate the equities of the wealthier Japanese. Some means had to be found to monitor who was selling what to whom, and the stock exchange kept records of transactions. But nothing Cherne said succeeded in persuading MacArthur, who was a nineteenth-century populist with an aversion to moneychangers, Wall Street, and "Eastern decadent devices."

MacArthur's second objection was to Cherne's recommendation to institute the plan by fiat. MacArthur intended to present the plan to the Japanese Diet for consideration. According to Cherne's account, MacArthur believed that this action had to be "taken by the Japanese government. They've got to learn to govern themselves. One of my objects is to build a democracy which functions here." Cherne reported that while he was in total agreement with MacArthur's purpose, he believed that the Diet would debate the matter for months; assets had to be confiscated or they would disappear very quickly. MacArthur understood the risk, but he was convinced that the Japanese must learn to think for themselves. MacArthur had made up his mind and that was the end of the matter.[24]

Cherne's group finished the tax plan on schedule and MacArthur approved it—or so Cherne thought—and the revised tax law was submitted to the Japanese Diet. For ninety days, the Communist labor union paralyzed the effort to confiscate the equities of the wealthiest Japanese. The Communists masterminded this, reported Cherne years later, to increase the perception of injustice, cause anarchy and economic dislocation, and thus better their prospects. The Communists did not want social or agrarian reform: "they wanted exactly the opposite." During this time, as Cherne had predicted, a large portion of the equities passed into other hands and were no longer readily accessible for confiscation when the law passed.[25]

Before Cherne had arrived in Japan, MacArthur had received a request from the Chinese Government for an American economist to help deal effectively with the Chinese economic catastrophe. The request had been made by T. V. Soong, who was very close to the Chinese leader Chiang Kai-shek, then engaged in a civil war with the Communists led by Mao Tse-tung. On the day of Cherne's arrival MacArthur asked him to accept the assignment. Cherne, who knew nothing about China, stalled, telling MacArthur that he would visit Soong in Shanghai for a weekend to see what he could do. At the same time, Cherne asked Leon Henderson what to do. Henderson responded that it would be almost impossible to succeed under these circumstances, because Soong's family was the problem.[26]

When Cherne was asked if he'd had plague shots, he said no and was refused permission to depart. As it would take two weeks for the shots to take effect, Cherne refused to go to Shanghai and made plans to return to the United States. While waiting for military transportation, Cherne met with several correspondents, whom he briefed "off the record" about his tax plan. Shortly thereafter, Cherne's commentary was cited in several American newspaper articles, including the *New York Times*. Cherne returned home on May 21, 1946. Neither the citations nor Cherne's return to the United States pleased MacArthur.[27]

Cherne's several letters thereafter to MacArthur received no reply. However, he continued to communicate with others whom he had met in Japan. He was upset to hear that his revised tax plan was revised again. MacArthur denied that he had ever approved Cherne's plan. So the plan was revised some more. Then it was altered again. When the bill finally passed the Japanese Diet in September 1946, not a single aspect of Cherne's original tax program remained.[28]

After returning from Japan, Cherne immediately went on the Bessie Beatty radio program and others to discuss his trip. During the summer, he regularly visited Grossinger's—a Jewish resort hotel in the Catskills, then a mecca for Broadway and Hollywood stars. As soon as an airport opened near Grossinger's, Cherne flew up as a passenger from New York. After a month of commuting, he took flying lessons. By the end of the summer, he flew solo.[29] One of his passengers was Eleanor Roosevelt, whom Cherne had met on the Freedom House board. They remained close friends and saw each other regularly thereafter.

Another person Cherne took up in his airplane was Bill Casey, just back from serving in the OSS during World War II. Unfortunately, on this trip Cherne forgot to replace the gas cap when he filled up and the tank quickly lost fuel. Cherne managed to get the plane down, but Casey refused ever to fly with him again. Another anxiety-producing experience occurred when his plane's engine stopped in midflight. Cherne was able to restart the engine, but he decided never to pilot his own plane again.[30]

During the 1940s, Cherne continued to work as a commentator for a television program at WOR Mutual. When 1948 rolled around, WOR asked Cherne to cover the Democratic and Republican Conventions. MacArthur attended the Republican convention, but, as Cherne had predicted, was not even considered for the nomination. At this convention, and also at the 1952 Republican Convention, MacArthur refused even to acknowledge Cherne.

The International Rescue Committee

Aaron Levenstein retained his links to the Socialist Party and by 1946 served on its National Executive Committee. Through the Socialist Party, Levenstein met Sheba Strunsky and Hollingsworth Wood, both members of the board of the International Rescue and Relief Committee (IRRC). Strunsky and Wood were looking for businessmen to add to the IRRC's board. The IRRC had had an illustrious but complex history. Two years after the creation of the European-based International Relief Association (IRA) in 1931, the *New York Times* announced the formation of an American counterpart founded by Albert Einstein, who had arrived in the United States in 1933. Soon thereafter, John Dewey, the philosopher and educator from Columbia University, and Reinhold Niebuhr, one of the foremost Protestant theologians in America, formed the American committee of the IRA. The purpose of the European organization was to assist "victims of civil oppression in many lands without reference to religious or political faith." The purpose of the American committee, chaired by Amos Pinchot, was to solicit funds to assist refugees suffering as a result of Hitler's regime. The money raised was sent to Mayor Charles Hueber of Strasbourg, France, the treasurer of the IRA.[31]

Among the founding members of the American committee, in addition to Dewey and Niebuhr, were Sterling Spero, political scientist and educator from New York University; Upton Sinclair, socialist politician and writer; Bryn Hovde, then of the University of Pittsburgh, who later helped establish the New School for Social Research (which hired many German refugees) and David K. Niles, then at Ford Hall Forum in Boston and subsequently administrative assistant to Presidents Roosevelt and Truman. Other prominent Americans who joined the board included David Dubinsky, president of the International Ladies Garment Workers Union, William Borah, senator from Idaho, and Jay Lovestone, a former leader in the Communist Party who had broken with Moscow during the 1920s and became a top American Federation of Labor thinker.[32] Although not a member of the board, one of the volunteers who helped place refugees in colleges and university positions was Peter F. Drucker.[33]

The European International Relief Association was antifascist and supported the Loyalists fighting against General Franco who received aid from Mussolini and Hitler during the Spanish Civil War. The Loyalists, on the other hand, received assistance from the Soviet Union. When the war turned against the Loyalists, the IRA helped resettle the left-wing refugees flooding out of Spain. At the time, Cherne was aware of the American committee of the IRA and supported its efforts on behalf of the Loyalists.[34] The European IRA moved to Paris and finally disintegrated when the German military marched into France in May 1940.

The 1940 armistice between Nazi Germany and Vichy France required that the French arrest and return all refugees who had escaped from German-occupied Europe. This imperiled thousands of refugees who had fled to Vichy-controlled France. On June 25, 1940, the American Friends of German Freedom held a luncheon in New York. Reinhold Niebuhr appealed for contributions and $3,500 was raised. A new American group, the Emergency Rescue Committee, was formed specifically to spirit political, religious, and intellectual leaders out of German-occupied Europe.

Varian Fry, an American who spoke French and was then the Headline Book series editor of the Foreign Policy Association in New York, was selected to establish an escape route for prominent refugees believed to be trapped in southern France. At the time, confusion reigned in Marseilles. The Gestapo had not yet arrived, but the Vichy French officials refused to issue exit visas. However, they paid little attention to refugees who possessed foreign visas. In Marseilles, Fry teamed up with others, including Carel Sternberg, a young Czech refugee student who had escaped Paris on a bicycle just ahead of the German Army. The group forged papers, smuggled refugees to the Spanish border, and acquired transit visas through Spain and Portugal. At least two thousand prominent leaders were rescued by this operation during its thirteen-month existence, including the political philosopher Hannah Arendt, the Russian artist Marc Chagall, the sculptor Jacques Lipchitz, the German Surrealist painter Max Ernst, the harpsichordist Wanda Landowska, and the writer Franz Werfel and his wife Alma Werfel, who escaped with her husband's draft manuscript of what became *The Song of Bernadette*.[35] After thirteen months, the Marseilles operation was raided and closed by the French Vichy police; Fry and others barely escaped.

Despite their world-famous talents, getting these refugees into the United States was not an easy task. The Secretary of the Department of Labor, Frances Perkins, recognized that those brought into the United States by the ERC were a national treasure, but the immigration statutes were hostile to individuals with attitudes that diverged from mainstream Americans, such as those who believed in socialism or radicalism.[38] But the

ERC found that persistence paid off and most refugees entered the United States eventually.

Among the leaders of the Emergency Rescue Committee were H. William Fitelson, a young lawyer who would become prominent as an attorney in theatrical and publishing law, and Joseph Buttinger, who was an Austrian émigré. Buttinger had been born on an impoverished Bavarian farm, but after finishing elementary school, he went to work in an Austrian glass factory. Subsequently, he became leader of the Austrian Socialist youth movement. By the age of twenty-four, he was a secretary of the Social Democratic Party, an ally of the Austrian labor unions. He was imprisoned for several months in 1934 and became the leader of the Socialist underground and a top leader of the anti-Nazi movement in Austria.

Buttinger met and married Muriel Gardiner, a wealthy American student who became a noted psychoanalyst. As an American citizen, Gardiner could easily serve as a courier. As the Gestapo was closing in on their operation, the Buttingers escaped Austria and settled in Paris. Several months before France fell to Germany, the Buttingers moved to the United States.[36]

Gardiner later wrote about her experiences in her memoir, *Code Named Mary*. Her experiences were strikingly similar to those described in Lillian Hellman's best-selling memoir *Pentimento: A Book of Portraits*, upon which the popular movie *Julia* was based. Hellman refused to identify the real Julia, but portrayed her as a childhood friend who died working in the Austrian underground in 1938. Gardiner had never met Hellman and no one in the Austrian underground remembered any other American woman who assisted them during that period other than Gardiner. However, Hellman and Gardiner did have a common friend to whom Gardiner had related her pre-World War II experiences in the Austrian underground. When this matter was brought to Hellman's attention, she denied that the model for her "Julia" was Gardiner, then refused to answer any further questions.[37]

Before the war, the ERA and the IRA had been funded by public subscription generated by antifascist fervor. During the war, they were funded by the National War Fund, similar to today's United Way. In 1942 the two groups merged to form the International Rescue and Relief Committee (IRRC). An early leader was Ernst Reuter, who had been a member of the Communist Party in Germany after World War I. He knew Lenin and had worked for Joseph Stalin. Reuter broke with the Communists and became a prominent Social Democrat. Forced into exile when Hitler took power, he moved to Ankara, where he established refugee programs for the IRRC. He operated throughout World War II, assisting refugees unable to make it to the United States or the United Kingdom. After the war, Reuter returned to Berlin and was the first appointed mayor of the part of city occupied by the Western Allies.

After the war, those left on the board were those opposed to Communism, including many Socialists and ex-Trotskyites, who were leery of working with capitalists. With Levenstein's intervention, Strunsky and Hollingsworth had approached Cherne to join the IRRC's board as their first businessman. They wanted to use his name to attract others. Cherne consented and spent little time working on the organization's programs. His only early claim to fame was his recommendation that the organization shorten its name to International Rescue Committee (IRC), which it did.[39]

By 1950, Cherne wondered if his best days were behind him. He had not written a book in five years. His invitations to speak at major conferences had declined, and his article submissions to magazines were rejected. Although he occasionally appeared on television programs, his weekly radio engagements had ended. He spent little time in Washington developing new contacts, and other organizations competed successfully with the activities of the Research Institute. Carl Hovgard was deeply concerned with Cherne's productivity and commenced an extended series of discussions with accompanying memos.[40] In the midst of these discussions, events occurred in Eastern Europe that were soon to change Cherne's life.

Post–World War II Eastern Europe

In the final months of World War II, the Soviet Union occupied much of Eastern Europe and installed totalitarian Communist regimes, called "people's republics," which were supported externally by Soviet troops and a formidable array of internal secret police forces. Winston Churchill delivered a speech in Fulton, Missouri, in March 1946, in which he said: "From Stettin in the Baltic to Trieste in the Adriatic, an iron curtain has descended across the continent. Behind that line lie all the capitals of the ancient states of central and eastern Europe—Warsaw, Berlin, Prague, Vienna, Budapest, Belgrade, Bucharest and Sofia. All these famous cities and the populations around them lie in what I must call the Soviet sphere."[41] Thus Churchill publicized the phrase *Iron Curtain*.

In divided Berlin, Ernst Reuter, the representative of the IRC in Turkey who had been appointed mayor by the Western allies, was elected mayor of the entire city. The Soviets vetoed the election. On June 7, 1948, France, the United Kingdom, and the United States agreed to unite their three occupation zones and create a unified western Germany. Seventeen days later the Soviets retaliated by blockading the western sectors of Berlin deep inside the Soviet zone of Germany. They stopped all land traffic, including trucks and railroad trains carrying supplies to the city. If the allies used military power to insist on their right of access to Berlin, it might well have meant war with the Soviet Union, a war for which the western allies were unprepared. Reuter, fearful that the Western powers would cave in to Soviet demands to leave Berlin, asked Berliners to demonstrate their support for the allies. More than 300,000 Berliners rallied and voiced their support.

Rather than abandon West Berlin or precipitate a war with the Soviet Union, the Western Allies responded with an unprecedented airlift, delivering—week after week and month after month—food, fuel, and supplies needed by West Berlin's three million residents. Cherne, who had chaired the IRC's Executive Committee since 1948, visited Berlin and offered the IRC's willingness to assist General Clay. Cherne, along with the polar explorer retired Rear-Admiral Richard E. Byrd, Harvard University's president James Conant, and the former head of the OSS, William J. Donovan, led a national fundraising campaign on behalf of beleaguered West Berlin. The IRC generated tens of thousands of dollars in donations from Americans.

Throughout the winter, the Soviets doggedly maintained their blockade and the Western allies continued their airlift, confounding the critics who predicted failure. Fearful that the Berlin crisis could easily escalate into war, President Truman announced his intention to provide military aid to Western European countries in January 1949. Three months later, the North Atlantic Treaty Organization (NATO) was created to defend Western Europe against a potential Soviet invasion. As aid poured into Berlin, the Soviet leaders concluded that they could not eject the allies from Berlin with the blockade. They also concluded that the Berlin airlift was a solid allied propaganda victory. Failing to achieve their objective, the Soviets lifted their eleven-month blockade on May 12, 1949.

The Soviet Union did not give up their ambition to gain control of West Berlin. In 1950, Soviet and East German authorities organized East German youth to march into West Berlin and take over the city. The IRC worked closely with Mayor Reuter to counter this new thrust. The IRC's "Project Berlin" sent 4,224,000 pounds of milk, butter, and cheese for free distribution and offered these supplies—scarcities in East Germany—to all Berliners. The expected invasion did not materialize, perhaps because the Communist authorities were not interested in East German youth picking up scarce supplies distributed in West Berlin.[42]

Germans living in the Soviet zone of occupation continued to flee to West Berlin. In 1951 alone, 165,000 refugees from East Germany escaped to the West.[43] Unfortunately, the IRC was in tight financial straits in 1951. IRC staff member Richard Salzmann rallied supporters to meet the immediate financial crisis, but it was not enough. To make matters worse, IRC's board chairman, Reinhold Niebuhr, suffered a mild stroke and stepped down from his position. The IRC's board was convinced that the problem of political refugees from totalitarian societies had not diminished. While the IRC's board was persuaded of this, they saw no indication that the American people had the slightest awareness of refugees' problems nor shared an interest in them. Cherne was appointed chairman for an anticipated six-month stint, during which time he was expected to either phase out the organization or discover—though it seemed unlikely—a sound financial basis for continuing its work. To the surprise of many, Cherne managed to revive the IRC. A key factor was his extraordinarily successful approach to foundations. Lessing Rosenwald, who had helped resettle displaced persons in the aftermath of World War II, committed $100,000 and agreed to approach the Ford Foundation, which subsequently provided an additional grant of $500,000.[44]

These funds came at the right time, for refugees streamed out of East Germany in ever greater numbers. In 1952, the number of refugees entering West Berlin rose to 182,000. Cherne again traveled to Berlin to survey the situation. By January 1953, as many as 6,000 refugees a day were pouring into West Berlin. Berlin was still a war-shattered city: it had few facilities or resources to care for these new refugees. The winter of 1952–53 was brutal; the refugees arrived in deep snow and were housed in buildings and warehouses that were heavily damaged by the war. Unusable for anything else, they still had sufficient walls and ceilings left to shield people from the weather.[45] With the active encouragement of President Eisenhower, Cherne worked closely with Reuter to organize refugee shelters in Berlin and to mobilize substantial aid in the United States and Western Europe.[46]

Stalin died on March 5, 1953. The new Soviet leaders encouraged Walter Ulbricht, the Communist leader of East Germany, to liberalize his policies and stop enforced industrialization. Ulbricht ignored the advice and established new work quotas in June 1953. On June 16, a large demonstration of East German workers rallied in favor of lifting the quotas. The American radio station in Berlin broadcast the workers' demands. On the following day, East Germans rose up against Soviet and Communist control in Berlin and other cities.[47] During the following days, 400,000 East Germans demanded better working conditions. These demonstrations metamorphosed into demands for political reforms as well, but Soviet tank units crushed the rebellion. Tens of thousands of East Berliners escaped into West Berlin, totaling 330,000 by the end of the year.

In West Berlin, 300,000 people were out of work; but conditions were even worse in East Berlin. Reuter again appealed for aid and Cherne flew to Berlin to help establish new IRC programs to feed and resettle the new hoard of East German refugees. Cherne returned to Berlin again in the fall to deliver two million pounds of butter. East Berliners came to West Berlin and smuggled their butter across the border.[48] Cherne sent a radiogram to the Institute reporting on the situation; upon receipt in New York it was copied and mailed out to Institute members as a message "from the edge of the Iron Curtain." In one missive he reported that the Soviets had been badly hurt by the events in East Germany, yet he predicted that there would be no liberation of Eastern Europe any time soon.[49]

On one trip to Germany that year, Cherne and Richard Salzmann ventured into East Berlin. The two men wandered the streets, snapping tourist photos, which was illegal in East Germany. They were spotted and apprehended by the East Berlin police. Cherne demanded that they be taken to a Russian officer, because the East Germans had no direct relationship with the United States. The police located one and Cherne told him that they were tourists and gave him the film. The officer returned the camera; Cherne and Salzmann high-tailed it out of East Berlin.[50]

Another tourist in Berlin in 1953 was Daniel Patrick Moynihan, a student who had taken a break from his studies and traveled in Europe for a year. He did not meet Cherne or Salzmann in Berlin, but when he returned to the United States, he applied for a job at the IRC. Cherne interviewed and hired him to direct the IRC's public relations program. Moynihan, who had no background in public relations, performed well before he returned to complete his education.[51]

Upon Stalin's death, Reuter had urged maximum exploitation of the period of uncertainty in the Soviet Union. He believed that during power transitions, totalitarian societies were vulnerable. He and Cherne believed that this was especially valid with the death of Stalin, who held all the reins of power tightly in his own hands. Although Eisenhower had campaigned in 1952 on the theme of rolling back Communism in Europe, he made no progress in this area in 1953. Reuter and Cherne believed that through inaction the United States gave the Soviet Union a year in which to get its house in order. Stalin's death had indeed unleashed a power struggle among the Soviet Union's leadership. The chief of the Soviet secret police, Lavrenti Beria, was shot by an agent of a coalition of prominent Communist leaders. Parallel struggles erupted in the Soviet military, the Communist Party, and the Central Committee. As a result, the Soviet Union went through a succession of heads of state. Georgi

Malenkov took power at first, while Nikita Khrushchev entrenched himself behind the scenes.[52]

Eisenhower and Khrushchev met at Geneva in 1955. At this summit, the United States made a unilateral pledge not to initiate war. The pledge was designed to ease the minds of leaders such as Jawaharlal Nehru, the first prime minister of postcolonial India. The Eisenhower administration wanted to demonstrate to the weaker and neutral nations of the world, as well as to Western public opinion, that the United States was not the warmonger portrayed in Soviet propaganda. A second purpose of the Geneva agreements was to cut the U.S. national budget—the only major opportunity for savings was in military expenditures. So President Eisenhower undertook a succession of missions and negotiations designed to achieve the "peaceful coexistence" proposed by Khrushchev. The atmosphere in Geneva was euphoric. One Eisenhower administration negotiator, Charles Wilson, returned to the United States in advance of the secretary of state and, immediately on embarking from the plane, informed the American people that peace had been achieved in our time and that the military budget could now be reduced.[53] Cherne was opposed to peaceful coexistence. He believed that it was better to keep pressure on the Soviet Union and its Communist allies.

Along with Khrushchev's "peaceful coexistence" campaign with the United States, the Soviets put into high gear a program to force redefection to the Soviet Union of refugees in the United States and Western Europe. To achieve their ends, the Soviets used a variety of methods, including blackmail and hostage pressure on families still in the Soviet Union or Communist Eastern Europe. Cherne persuaded General Donovan to form an IRC Commission to investigate and publicize this redefection campaign. Cherne hoped that the Commission, by making the facts public, might help to blunt the campaign. Cherne himself served as vice chairman of what became known as the Donovan Commission.[54]

Poland

In 1955, Khrushchev had deposed Malenkov in the Soviet Union and become the undisputed leader in the Kremlin. Once in control, Khrushchev stunned the Communist world in February 1956 by denouncing Stalin and Stalinism in a secret address before the Twentieth Party Congress in Moscow. Khrushchev's speech was followed up with an anti-Stalinist campaign in the Soviet Union. The speech was acquired by the Central Intelligence Agency, which, after extensive internal debate, leaked it to the *New York Times*.[55] It was subsequently broadcast into Eastern

Europe by Radio Free Europe, a radio station financed mainly by the Central Intelligence Agency.

Khrushchev's speech and the anti-Stalinist campaign in the Soviet Union reverberated throughout Eastern Europe. When Polish workers in Poznan went on strike against wage cuts and demanded better working conditions, the strike quickly snowballed into protests against the authoritarian Polish leaders. Polish troops, sent into Poznan to quell the protests, massacred over seventy strikers. This led to severe internal criticism of the Polish Communist leadership, resulting in its replacement by a reformist faction headed by Wladyslaw Gomulka, recently released from prison where his Stalinist predecessors had incarcerated him. Khrushchev was outraged by this unapproved shift and flew to Poland; he concurrently ordered Soviet occupation forces in Poland to march on Warsaw. After a heated exchange with Gomulka, Khrushchev relented. On October 19, the Soviet and Polish leaders compromised: Poland received a promise of some Soviet troop withdrawals, internal economic liberalization, and limited democratization in return for a Polish promise to remain a firm ally of the Soviet Union. These dramatic developments were monitored closely by reformers within the Hungarian Communist Party, who now demanded the same concessions the Poles had achieved.

Refugees as Weapons

Cherne's attraction to working with refugees was many sided. He was of course compassionate for their plight and wanted to assist them. Political refugees pointed to the weakness of totalitarian political systems. Despite all their propaganda, people in authoritarian countries would do almost anything to leave these "workers' paradises." In addition to their propaganda value, many refugees were from the best-educated layer of their societies. Cherne believed that these exiles deprived the authoritarian system of their talents while, if properly resettled, they could greatly enhance their adopted countries. Hence, for Cherne, refugees were a political weapon. As he believed that the Soviet Union and Communism were the greatest post-World War II threat, he was more concerned with helping refugees who were escaping from the Communist countries.

When the election year of 1956 arrived, however, the IRC was again in dire financial shape. Early in the year, charitable giving to the IRC plummeted as newspapers, radio, and television focused almost exclusively on the presidential election and related campaign news, and the old story of the plight of refugees in Europe and Asia faded from view. By the summer of 1956, the IRC had difficulty meeting its monthly payroll. By September, the IRC was on the verge of financial collapse. The executive committee of the board seriously discussed closing down operations, but dissension so plagued the meeting that no decision was forthcoming. After the meeting, Cherne tried to mend fences among executive committee members so that they could reach a consensus to close the IRC at the following meeting. However, events unfolded in Hungary that would eventually conspire to save the IRC.

Epilogue

- One of the assistants Cherne selected to help him revise the Japanese tax laws, Hayato Ikeda, won election to the Japanese Diet in 1949, became the secretary general of the Liberal Party in 1954, and was instrumental in merging the Liberal and Democratic Parties in 1955. Five years later he became prime minister of Japan, a position he held until 1964.

- Kiichi Miyazawa, who also served on Cherne's staff, was elected to the Japanese Diet in 1953, and served as foreign minister and finance minister, becoming prime minister in 1991. Unable to achieve reforms, the Liberal-Democratic Party split and lost its majority, and Kichi resigned. However, he was so respected internationally and domestically that Prime Minister Obuchi called him back in 1997 to serve as finance minister.

- Upon reflection, Cherne concluded that MacArthur intentionally surrounded himself with yes-men, who were often second-rate thinkers. While MacArthur was extremely intelligent, his vanity prevented him from working with anyone who was his intellectual equal. Those who differed with MacArthur either remained silent or soon departed. Cherne believed that MacArthur risked destroying himself through this behavior and was not surprised when President Truman fired MacArthur as commanding general of the American and U.N. forces during the war in Korea for insubordination. Cherne "very warmly approved" of President Truman's action.[56] Years later, though, Cherne declared that Douglas MacArthur was "the most extraordinary mind" he had ever run into.[57]

- Daniel Patrick Moynihan, whom Cherne had hired in 1954, returned to Syracuse University to complete his doctorate the following year. He became a professor at Harvard University and served as a White House advisor to Presidents Kennedy, Johnson, and Nixon. Moynihan also served as U.S. ambassador to India and as the U.S. ambassador to the United Nations. He was elected to the U.S. Senate in 1976, where he served until his retirement in 2001. He and Cherne remained close friends for the remainder of Cherne's life.

- Refugees continued to flow out of East Berlin into West Berlin. To stop the refugees, the Soviets and East Germans built a wall separating East and West Berlin in 1961. On the second anniversary of the construction of the Berlin Wall, Cherne organized a major effort to remember the event: four national television networks interrupted their normal programming to mark the first anniversary of the Berlin Wall and church bells tolled across the country. The mayor of West Berlin, Willy Brandt, issued a plea to tear down the wall read in the United States, and at Cherne's instigation, Robert Kennedy, the President's brother, issued a similar plea in the United States.[58]

- Cherne received the Commander's Cross of the Order of Merit from the Federal Republic of Germany, awarded on August 21, 1958. The citation reads in part: "As early as 1945, when it was very unpopular to do so," Cherne "came out strongly for the preservation of the German economic potential in Mid-Europe."[59] He also was made a Chevalier of France's National Order of the Légion d'Honneur, and was awarded the United Nations's Gold Medal of Peace.[60]

Chapter 4

Combusting Spontaneously

In the flaming days of late October, something happened that changed my life, and it is changing your life, too. I was one of the first to cross the border and reach Budapest in the brief hour of Hungary's liberation. I saw freedom burning in a nation, and in the light of those flames I caught a glimpse of epic things to come—changes which can touch the lives of everyone.

—Leo Cherne, 1956.[1]

Prologue

Soviet military forces occupied Hungary at the end of World War II. Stalin imposed a coalition government on Hungary at first, but in 1948, he installed Matyas Rakosi, a savage Communist dictator. The Soviet Union assisted Rakosi in developing a totalitarian state with a large Hungarian army supported by a powerful secret police force, the AVO (State Defense Section). The AVO's 50,000 operatives, assisted by another 80,000 informers, ruled through terror. Most Hungarians feared the AVOs, who operated one hundred concentration camps and routinely arrested, tortured, and imprisoned dissidents. The most famous imprisoned Hungarian was the Roman Catholic primate of Hungary, Jozsef Cardinal Mindszenty.

While a power struggle was underway in the Kremlin after Stalin's death in 1953, hardline Communist regimes weakened throughout much of Soviet-controlled Eastern Europe. Malenkov approved Imre Nagy as premier of Hungary. Nagy, a lifelong Communist, was viewed as a reformer in comparison with his predecessor. Nagy, however, was replaced first by Rakosi and then by Erno Gero, whom the Hungarians considered a carbon copy of Rakosi.

Many Hungarians were enthralled by the unfolding liberalizing movement in Poland in 1956. Despite continued deep fear of the secret police, criticism of the Communist leadership increased during that summer. A few days after the Polish Communists gained some internal autonomy from the Soviet Union, Hungarian intellectuals and students demanded similar reforms and threatened to demonstrate if their demands were not met. On the evening of Monday, October 22, students at the Budapest Technical University took another unprecedented step when they used the university's printing press to duplicate a statement composed of "16 points" for reform of the Communist system. The statement called for a peaceful march to City Hall the following evening to express sympathy for the new Polish Communist reforms. Initially, the flustered Ministry of Interior granted permission, but then rescinded it. The students and faculty protested and the ministry reversed its ban. Gero announced that he would address the Hungarian nation that night. When the factories let out, thousands of students and workers gathered at City Hall and waited to hear Gero. He defended the Soviet military occupation of Hungary and expressed no sympathy for the demands of the protesting students, whom he branded as traitors. Gero threatened to crush future demonstrations.

Outside Budapest's City Hall, the milling group—now composed of a wide spectrum of students, intellectuals, and workers—was incensed by Gero's speech. Two thousand marched on the radio station to request equal time to rebut his accusations. The orderly demonstrators arrived at the station and sent in a delegation. The AVO agents, surrounding the station, arrested the delegation and fired on the unarmed demonstrators. This triggered what Cherne later called "spontaneous combustion." The senseless firing on Hungarians ignited long pent-up hatred against the regime. Students, workers, and intellectuals banded together to fight the AVO. Fighting spread throughout the city. Gero's Communist regime lost all legitimacy when he requested Soviet military intervention to end the rapidly growing revolt. On the morning of October 24, two Soviet mechanized divisions with ten thousand soldiers streamed into Budapest. Two additional Soviet divisions stationed in Romania were deployed into Hungary. When the AVO again fired on demonstrators outside the parliament building, Soviet troops joined in, resulting in an estimated one thousand casualties. This stoked open rebellion against the AVO forces and Soviet troops. In the afternoon of Wednesday, October 2, Hungarian police refused to fire on demonstrators, and many joined the uprising. Hungarian army units were called in to support the AVO and Soviet troops. Many Hungarian soldiers—among them a tank battalion led by Colonel Pal Maléter—joined the rapidly growing uprising.

The leaders of the Hungarian Communist party frantically reinstated Nagy as premier. On orders from Moscow, they selected a hardliner, János

Kádár, as head of the Hungarian Communist Party. Nagy and Kádár at first vacillated, but then announced they would negotiate the removal of Soviet troops from Budapest. Nagy appointed Maléter as defense minister in charge of all Hungarian forces. After a lengthy Politburo meeting in Moscow, Khrushchev dispatched Anastas I. Mikoyan, the deputy premier of the Soviet Union, and the Soviet ambassador to Hungary, Yuri V. Andropov, to enter into negotiations with Nagy to create similar arrangements in Hungary to those previously agreed upon with Gomulka in Poland. Despite the negotiations, fighting continued throughout Budapest.[2]

Beginning Response

News of the uprising was slow to reach the United States. As soon as the AVO forces fired on the Hungarian demonstrators on October 23, telephone connections between Hungary and the outside world were severed. Officially controlled Hungarian radio broadcasts made little mention of the unprecedented events unfolding on the streets of Budapest. But international reporters and journalists stationed in Budapest witnessed the uprisings and promptly scrambled to file their stories in Austria and Yugoslavia. As these stories circulated, more Western reporters flocked to Vienna and, in the ensuing confusion, slipped across the border into Hungary. Their articles, photos, and films captured dramatic incidents, but the primitive state of communications delayed their transmission, which only added to the confusion in the West. The *New York Times* published its first article about the October 23 events two days later. A small headline over two left-hand columns on the front page announced: "Police Fire on Hungarians Marching Against Regime." One demonstrator was reported killed. The following day, American newspapers featured major headlines declaring that an uprising was underway in Hungary.

When Hungary exploded, Bill Fitelson, a prominent New York lawyer and a member of IRC's Executive Committee, urged Cherne to initiate a national campaign that would demonstrate the support of the American people for the Hungarian freedom fighters. At the time, presidential elections were only a few weeks away. Fitelson suggested that Cherne contact the two presidential candidates to ask their approval of a symbolic American demonstration supporting the Hungarians. Fitelson had a joint proclamation in mind urging churches to toll their bells at a particular hour and asking Americans to stop work for a few minutes on the same day.

Cherne contacted aides to Dwight Eisenhower and Adlai Stevenson, but both had campaigned on platforms calling for peaceful resolution of conflicts with the Soviet Union. Neither wanted to look warlike at that stage of their campaigns.[3]

The news from Hungary became more dramatic. On Thursday, October 25, the *New York Times* headlines disclosed **"SOVIET UNITS QUELLING REVOLT IN HUNGARY, BUT SOME RIOTING CONTINUES IN BUDAPEST."** Friday's headlines blared that a **"NEW DRIVE ON BUDAPEST REBELS PRESSED BY NAGY GOVERNMENT."** Soviet tanks fired on unarmed Hungarians. Saturday's headlines roared: **"HUNGARIAN REVOLT SPREADS, NAGY TOTTERS; THOUSANDS IN ARMY FIGHT SOVIET TROOPS."** The Hungarian revolutionaries commandeered radio stations and commenced broadcasting reports of events in Budapest and fervent pleas for assistance. The Voice of America and Radio Free Europe (RFE), a CIA-financed operation that had been established to encourage a spirit of nonviolent, anti-Communist resistance in Eastern Europe, increased broadcasting into Hungary and other Communist countries in Eastern Europe. RFE reported extensively on the Hungarian uprising and rebroadcast radio reports emanating from local freedom fighter–controlled stations in Hungary, some carrying exaggerated reports of Western reaction. These broadcasts led many Hungarians to the belief that the United States was moving toward intervention.

In fact, no such move was ever contemplated in Washington. The revolt caught the U. S. government completely off guard, and no one knew how best to respond to the events unfolding in Budapest. Complicating U.S. policymaking was the absence of a U.S. ambassador in Hungary. The main reason for the paralysis in the State Department was the prevailing belief among the American foreign policy community that a revolt in Soviet-occupied Eastern Europe was not even remotely possible. Experts assumed that Communist regimes controlled their people so systematically through propaganda and terror that rebellion was unthinkable. Because the youth of Eastern European countries had been particularly targeted by Communist propaganda, American leaders were even more surprised by the fact that Hungarian young people had led the demonstrations. Most believed that the youthful disturbances would not amount to much and some feared that the students were moving too fast. However, the uprising that started as a small student demonstration mushroomed quickly, engulfing Budapest, then spreading throughout the country. By Saturday, October 27, most of southwest Hungary was under rebel control.

United Nations Security Council

The Soviets did not anticipate such a rebellion either, nor did they know how to respond. On Sunday, October 28, the Soviets formally agreed to leave Budapest, and began withdrawing that evening. A special session of the U.N. Security Council was held that evening. The Soviet ambassador argued that the United Nations had no authority to intervene in Hungary's internal affairs. Henry Cabot Lodge, the U.S. ambassador to the United Nations, described the atrocities committed by the Soviet troops in Hungary and requested that the Security Council demand an immediate withdrawal. He also strongly praised the freedom fighters. Lodge's comments were rebroadcast over Radio Free Europe and reinforced the Hungarian misconception that military support from the United States was imminent.

One observer at the U.N. Security Council session was John Richardson, who worked for the Wall Street investment banking house of Paine, Weber, Jackson & Curtis. Richardson was infuriated by America's failure to support the Hungarian rebels, who were fighting Soviet tanks with Molotov cocktails. Richardson phoned the IRC and reached Anna Matson, who was then special assistant to IRC's president Angier Biddle Duke, a former U.S. ambassador to El Salvador. Matson told Richardson that the IRC engaged only in humanitarian relief. He asked what he could do to assist the IRC with humanitarian relief for the Hungarians. Matson replied that the IRC wanted antibiotics to send to Hungary for the wounded. Richardson had no contacts in pharmaceutical manufacturing, but assured Matson that he would try. When they hung up, Matson assumed that she would not hear from him soon, if at all.

Half an hour later, Richardson phoned back, reporting that he had acquired antibiotics. Richardson explained to an incredulous Matson that after his first phone call, he had vaguely remembered the name of a drug company in his office building. He took the elevator down and walked into a branch office of Charles Pfizer & Company. He asked the receptionist if the company made antibiotics. She responded that Pfizer was the world's largest manufacturer of these drugs. After telling his story three times, Richardson was placed in contact with John E. McKeen, Pfizer's president, who promptly supplied $75,000 worth of Terramycin provided that Richardson could arrange transportation. So Richardson called Pan American Airways and the airline agreed to fly the medicine to Vienna free of charge, provided that Richardson could acquire proper clearances from the State Department and the Austrian Government. After a few more phone calls, he had obtained the proper clearances.

Matson inquired if Pfizer could arrange for a token shipment of drugs to be sent on the plane with Angier Biddle Duke, who was on his way to Vienna that afternoon. Pfizer agreed. Fifteen minutes before the afternoon flight to Vienna took off, a symbolic shipment of fifteen thousand vials of Terramycin was onboard the plane.

Richardson was not the only American who wanted to help the Hungarians. Another was John C. Whitehead, a Partner at Goldman, Sachs & Co. In the fall, Whitehead and his wife had decided to take a peaceful vacation in Austria. It was after the summer tourist season and before the winter ski season. As they breakfasted with a friend in a Viennese café, a disheveled young man burst through the door looking for their friend. This young man, a Hungarian freedom fighter, had escaped across the border. He excitedly announced that the Hungarians were fighting Soviet tanks in Budapest. If the Hungarians were to resist the Soviet onslaught, reported the freedom fighter, they needed radios with which to communicate and motorboats to outrun the Communist patrol boats. Whitehead became emotionally caught up in the Hungarian drama. He and his wife cut short their vacation and returned to New York. Forty-eight hours later, Whitehead was on a windowless Pan American cargo plane headed back to Vienna with radios donated by RCA and motors contributed by the Outboard Motor Company. Trucks were waiting for the plane in Vienna, and the equipment was handed over to the Hungarian resistance.

Cherne in Hungary

At breakfast on Monday, October 29, IRC's Chairman Leo Cherne held a strategy session with Angier Biddle Duke and Harold Oram, IRC's fundraiser and organizational strategist. That morning the *New York Times* had reported that the rebels held key Hungarian cities and that the Soviet military had agreed to withdraw from Budapest. The breakfast group decided to rush Duke to Vienna to establish an IRC field office for humanitarian purposes in Budapest. Even a symbolic private American presence in Budapest might deter further Soviet military attacks. Oram issued a press release announcing that Duke was headed to Vienna and that General Lucius Clay was going to spearhead a fund-raising drive in the United States for the Hungarians. Cherne returned to his office and at 10:30 A.M. received a telephone call from Duke, who reported that he had reserved a seat on the 4:00 P.M. flight to Vienna. After brief contemplation, Cherne decided to join Duke in flying to Austria. His wife threw a few things into a bag, which his secretary picked up from his home, while Cherne frantically finished up some business at the Research Institute of America. As the IRC had no money, both men bought their own tickets and paid their own expenses. Oram dashed off a revised press release covered in the *New York Times*, proclaiming that Duke and Cherne were on their way to Hungary with the Terramycin.

To give the departure some visibility, a press conference was conducted at Idlewild Airport (subsequently renamed John F. Kennedy). It had been arranged by Richard Salzmann, IRC's public relations director, and Dickey Chapelle, a photojournalist then working for the Research Institute of America. Chapelle had pitched *Life* magazine to do a story on IRC and the Hungarian refugees, but the editors of *Life* refused to up-front the costs of the travel. Chapelle accompanied Cherne to the airport and asked if the IRC would cover the costs of her proposed trip to Hungary. Cherne liked the idea but he told her to get permission from Duke for her expenses.[4]

At Idlewild, reporters snapped photos of workers loading Pfizer's Terramycin on the plane and asked Cherne and Duke a couple of questions. Few newspapers covered their departure. Their flight was uneventful, and they arrived in Vienna the evening of October 30. They were met by Marcel Faust, who directed IRC's Vienna office. Faust was born in Austria, but had fled when German troops occupied the country in 1938. He came to America via France in 1940 and assisted the efforts of the International Relief Association, one of the predecessor organizations to the IRC. He became an American citizen and after the war worked for the American civil administration in Germany. In 1946 he opened the IRC's Vienna office, which assisted refugees from Eastern Europe, particularly those from Hungary who escaped during the late 1940s and the 1950s. When the uprising broke out in Budapest in 1956, he visited the Hungarian border to acquire as much information as possible about the events then underway.

Faust also had arranged for previously exiled leaders of Hungarian political parties to greet Cherne and Duke when they arrived at the Vienna airport. These leaders presented Cherne and Duke with a handmade decoration displaying the colors of the pre-Communist Hungarian flag in thanks for their willingness to help. Unfortunately, no one in Vienna had much knowledge about what was happening in Hungary and no one knew whether it was still possible to cross the Austro-Hungarian border.

Cherne's hotel phone rang the following morning at 6:30. The caller announced that the border was open. As both Cherne's and Duke's passports specifically prohibited travel to Hungary, Duke decided to visit the

American Embassy in Vienna to request special permission to visit Budapest. The American ambassador to Austria, Llewellyn Thompson, denied Duke's request and strongly discouraged him from traveling to Hungary illegally. As a once and future ambassador, Duke heeded Thompson's advice. Cherne, having prudently avoided participation in Duke's visit to the embassy, decided that Thompson's directive did not apply to him. So, Cherne and Faust packed the medicine into Faust's battered white 1954 Chevrolet convertible. They also took thirty loaves of bread, twenty rolls of bandages, and eight parcels of clothing contributed by an Austrian workers' welfare organization. They draped a homemade red cross flag on the car's radiator, wedged themselves into the front seat, and headed for the border. The one thing they failed to pack was food for the journey. At a roadside Austrian fruit stand they picked up a bunch of bananas and a few bags of peanuts. Cherne cabled the IRC from Nickelsdorf to make a public appeal for massive relief supplies, although no Hungarian refugees were as yet fleeing into Austria. In fact, the reverse was true. Refugees who had previously fled Hungary and lived in Austrian refugee sites, piled into trucks heading toward Budapest to join the uprising.[5]

Unfortunately, neither Cherne nor Faust spoke the Hungarian language. Faust spoke German with the Hungarian border guards enough so that they were permitted entry. After crossing the border, Cherne asked Faust when he had last been in Hungary. Faust responded that he had never been in Hungary. Shocked, Cherne again asked: "You mean you've been in Vienna all these years and you've never been to Hungary?" Faust responded negatively. Fortunately, the intrepid travelers did not have to worry about getting lost. Hungary did not have an elaborate highway network and the road to Budapest was congested with trucks packed with exiled Hungarians and relief supplies from Germany, Belgium, France, and Austria.

The first large city Cherne and Faust entered was Györ, then in the throes of tumult. Soviet soldiers still occupied parts of Hungary and they remained on the outskirts of Györ. Inside the city, Hungarians had emerged from their homes to converse freely about the momentous events unfolding in Budapest. Györ residents were unable to tell Cherne and Faust whether the road to Budapest was blocked by the Soviets; but the situation was so confused that they had a good chance of making it without serious difficulties.

While Cherne and Faust were on their way, critical events were underway in Budapest. Soviet forces withdrew from parts of Budapest, but they entrenched themselves outside the city, awaiting orders. Rebel forces stormed the AVO headquarters and Communist Party offices. When AVO agents were apprehended, many were executed on the spot in retribution for the terror they had inflicted on the Hungarians over the previous eight years and for the killings during the preceding few days.

Twelve miles outside Budapest, Cherne and Faust encountered Soviet tanks blockading the road. Soviet soldiers searched their car looking for weapons. When the soldiers found only medicine, clothing, bananas, and bread, Cherne and Faust were permitted to pass. The most dangerous moment came when they were stopped at a Hungarian roadblock ten miles outside Budapest. It was manned by young boys, some armed with machine guns. One ripped open the car door and shoved a revolver into Cherne's ribs. The boy did not understand one word of English or German. Cherne repeated what he believed to be a universal word, "medicinen, medicinen," hoping this would convince the youth to let them go. Only later did Cherne learn that the word has no meaning whatsoever in Hungarian. With the gun still jabbed into his ribs, Cherne frantically pointed to the clothes, bread, and the cartons labeled "Terramycin, Chas. Pfizer & Co." But Charles Pfizer & Company was unknown in Hungary, and Terramycin was equally obscure. After extended discussion among the freedom fighters, the boy with the gun finally backed off and permitted the two to enter Budapest.

Cherne in Budapest

Although the drive from Vienna to Budapest is only 170 miles, it took Cherne and Faust six hours to traverse the distance. They arrived after nightfall. The electricity was off, and candles filled the windows of private homes and apartments in accordance with Hungarian custom in observance of All Soul's Day and as a sign of solidarity with the Hungarian freedom fighters. Cherne and Faust lost their way a couple of times, but passersby eagerly provided directions to the American Embassy.

As they drove through the dark city, Cherne and Faust invariably found Hungarians who spoke German. When they found out that Cherne and Faust had just arrived from Austria, everyone wanted to hear about the attention events in Hungary were receiving in the West. These men also asked what assistance the United States and the United Nations were going to send to Hungary. Cherne had no real expectation that the United States would do very much, and he said so. With neutral Austria separating American military forces in Germany from Hungary, sending troops would have been very difficult. As conscious—and resigned—as the Hungarians were about the inability of the United States to intervene militarily, their expectations for United Nations support were high. Their radios were tuned to Western broadcasts (European broadcasts, Voice of America, or Radio Free Europe) to keep them updated about potential U.N. actions. At each stop, Cherne tried to moderate unrealistic expectations that the United Nations would send troops. While many Hungarians were well informed about the U.N. limitations, their mingled anxiety and euphoria conjured up in their minds a vast and powerful international agency with a military force capable of rescuing them from the Soviets.

As Cherne and Faust neared the center of the city, they found more destruction: unrigged electric trolley cables, destroyed trucks and tanks, rubble and debris. At one corner where Cherne and Faust stopped for directions, tanks rumbled through the intersection less than fifty feet away. They finally found themselves surrounded by public buildings, totally blacked out. At a square where some of the heaviest fighting had occurred, Faust carefully maneuvered their car through broken glass, uprooted cobblestones, and a labyrinth of electric wires. Fearing that some of the power lines might still be live, the two sat very carefully on the upholstered seats without touching any metal. Corpses lay where they had fallen. The one unscarred building had a metal plaque designating it as the American Embassy. Finding the gate closed, locked, and barred, they hammered on it and yelled for someone to let them in. To their relief, their raucous banging and shouting finally attracted the attention of the gatekeeper. Cherne and Faust explained their mission to him and he went off to find somebody to assist them. After a long wait, an official listened to their story, but was neither pleased to find two Americans on the embassy's doorstep at 10:30 at night nor very helpful in giving assistance to locate lodging. The Embassy official encouraged them to stay at the Duna hotel in the center of the old city. He did not recommend Cherne and Faust return to the embassy the following day.

Although the Hotel Duna was only two miles from the embassy, it was an emotionally exhausting drive, interrupted with stops by trigger-happy young freedom fighters patrolling the city against the return of Soviet soldiers, and hunting for the hated AVO. More and more, the streets were blocked by debris, glass, broken pavement, and destroyed vehicles.

When Faust and Cherne finally found the Hotel Duna, bedlam reigned inside. The lobby was crammed with excited reporters from European wire services and newspapers. All available seats in the lobby were already occupied by people sleeping upright. With difficulty, Cherne and Faust pressed their way forward to the desk clerk, who reported that no rooms were available. No one could offer any idea where Cherne and Faust might spend the night. Exhausted, cold, and hungry, they proceeded to the restaurant, but found no food. A shot of whiskey would have been welcome, but there was no liquor either. They did manage to get some coffee. While wandering around in the restaurant, Faust ran into people he knew and managed to find some left-wing intellectuals. Some were members of the Congress for Cultural Freedom, an anti-Communist network centered in Paris, subsequently identified as a CIA creation. In the midst of excited talk of the momentous developments around them, Faust acquired directions to another hotel that might be able to accommodate them. Refreshed by the coffee, they reluctantly left the Duna Hotel and once again began feeling their way through the blacked-out city. Unfortunately, the hotel they were seeking had no identifying sign. Finally they got directions from a fierce-looking but helpful group of young freedom fighters armed with tommy-guns.

Cherne and Faust parked amidst the rubble of the hotel's facade, which had been shattered by cannon fire. The small lobby, illuminated only by candlelight, was in complete disarray. Furniture was upended and the walls were riddled with gunfire. Toward the rear of the lobby was a shabby wreath of flowers with a crudely handwritten placard paying tribute to the desk clerk, who had been shot and killed only three or four hours earlier as the Soviet soldiers, who had occupied the hotel, departed. The proprietor behind the desk explained that, while rooms were vacant, the hotel had no heat and few unbroken windows. Most doors were shattered. Cherne and Faust accepted the offer of a room sight unseen and returned to their car to pick up the Terramycin. The proprietor helped them sheet the broken windows to impede the cold howling wind. The beds, though old and lumpy, were feather-quilted and promised warmth.

Too excited to sleep, Cherne and Faust wandered the halls. They found a couple of Faust's old anti-Communist friends and swapped the latest rumors. One offered a drink from a bottle of whiskey. Cherne and Faust finally settled into bed. Four hours later, they were awakened by bright sunlight streaming through the window sheets. They left the hotel with the goal of establishing contact with the headquarters of the freedom fighters and the leaders of the long-suppressed Democratic political parties. Budapest in broad daylight was a shocking sight: streetcar cables, power lines, and telephone wires heaped spaghetti-like on streets littered with wrecked vehicles, broken glass, cobblestones, and occasional bodies. Sandbags, rocks, and bricks protected machine-gun nests manned by Hungarians, some of whom had remained in position for days. Few vehicles moved except for tanks and jeeps manned by Hungarians, and trucks filled with volunteers from the countryside, pouring into Budapest by the thousands to support the revolution. Freedom fighter patrols filled the streets and combed the city, hunting AVOs. Frightened men were hustled out of hallways and pulled from sewers with their hands clasped behind their heads, guns pointed in their backs.

Cherne photographed what he saw. Public frenzy was great in Budapest, but so was discipline. Cherne saw no looting. Although store windows were broken, the merchandise behind the shattered glass remained untouched. The only premises emptied or looted were the Communist Party offices and propaganda centers. With the AVO on the run, Budapest residents freely raided the Communist bookshops and newspaper offices. Hungarians in a human chain carried out the books, pamphlets, magazines, papers, and leaflets and torched them in the streets. Cherne's photos of these bonfires were subsequently published by the *New York Times*, *Life*, and other American publications.

Two English-speaking students who attached themselves to Cherne and Faust proved to be invaluable guides. One of the young men was the president of a Hungarian student organization; the other, an architecture student. They helped Cherne and Faust locate the headquarters of the freedom fighters in a section of Budapest filled with overturned trolley and railroad cars. Mangled antiaircraft guns with barrels at odd angles, used as anti-personnel weapons, cluttered the street. Many buildings had gaping holes from rocket and cannon fire. Hungarian flags—with the hammer and sickle motif torn away from the center—proudly waved everywhere.

Cherne, Faust, and their new guides, unable to navigate the car through the rubble, proceeded on foot, led by the student guides. They trekked through large workers' apartment buildings, into a cellar and then up a narrow set of stairs, emerging into a courtyard populated with volunteer students and workers engaged in military training. A long line threaded into a building. When word spread that Americans had arrived, everyone made way. Outside the headquarters was a machine gun emplacement manned by two exhausted boys with tommy-guns and a man in civilian clothes. Finally, Cherne and Faust walked up the stairs past a long line of freedom fighters waiting for orders, and were ushered into a small room packed with people. For the first time they saw the leader— a twenty-one-year-old woman. Cherne and Faust explained their mission, and the freedom fighters expressed their gratitude. Helpers accompanied them back to the car to pick up one carton of Terramycin, presented both as a token of American private support, and as much-needed medication for a few of the thousands who had already suffered injury. Cherne photographed the young woman, who would be killed four days later.

Cherne and Faust next went to the headquarters of the newly organized Democratic Socialist Party, located in another shell-scarred building. Here, too, they found a large mob milling outside. Cherne and Faust were taken up to the top floor, where they met four party leaders. The Socialist party leaders knew about the IRC, as it had been frequently attacked by Communist propaganda organs, thus enhancing IRC's reputation. The IRC was also known for the actual role that it played in saving thousands of antifascist union leaders during World War II, and for its vigorous anti-Communist position after 1945. Cherne apologized for the meager supply of Terramycin, clothing, and bread that they had been able to bring in the car. The party leaders were nonetheless happy to receive the symbolic gifts. Thirty men marched to Faust's car, and in solemn procession each carried a loaf of bread back to the party offices. Cherne made commitments for future shipments of supplies from America.

Cherne and Faust then proceeded to the party headquarters of Zoltan Tildi, a distinguished, longtime anti-Communist political leader. When Cherne and Faust arrived, they were told that Tildi had left to visit Cardinal Mindszenty, who had just been freed from prison. No one knew the exact whereabouts of the Cardinal. Cherne and Faust continued to the Catholic cathedral, where they were told the Cardinal might be at his residence on the other side of the Danube, a part of the city still largely in Communist hands.

It would have been unlikely that Mindszenty would have taken refuge in a part of the city still occupied by the Soviet forces. Nevertheless, Cherne and Faust decided to forge ahead. They found an undamaged bridge that took them across the river and started to wind their way up a fairly long hill. They halted at a roadblock clogged with motorcycles and vehicles amidst a great deal of confusion. Their Hungarian guides explained why Cherne and Faust urgently wished to find the Cardinal. The freedom fighters advised them not to go to the Cardinal's residence, because snipers were still in position in that part of the city. Even though they heard gunfire, Cherne and Faust decided to continue their journey. That quarter of the city was deserted, and they saw no snipers. Eventually, they found the Cardinal's residence. Cherne and Faust pushed their way through to a locked gate, where they learned that Zoltan Tildi and General Maléter, the new commander of the Hungarian forces supporting the rebellion, were inside meeting with the Cardinal.

Cherne and Faust returned to their car and picked up the remaining Terramycin. Word of their arrival reached the Cardinal's staff, and a priest came to the gate; the Hungarian guides explained that the Americans carried medicine for the Cardinal's use. Cherne and Faust were pushed closer to the iron gate to talk to the priest, who agreed to convey their message to the Cardinal. As they waited, Tildi and Maléter came out of the Cardinal's residence. While the gate was still open, Faust and Cherne elbowed their way into the courtyard, where the priest they had met at the gate escorted them into a room off a large open entranceway. They sat down and again explained why they wanted to see the Cardinal. The priest responded that the Cardinal was terribly tired and asked them to wait in the debris-strewn courtyard. In the courtyard were some forty photographers and television cameramen. Freedom fighters sat on the surrounding walls, which were pocked-marked by bullets and shells.

It was an icy cold day, but a quiet, repressed excitement filled the courtyard as a microphone was set up about ten feet from the doorway. Cardinal Mindszenty, in a black cassock and skull cap, slowly walked into the courtyard. Cherne saw that he was a striking figure, but terribly exhausted. The Cardinal slowly read a statement that he held in his hand. Cherne was not sure if the pace was deliberate or a reflection of a shattered man, permanently wasted by years of imprisonment and torture. When Mindszenty finished reading his statement, Cherne picked up the boxes of Terramycin and worked his way forward. Cherne later confided that, as a Jew from New York, he had no clue as to what he should do in the presence of a Catholic Cardinal who had just been liberated from years inside a Communist prison. According to Faust, though, Cherne was smooth and forceful in his presentation to the Cardinal. In English Cherne stated that the Terramycin was a symbol of the American people's concern for Hungary, and particularly for those Hungarians who had been tortured, killed, and imprisoned. Cherne then gave the cartons to the Cardinal. The Cardinal asked Cherne to convey his deepest gratitude to the American people for their support and for what he hoped would be America's support for the struggle for Hungarian freedom in the days to come. Having made his statement, the Cardinal then turned the cartons over to an assistant and retired into the building. The entire event was filmed by European film crews and repeatedly broadcast on newsreels in Europe during the following days.[6]

After the meeting, Cherne concluded that it was time to leave Hungary. He offered to take the two guides to Vienna and they readily agreed. Faust had come to Hungary with blank Austrian travel documents which he then proceeded to fill in to permit the guides to exit Austria. On their way out, Faust drove to a farmhouse outside of Budapest to meet another Hungarian leader. Leaving the farmhouse, the foursome had to travel by back roads to reach the main road. When they crossed the border into Austria, they were informed that Soviet forces had encircled Budapest and closed all major roads out of the city. Only because they traveled part of the way via a circuitous route did they make it out. Had they taken the main road, they would likely not have made it.

Once in Austria, Cherne dispatched the first of several cables announcing his return from war-ravaged Budapest, reporting that he had slipped out fifteen minutes before the Soviets closed the border. He reported that Budapest was an unlighted city of two million people filled with broken glass, burned, tilted trolleys, exploded tanks, overturned trucks, and bodies. Trigger-happy youngsters with tommy-guns roamed the darkness. Groups ferreted out suspected members of the Hungarian secret police, and upon finding them, hanged them on lampposts, thus avenging years of oppression.

Churning up a Whirlwind

Cherne left on the earliest possible flight out of Vienna and arrived in the United States on Saturday, November 3. He had cabled his arrival time to Harold Oram. Oram, Salzmann, and Chapelle had been working constantly since Cherne's departure to publicize the trip and IRC's activities. When they knew Cherne's time of arrival, they set up a press conference for him. As Cherne was one of the few Americans known to have visited Budapest and returned to tell the tale, he was news: the press conference was covered by all major newspapers, including the *New York Times*. At the news conference, Cherne reported on his trip and his conversation with Cardinal Mindszenty. He estimated that seven to ten thousand Hungarians had died in the uprising. The following morning, Cherne, Oram, and Gilbert Jonas, an Oram staffer in charge of the IRC's account, discussed their next move. Oram concluded that Cherne needed to appeal to a national television audience. They quickly checked the program listings; but in 1956 the only live, national television show on Sunday was Ed Sullivan's variety show, which did not do interviews on international issues and did not air humanitarian appeals. Jonas was assigned the task of convincing Sullivan to change policies. Jonas proceeded to the Delmonico Hotel, where Sullivan was preparing his show for that evening. When the hotel room door opened, Jonas saw Sullivan in the back and shouted that he had a message for Ed Sullivan from Cardinal Mindszenty. That caught Sullivan's attention. After listening to Jonas, Sullivan invited Cherne to attend the evening's show, and promised that, if time permitted, Sullivan would ask Cherne to say a few, brief words.

That night, time did permit Cherne's participation and Sullivan questioned him for more than four minutes on the air. Cherne spoke dramatically about his trip to Budapest while holding up the shredded and soiled flag with the hastily improvised red cross. He told of the deeds of brave Hungarians and conveyed the thanks of Cardinal Mindszenty for the assistance of the International Rescue Committee and the American people. Sullivan closed with an appeal for financial support of the IRC, asking viewers to send in at least a dollar apiece. This appeal generated $455,000 in donations, which was unprecedented in television history up to that date.

Not everyone was happy with Cherne's appearance on the Ed Sullivan Show. Shortly afterwards, Cherne received an irate message from the head of the American Red Cross that Cherne had taken an unauthorized liberty in using the Red Cross symbol. Cherne explained that he had used it because it was the world's best known symbol reflecting a mission to dispense medicine, food, and clothing. He had not claimed he was representing the Red Cross in Hungary or on the Ed Sullivan Show, and he did not believe that he had dishonored the symbol.

Although the trip was unauthorized and technically he had violated regulations against travel to Hungary, no American officials ever made the slightest effort to raise these issues. On the contrary, representatives of several agencies of the U. S. government, including the CIA and the United States Information Agency, asked to debrief Cherne in the days that followed his return. He also briefed Max Rabb, the President's Counsel for the Cabinet. Rabb in turn introduced Cherne to Sherman Adams, President Eisenhower's Chief of Staff.[7] Rabb and Adams conveyed Cherne's assessments to President Eisenhower. All were very eager to have Cherne's observations, but none were particularly interested in his recommendations. As a result of these briefings in Washington, Cherne became convinced that within the Eisenhower administration a wide rift separated the "activists," who supported some kind of intervention in Eastern Europe, and the "pacifists," who supported "peaceful coexistence" with the Soviet Union and the Communist world. Cherne privately chastised the U. S. government for refusing to recognize the Nagy government, for neglecting even to engage officially in any humanitarian relief mission for the freedom fighters, and for failing to demand that United Nations observers be rushed to Budapest.

In Hungary, on Saturday, November 3, Pal Maléter, under a flag of truce, had opened discussions with Soviet generals for the withdrawal of their troops from Hungary. In the midst of the negotiations, he was detained by the Soviets and he disappeared. He was subsequently shot. Early the following morning, fifteen Soviet artillery and infantry divisions with six thousand tanks stormed into Budapest, shelling the resistance into submission. By noon, Soviet forces occupied all the important intersections and buildings in the city. In heavy street-to-street fighting, Soviet forces destroyed one pocket of resistance after another. Cardinal Mindszenty took refuge in the American embassy. Nagy was granted sanctuary in the Yugoslav embassy, and the Soviets installed Kádár as head of the Hungarian government. On November 6, the rebel radio station broadcast its last message. The following day, Soviet troops tried to wipe out the remaining pockets of resistance. However, some freedom fighters fought on, defending Budapest from house to house. While the fighting continued, thousands more Hungarians fled to Austria.[8]

As refugees began their exodus, the International Rescue Committee sent out a somewhat ambiguously titled "Emergency Appeal to Help Free Hungary," signed by six prominent Americans. It announced a drive to raise one million dollars for the purchase of medicine, ambulances, hospital supplies, food, and clothing. The appeal mentioned the $200,000 worth of drugs given by Pfizer and asked every American to make contributions. The signers of the appeal were Lucius D. Clay, the former military commander in Germany, then chairman of Continental Can Company; Admiral Richard E. Byrd; General William J. Donovan, then a partner in the New York law firm of Donovan, Leisure, Newton, and Irvine; Henry Luce, president of Time-Life-Fortune publications; Carl Spaatz, ex-chief of staff of the Air Force; and Herman W. Steinkraus, a prominent Republican businessman who was a former president of the U.S. Chamber of Commerce and president of Bridgeport Brass. The emergency appeal generated $200,000 in cash and checks during the first twenty-four hours. Contributions varied from $1 from individuals to $5,000 from corporations. It was an astonishing financial response from the American people, but the letters that came with the donations were even more heartwarming. "This is from me and my parents," said one letter accompanying three $1 bills. "We hope it will be of some help to a brave people who are fighting our battle, too."[9]

On November 5, Cherne spoke about his experiences in Hungary on the "Tex & Jinx Show" on radio. The following day he spoke on WOR's Martha Deane Show and the Home Show on television. On November 7, he spoke on "Meaning of Revolt in Hungary," to the Council on Foreign Relations.[10]

On November 8, five days after Cherne's return from Budapest, the IRC organized a rally for the Hungarian cause at Madison Square Garden. The organizers included Monsignor Bela Varga, the anti-Communist former leader of the Hungarian Peasant Party who had served as the last president of the Hungarian Parliament before the Communist takeover in

1948. As the date drew near, the organizing committee became worried about attendance, so they offered Varga free tickets for Catholic college students to fill the upper balconies. More than twelve thousand participants attended the mass rally to "End the Massacre." The program started well. General Clay served as master of ceremonies and introduced speakers, including Clifford Case, a Republican senator from New Jersey; Jacob Javits, the senator from New York; and Varga. President Eisenhower, having handily won reelection, sent a telegram to the rally that was read to cheers from the audience when he strongly protested the Soviet invasion. In the telegram, he announced that he was allowing 5,000 Hungarian refugees to enter the United States, the maximum possible under U.S. law at the time. The next speaker was Anna Kethly, the newly appointed Hungarian minister of state and the highest-ranking Hungarian official not in Soviet hands. She had been friends with Joseph Buttinger before World War II, but had remained in Hungary when the Communists took over. Varga considered her to be a Communist and may have instructed the students in the balconies to treat her as such. Whatever the reason, the students reacted negatively when she began her speech and derided her when she mentioned the code words *peaceful coexistence* with the Soviet Union. For many in the audience, the phrase *peaceful coexistence* was a Communist slogan implying that the United States should not oppose the Soviet Union. The strongly anti-Communist audience booed her, and General Clay lost control of the crowd. Before the event turned into a disaster, Cherne rose to the lectern, quieted the audience with his eloquence, and lectured the students about the importance of free speech. The most poignant moment came when Cherne held up a tag and reported that it had been removed from a boy at the Austrian frontier a few hours before, one of three thousand children who wore similar tags. It read: "We are sending you (the boy's name). He is only nine years of age. We send him to you as we fight. Please be good to him. God bless him and you." The rally generated another $400,000 for IRC's Hungarian refugee programs. Similar rallies were held in Boston and other cities.

With tens of thousands of refugees fleeing into Austria, the IRC sent a delegation to Vienna. The delegation was composed of General Donovan, Herman Steinkraus, and Claiborne Pell, then an executive at the Bell Syndicate and an IRC vice president. William vanden Heuvel, an assistant to Donovan, served as rapporteur. In Austria they met Congressman Francis E. Walter, who had previously sponsored the U.S. immigration law that limited the number of refugees to five thousand per country. On November 18, the delegation arrived in Vienna. The following day, they visited the bridge at

Andau and watched thousands of refugees fleeing into Austria. Three days later, the bridge itself was destroyed by Soviet tank fire, but the canal was only four feet deep at that point and refugees waded through the icy water to safety on the Austrian side of the border. Returning to Vienna, the delegation ran into James A. Michener and his wife Mari. Michener was on assignment with *Reader's Digest* to cover the exodus of refugees from Hungary. Vanden Heuvel took Michener to Andau, where more refugees fled via a wooden footbridge over the Einser Canal, hastily constructed by Austrian students, making it easier for refugees to cross. Michener took copious notes and subsequently interviewed Cherne and other members of the IRC. Michener made the crossing point famous the following year with the publication of his book, *The Bridge at Andau*.[11]

Included in Michener's book was the saga of Dickey Chapelle, who took a leave of absence and received $3,000 from the IRC to travel to Hungary for the *Life* magazine story. Faust was not overwhelmingly happy to see her: he had plenty to do and was not pleased with the idea that Chapelle intended to cross the Hungarian border illegally; but he did supply her with Austrian documents to serve as a cover in case she was apprehended in Hungary. Chapelle became friends with the Micheners and they frequently visited the bridge at Andau. Chapelle crossed the Austrian-Hungarian border fifteen times, tracing and photographing the route that the IRC's medical supplies followed from Austria to the freedom fighters in Hungary. *Life* magazine published two of her photographs on December 3. On her fifteenth trip, Chapelle headed for Budapest. Two days later, she was caught and jailed by Soviet forces. The Micheners worked for her release, as did her ex-husband, Anthony Chapelle. Cherne maintained that he had cautioned her against going to Budapest. Dickey Chapelle later declared that she had been told by both the editors at *Life* magazine and the leaders of the IRC that, if she were captured, they would deny that they had sent her into Hungary. Unable to communicate with her while in prison, neither group admitted that she was engaged in an assignment for them. After six weeks of interrogation, and thanks to the intervention of the officer in charge of the U.S. embassy in Hungary, Chapelle was expelled from Hungary. She returned to her job as press liaison for the Research Institute. However, she believed that Cherne had not spoken out forcefully enough on her behalf. A few weeks later she resigned and turned to freelance work.[12]

Meanwhile, Hungarian refugees were flooding into Austria. On a single November day, 9,000 refugees exited Hungary. By the end of November, 100,000 Hungarian refugees had arrived in Austria and Germany, and more were arriving daily. The delegation returned to the United States and promptly issued a report, the *Sorrow and Triumph of Hungary*, pointing out the refugee crisis that could well turn into disaster if not adequately addressed. Specifically, the report recommended that the IRC appoint a single director to coordinate all European refugee efforts and urged that a half million dollars be committed to help the refugees. Joseph L. Buttinger, then the IRC's vice president, was appointed European Director. Buttinger had served a similar function for the IRC in Indochina in 1954. The money was transferred to Vienna, and Marcel Faust put it to work assisting thousands of refugees.[13]

Armed resistance to Soviet forces finally crumbled in Budapest on November 15, but a general strike gripped Hungary for weeks thereafter. An estimated 8,000 Hungarians died during the revolution, and some 30,000 were wounded or injured. Another 10,000 were rounded up by the Soviets; 300 of these were executed and the rest were deported to slave labor camps in the Soviet gulag; another 35,000 were thrown into Hungarian prisons. Nagy, who had sought refuge in the Yugoslavian Embassy, was given a safe conduct pass by the occupying Soviet forces. But when he left the Embassy, he was kidnapped, imprisoned, and shot by Soviet operatives.[14]

In the United States, Cherne continued to speak out on Hungary and the refugees. He flew to Los Angeles where he spoke to the National Paint, Varnish and Lacquer Association Convention; the following day he addressed the Overseas Press Club in New York. On November 28, he spoke at the World Affairs Council of Philadelphia on the "Current Crisis in Hungary."[15] On December 4, he addressed the National War College on "Iron Curtain Situation—Observations in Hungary." On December 6, he attended the "Second National Conference on Exchange of Persons" in Chicago, where he reported on events in Hungary. On December 23, a 90-minute special "Dumont Salute to Hungary" was aired on television, with a star-studded roster featuring Sammy Davis, Jr., Burgess Meredith, Edward G. Robinson, and Shelley Winters. Viewers were entertained by calypso singers and Hungarian dancers. In the middle of the program, Cherne appealed for contributions to help the Hungarian refugees. More money poured into the IRC coffers.

Concurrent with his speaking engagements, Cherne conducted press conferences, encouraged interviews with radio, magazine, and newspaper reporters, and cranked out a stream of eye-witness accounts that gave high visibility to the Hungarian Revolution and the IRC's efforts, including articles in the *New York Journal American*; "I Spoke with Cardinal Mindszenty" in the *National Catholic Weekly Review*; and "From Inside Hungary, 30 Days that Shook the World" in the *Saturday Review*.[16]

By the end of 1956, the IRC had raised nearly $2.5 million. In addition, supplies and services were contributed by American corporations to assist the refugees. Pfizer eventually gave a total of $220,000 in medical supplies. Gerber supplied baby food, Pitman-Moore donated polio vaccine, and General Electric committed X-ray machines worth $25,000. Leopold Silberstein, President of Penn-Texas Corporation, offered 1,000 jobs plus homes and training for the incoming refugees. The International Ladies Garment Workers Union furnished 100,000 garments estimated to be worth $80,000. The Medical Society of the State of New York donated $5,000. Protestant churches committed $2 million. The New York Fund for Children contributed to the IRC to assist Hungarian children. All these contributions were collected in addition to the extensive refugee assistance generated by the Red Cross and other traditional relief agencies.

By December 12, more than 130,000 Hungarians had arrived in Austria and 50,000 more were dispersed throughout the rest of Europe. President Eisenhower took advantage of a loophole in U.S. immigration law by admitting 15,000 additional Hungarian refugees as "parolees." These refugees were flown to the United States in Operation Safe Haven, the largest airlift since the Berlin blockade. The 15,000 ballooned to 21,000 by the end of the year. The IRC, still thinly staffed, initially sponsored 500 of these refugees. Other humanitarian organizations, including the National Catholic Welfare Conference, the Hebrew Immigrant Aid Society, the United Ukranian Refugee Committee, and several Protestant groups, did more. Even these efforts fell short as refugees continued to flee Hungary, 200,000 in all. The United States eventually absorbed 40,000 of them.

In 1957, the Hungarian Revolution receded in the news stories; but the refugees did not fade away. Long after the revolution, the IRC and other relief organizations continued to resettle refugees. In diminishing numbers, refugees continued to arrive in the United States through 1958. Congress enacted a law granting retroactive admission to parolees. Most became American citizens.[17]

For Cherne, his involvements with Hungary and his efforts on behalf of the refugees were fortuitous. He had decided instinctively to fly to Austria on behalf of the IRC when there were not yet any refugees. He chose not to heed the directive of the American ambassador to Austria to stay away from Hungary. At the Hungarian border, the confusion was so great that it was possible to cross a highly fortified frontier simply by driving down a main road. He arrived in Budapest just as the Soviet troops were withdrawing and fighting had ebbed. He just happened to be in Budapest when Cardinal Mindszenty was released and almost by accident spoke with him. Cherne left Hungary just as Soviet troops surrounded Budapest and closed the border. Had he left a day later, the story might have turned out quite differently. As usual, Cherne's timing was impeccable.

No one was better equipped to exploit these unprecedented events than Cherne. He was willing to leave his work and home on the spur of the moment and fly at his own expense to Austria. He took personal risks in Hungary that others had preferred to avoid. While his adventure in Hungary was personally revealing, more important was the whirlwind campaign Cherne undertook upon his return. His previous television experience permitted him to shine on the Ed Sullivan Show. His expertise as a war correspondent and a reporter helped prepare him to present his personal adventure in a way that made it nationally newsworthy. Moreover, he converted this visibility into successful fundraising opportunities for the IRC. These funds in turn assisted tens of thousands of Hungarian refugees. And, while the IRC had been financially destitute and on the verge of collapse in September 1956, Cherne's fundraising activities stabilized its finances by November and catapulted the IRC to the status of a world-class organization by December. It became the largest refugee relief organization in the world.

Even more significant, Cherne saw the light of freedom burning brightly in Hungary. Despite the brutal suppression of Hungarians after the revolution, the flame was never extinguished. Cherne had caught a glimpse of epic things to come. Although the fall of the Berlin Wall and the subsequent establishment of non-Communist nations in Eastern Europe was still thirty-three years in the future, these changes were heralded by the Hungarian revolt. These events eventually did touch the lives of everyone.

The Hungarians remembered Leo Cherne and his role in those events. For his support of the Hungarian refugees, Cherne was honored by the former Budapest Mayor Joseph Kovago on behalf of the Hungarian Government in Exile on November 19, 1958. For his support of Hungarian freedom, Cherne was awarded the Officer's Cross of the Order of Merit by the new democratic government of the Republic of Hungary on November 17, 1992.

Epilogue

- Marcel Faust remained the IRC's director of operations in Austria until his retirement in 1998.

- Angier Biddle Duke remained president of the IRC until 1960. He subsequently became U.S. ambassador to Spain, Denmark, and Morocco.

- The U.S. ambassador to Austria, Llewellyn Thompson, who had faithfully reflected U.S. policy in discouraging Duke's visit to Budapest, was one of America's top Soviet experts. President Eisenhower appointed him ambassador to the Soviet Union in 1957, a position to which he was reappointed by President Kennedy in 1962.

- The U.S. ambassador to the United Nations, Henry Cabot Lodge, whose words of praise for the freedom fighters had been interpreted as evidence of U.S. support, was selected by Richard Nixon as his vice presidential running mate in the 1960 election. After their defeat, President John F. Kennedy appointed Lodge U.S. ambassador to South Vietnam.

- William vanden Heuvel, General Donovan's assistant, was appointed the U.S. representative, United Nations European Office, Geneva. He has remained on the IRC's board and currently serves on its executive committee.

- The Soviet ambassador to Hungary, Yuri V. Andropov, later became the head of the KGB, the Soviet secret police. He became premier of the Soviet Union in November 1982, but died in office in 1984, setting the stage for the rise to power of Mikhail Gorbachev.

- Following his return from Budapest in 1956, Cherne invited John Richardson to join the board of the IRC where he has remained ever since, except during assignments as CEO of Radio Free Europe in the 1960s and as assistant secretary of state in the 1970s. In 1957, he and his wife took into their family a Hungarian refugee girl who had crossed the bridge at Andau alone on December 31, 1956.

- A State Department official informed John C. Whitehead that his gift of radios and outboard motors to the Hungarian resistance violated American law. The same official encouraged Whitehead to meet Leo Cherne. Cherne invited Whitehead to join IRC's Board. Whitehead became co-chairman of Goldman Sachs in 1976 and deputy secretary of state under George Schultz in 1985, retiring three years later. Whitehead succeeded Cherne to serve as chairman of the IRC from 1992 until he resigned in 1999.

- Claiborne Pell, a member of IRC's delegation to Austria in 1956, spent the next year of his life working with the Hungarian refugees for no salary. He became a director and an officer in the IRC. He returned to Rhode Island in 1957 and ran for the U.S. Senate in 1960, where he served for the next thirty-six years. As a senator, he eventually became the chairman of the Senate Foreign Relations Committee. He and Cherne remained associates for the remainder of Cherne's life.[18]

- Monsignor Bela Varga, who had been the last president of the Hungarian Parliament before the Communist takeover in 1948, returned to give the opening address to the first freely elected, post-Communist Hungarian parliament in 1990. After his speech, he wrote to Leo Cherne about this most unforgettable experience. On Varga's deathbed two years later, he said he considered this speech the crowning event of his life.

- When Leo Cherne began having difficulty walking in the 1990s, he visited a physical therapist at New York University's Medical Center. Entering the doctor's examining room, he started to introduce himself. Dr. Valerie Lanyi interrupted him, saying, "No need, Mr. Cherne. I know you well. You rescued me from out of Hungary back in those terrible days."[19]

Chapter 5

Uncovering Communists

In a democracy the liberty to speak, to write, to believe and politically influence is available even to the fool, the charlatan, the bigot, the fascist and the Communist. Why do we tolerate these threats to our institutions by the enemies in our house? We do it because we believe that democracy as a method can build a stronger and better community, because dissent is still the only source of change, of growth, of new social strength, of progress. That doesn't mean that every dissenter contributes to progress or justice. I know that the Communist uses the right of speech and press and political action with the intent to destroy those freedoms. But the one thing about the Communist I do not fear is that he will win in the battle of ideas or in the forum of political contest.

—Leo Cherne, 1947

Prologue

Before World War II, the Depression had shaken many Americans' faith in capitalism. Socialist, Communist, and other radical philosophies spread across the United States as numerous programs devised by the New Deal failed to improve the nation's economy. Some Americans were sympathetic to the Soviet Union, which seemed not to be suffering from the effects of the Depression. The American Communist Party mushroomed before the war, and some of its members became leaders in labor unions and employees in the federal government. During World War II, the Soviet Union was America's ally, and extensive propaganda supporting the alliance had been generated. Many Americans did not view the American Communist Party as a threat and hoped that the alliance with the Soviet Union would bring lasting peace after the war.

A few Americans actively spied for the Soviet Union before and during the war. Much of this activity was centered in the Soviet embassy in Washington, DC. Embassy officials received reports from informants in America, encrypted them into code thought unbreakable, and forwarded them to Moscow. Although the United States had broken the Japanese codes and the British had broken the German codes during the war, neither had the time nor resources to break the codes used by Soviet embassies.

After World War II the Soviet cryptographers committed a major blunder by reissuing these codes. This permitted American cryptographers to decipher messages dating back to the pre–World War II period. The project, code named VENONA, decoded the old messages, which demonstrated the extent of the Soviet espionage activities in the United States prior to and during World War II. Careful work identified Soviet informers, many of whom had been in government service. Those running the project made two important decisions. The first was the decision not to arrest the Soviet informers, so as not to jeopardize the ability of the United States to decode Soviet messages. Those informants still in the government were placed under surveillance. The second decision was not to inform President Truman, as they were afraid of leaks in his administration that would also alert the Soviets to VENONA.[1]

President Truman, in fact, took a strong anti-Communist approach throughout his administration. He urged the creation of the Central Intelligence Agency, which was established in the National Security Act of 1947. Well before the internal Communist menace was popularized by Joseph McCarthy, Truman required loyalty oaths of federal government officials and directed all federal departments to weed out known Communists and Communist sympathizers. His administration brought criminal cases against anyone who engaged in treason.[2]

Deeply worried that the economic conditions in Western Europe encouraged strong domestic communist parties and prevented the strengthening of the military necessary to defeat a potential Soviet external invasion, Truman sent Secretary of State George C. Marshall to Europe to survey the stagnating postwar economic situation. When Marshall recommended a recovery plan to give economic aid to war-torn European nations, Truman strongly supported the legislation, later called the Marshall Plan. When Truman became concerned with possible Soviet aggression in Europe, he launched negotiations that led to the formation of the North Atlantic Treaty Organization (NATO). Truman subsequently made military commitments to Greece and Turkey and resisted Soviet attempts to oust the Western allies from Berlin.

While these actions assisted Western Europeans to fend off the twin threats of Soviet armed power and internal Communist movements, Truman was less successful in Asia. He could not prevent China's collapse to the Communists in 1949. Although Truman stopped Communist North Korean aggression, he was unable to win the war in Korea, which broke out in

1950. However, Soviet actions in Europe, China's collapse to an internal Communist force, and North Korea's unprovoked military attack on South Korea convinced many Americans that the Communist threat was real. As the Cold War intensified, membership in the American Communist Party declined. By the mid-1950s, the Communist Party's influence was limited to a small intellectual circle.[3]

Cherne's Anti-Communism

Cherne's parents had been radical Socialists, and Cherne retained an affection for turn-of-the-century Socialism. His parents were particularly interested in social democracy. Cherne was sent during two summers to the upstate New York Camp Kinderlin, which was semi-Socialist in philosophy. Shortly after his time there, it was taken over by Communists, who used the camp to indoctrinate youth. Several members of Cherne's family who were exposed to the same environment did become Communists. But Cherne's immediate family took the opposite position and were in the anti-Communist camp. His parents were particularly concerned with Communist infiltration of labor unions.[4]

Prior to World War II, Cherne believed that the fascist threat exemplified by Hitler was the most serious menace, but he also attacked Communism and the Soviet Union. As the war drew to a close and fascism was defeated, Cherne turned his attention to the Soviet Union and the American Communist Party. His concern was highlighted by several experiences. The first were explorations in Europe in the autumn of 1945 and Japan in the spring of 1946 (covered in Chapter 4). The European mission convinced him that the United States faced a major challenge from the Soviet Union and that Europe was too weak to resist a Soviet invasion. Several European countries had large domestic Communist parties, which also posed threats to the survival of democracy in those countries. While Cherne was in Tokyo, MacArthur had emphasized the growing Communist penetration of Japanese labor unions.

Cherne was also concerned with Communist infiltration of labor unions in the United States. During the war, he befriended Irving Stone, who had been thrown out of the Screen Writers Guild because he had tried to rid the union of Communist agitators.[5] Toward the end of the war, the Research Institute began a study of labor union membership in the United States. This study revealed significant Communist infiltration of some unions. Cherne believed that Communist penetration was a threat that needed exposure. The RIA study, titled *The Communist in Labor Relations Today*, directly attacked specific unions dominated by Communists and alerted businessmen to tactics Communists used to gain control of unions.[6]

Cherne sent copies of the study to prominent Americans, including Claire Boothe Luce, then a Congresswoman from Connecticut. She was delighted with it. Cherne also sent a copy to her husband, Henry Luce, owner of *Time* and *Life* magazines. He too was pleased with the report and *Time* magazine published a story on it.[7] This was the beginning of a lifelong relationship between Cherne and the Luces.

Other groups, however, were not happy with the report. For instance, the Screen Actors Guild had been identified as a union that espoused causes similar to the Communists. The Guild's governing board considered legal action against the Research Institute.[8] The threat of legal action resulted in Cherne setting up a meeting with Hollywood leaders on June 1, 1947, to discuss Communist penetration of the Screen Actors Guild and other segments of the movie industry. Among those Cherne met at this meeting were Cecil B. DeMille, Robert Montgomery, and Ronald Reagan, the future president of the guild.[9] This meeting convinced Cherne that the Screen Actors Guild was not under left-wing domination.[10] Three months later, Reagan, Montgomery, and others testified as friendly witnesses at the hearings of the House Committee on Communist Infiltration of the Hollywood Motion Picture Industry. One member of the House Committee participating in the hearings was a newly elected Congressman from California, Richard Nixon.

Spotting Communists

Cherne believed that the Communist threat was real and that Americans needed to be aware of it. In March 1947, he published an article titled "How to Spot a Communist." He believed that the problem was exacerbated by reckless anti-Communists who called anyone who disagreed with their thinking a Communist. Cherne was appalled by those who lumped together progressives, liberals, Socialists, atheists, world federalists, chronic dissenters, and New Dealers under the Communist label. For Cherne, a Communist was a real force that should not be obscured by a scattershot barrage. Communists were unlike other Americans, as they believed in the Soviet Union and a Soviet America: they accepted the doctrines of the dictatorship of the proletariat as practiced in the Soviet Union. A Communist placed duty to the party as the first priority and was "prepared to use a dictator's tactics of lies and violence to realize his ambitions," as Cherne put it.[11]

Cherne believed that the Communist menace to America was not their estimated 80,000 members or the possibility that they would ever win at the ballot box. Their real danger rested in their members' special ability to infiltrate legitimate organizations: "to confuse and capture, and then use the legitimate groups for the special purposes of the Communist Party." This gave them far greater strength than their mere numbers indicated.[12]

Cherne identified five different levels among the ranks of those on whom the Communists relied for their strength: (1) party members; (2) fellow travelers; (3) sympathizers; (4) opportunists who selectively supported Communist causes for some particular gain they could enjoy; and (5) front groups through which Communists operated. He offered several ways to determine who was a Communist. These tests related to international matters (Does the person criticize the Soviet Union or just the United States?) as well as domestic matters (Does the person promote a classless society by violently pitting one class against another?).[13]

Freedom's House

One actively anti-Communist organization was Freedom House, which had been founded in 1941 to coalesce groups that believed that America's participation in World War II was inevitable and necessary. Freedom House, a nonpartisan, anti-totalitarian nonprofit, promoted cooperation among organizations housed in the same building.[14] Its honorary chair was the First Lady, Eleanor Roosevelt. On its board was Wendell Willkie, who had opposed President Roosevelt on the Republican ticket in the 1940 presidential elections. Despite Willkie's campaign against Roosevelt, he strongly supported Roosevelt's foreign policy. In 1942, with the blessing of President Roosevelt, Willkie traveled around the world on a peace mission to allies in Latin America, North Africa, the Middle East, Europe, and Asia. He recorded his experiences and conclusions in his book *One World*, which sold 4.5 million copies during the next year.[15]

Cherne and Willkie became friends, and Willkie served as an off-the-record consultant to the Research Institute during the war. Cherne served as an unofficial liaison between Willkie and Roosevelt. When the 1944 presidential elections rolled around, Willkie was defeated in the early Republican state contests in part due to his pro-internationalist position. Cherne tried to persuade Willkie to run on the Democratic ticket as Roosevelt's vice presidential running mate in 1944. Willkie expressed interest, but Roosevelt did not.[16] When Willkie died unexpectedly in October 1944, Cherne wept. He later reported that Willkie's death affected him even more than the death of President Roosevelt six months later. Freedom House held a memorial for Willkie and Cherne was invited to attend. This may have been Cherne's first official connection with Freedom House.[17]

Cherne was officially invited to join the Freedom House board in January 1946. Ten months later he was a member of its executive committee.[18] Through the Freedom House connection, Cherne met many important people probably including Eleanor Roosevelt. It was also where he met Judge Robert P. Patterson, the former undersecretary of war. Cherne worked with him on promoting civil rights. In 1948 Cherne joined a Freedom House delegation, headed by Judge Patterson, to present Truman with the recommendations for the creation of a commission to investigate civil rights violations. The delegation urged the adoption of new laws concerning equal opportunity in employment, voting, education, and protection against mob violence. Truman valued the recommendations "very highly"; but most were not enacted into law until years later.[19]

The La Follette–McCarthy Campaign

Robert La Follette, Jr., of Wisconsin, had served in the U.S. Senate since 1925. La Follette had opposed American entry to World War II, but had little in common with the hardline isolationists, such as the America Firsters. He vigorously fought the Communists before and after World War II. In 1946, La Follette's committee examined penetration of the American Communist Party into targeted areas of American life. La Follette planned to investigate Communist influence in labor unions during the 1947 legislative session; but first he had to win reelection.[20]

La Follette was opposed in the Republican primary by one Joseph McCarthy, then a relatively unknown lawyer who had been elected a judge before World War II. Exempt from the draft due to his judgeship, he enlisted anyway. McCarthy flew several missions as a tail gunner during the war, but slipped at a party, broke his leg, and was discharged. In 1944, he ran for the Senate against Alexander Wiley and lost. He then began planning a run against La Follette in 1946. As Cherne and others later reported, McCarthy received a great deal of support from far-left labor groups, including some dominated by the Communist Party. Communists in Wisconsin provided support for McCarthy's campaign for the Senate, mainly because of La Follette's anti–Communist activities.[21] La Follette did not take McCarthy seriously, and remained in Washington until the last few weeks of the campaign. McCarthy won the primary by less than 6,000 votes, then went on to easily win in the general election against the Democratic candidate and took office in the Senate in 1947.

Should the Communist Party be Outlawed in the United States?

McCarthy's election surprised many observers. Cherne reported that he had received a call from a high-level unnamed FBI official suggesting that Cherne go after the new Senator from Wisconsin. An unnamed White House official told Cherne that McCarthy had a very fat FBI file, a file that, according to Cherne, later disappeared.[22]

Within a month of McCarthy's arrival in the Senate, he debated Cherne and two others on the topic of whether the American Communist Party should be outlawed. The debate was broadcast on the popular radio program "America's Town Meeting of the Air." Cherne took the position that the Communist Party should not be outlawed. "It serves the Communist party to outlaw them," he said.[23] He continued: "I believe in civil liberties because I know that you cannot kill any idea, good or bad, by suppressing it. You only drive it underground and out of your reach. I wish there was some way of forcing the Communists into the spotlight."[24]

McCarthy condemned Cherne's views. McCarthy insisted that the Communist Party was already underground and that it was supported by the infrastructure of a public organization: "I might point out that very recently the Communists who are on the government payroll have been ordered to destroy their membership cards in the Communist Party."[25] McCarthy accepted one of Cherne's central points: "I think a tremendous amount of damage has been done by calling a lot of good, serious liberals Communists. The word 'Communism' is such a libelous phrase that I believe it should be reserved only for those who should receive that type of defamation."[26]

After this debate, McCarthy said little about Communists for the next three years. But, as his career in the Senate had so far been undistinguished, McCarthy worried about his 1952 reelection bid. He needed a subject that would give him visibility. While dining with a group of friends on January 7, 1950 in Washington, DC, McCarthy raised the issue of a focus for his reelection bid. The group discarded quite a few before choosing Communism. "That's it," McCarthy is reported to have said. "The government is full of Communists. We can hammer away at them." At the time, the Alger Hiss case was in full swing, and the convictions and executions of Julius and Ethel Rosenberg were vivid in the public consciousness.

McCarthy's first speech against Communism took place before the Republican Women's Club in Wheeling, West Virginia, on February 9, 1950. In his speech he claimed that he had "a list of 205 cases of individuals who were either card-carrying members or certainly loyal to the Communist Party."[27] This number shifted in various speeches and he generally refrained from naming names. His vagueness led most commentators to believe that McCarthy was simply a demagogue who had exploited a powerful emotional issue at the right time. Recent commentators have proposed that McCarthy had gotten wind of the VENONA intercepts, perhaps even receiving the information from J. Edgar Hoover, director of the Federal Bureau of Investigation. However, by 1950, most of the spies noted in the intercepts had already left the government. Whatever the reasons for McCarthy's claims, the controversy generated wide national exposure.

McCarthy Meets the Critics

As his popularity grew, McCarthy became reckless. For instance, he accused George C. Marshall of treason in a rambling nine-hour Senate speech on June 14, 1951 and subsequently published a slightly revised version of his speech under the title of *The Story of George C. Marshall.*[28] Cherne revered Marshall as one of the great men of American history. Chief of Staff of the U.S. Army during World War II, he had led America to military victory during the war. President Truman then appointed Marshall secretary of state, and in this position, Marshall had helped save Western Europe from economic ruin by initiating the plan that ultimately bore his name. Marshall had gone on to serve as secretary of defense during the early phase of the Korean War.

McCarthy repeated his charges against Marshall in *America's Retreat from Victory*, published in late 1951.[29] In it, he further identified President Eisenhower as a chief collaborator in Marshall's conspiracy. To promote his book, McCarthy agreed to appear on a television program titled "The Author Meets the Critics." Very few in Washington were willing to criticize McCarthy at the height of his power. John Kaye McCaffrey, the moderator of the program, knew that Cherne had debated McCarthy before and so asked him to serve as a critic of McCarthy's book. Cherne relished the prospect and readily agreed. The show was broadcast live on television station WABD on March 20, 1952, from 10:30 to 11:00 P.M.[30]

Cherne came prepared. He had checked with each person or source quoted in *America's Retreat from Victory* and found that McCarthy had misquoted or misinterpreted most important citations. In his opening statement, Cherne refuted McCarthy's charges one by one, and then illustrated McCarthy's errors with a series of large posters as visual aids. When McCarthy denied Cherne's accusations, Cherne put McCarthy on the defensive by offering to make a wager: if McCarthy could find one misstatement in his opening comments, Cherne would willingly give $1,000 to the charity of McCarthy's choice. If McCarthy failed to do so, Cherne proposed that McCarthy give a like amount to a charity of Cherne's choice. McCarthy publicly accepted the offer, but then did not fulfill his part of the wager.[31]

Cherne's denunciation of McCarthy's defamation of Marshall was the first time anyone stood up to the Senator in a national forum.[32] The impact of the debate was powerfully reinforced when Henry Luce, the publisher of *Life* magazine, called Cherne the following day and asked for an article about McCarthy. The result was that *Life* published an abbreviated version of the debate, thereby reaching millions of Americans.[33]

Shortly after Cherne debated McCarthy on "The Author Meets the Critics," he was invited to speak on the influential Barry Gray radio show. Cherne asserted that McCarthy had received support from Wisconsin Communists in his 1946 campaign for the Senate. As McCarthy had denounced others for receiving Communist support, Cherne declared he was deeply offended by McCarthy's tactics, which demonstrated "a pattern of dishonesty, of diabolic cynicism, of the most brutal and calculating distortion of the truth." After making these and other accusations against McCarthy, Cherne willingly volunteered to debate Senator McCarthy "at any time of his selection, at any time he requests in any place he finds most friendly and I should enjoy nothing more than continuing that which we only scratched the surface of in 'Author Meets the Critics.'" At the end of the program, Barry Gray stated that "this night will go down in history as one of the great nights of our broadcasts."[34]

Cherne's challenges rattled McCarthy, who responded, "Why are you doing this to me? You hate Communists." Cherne responded, "Yes, that's why I'm doing it." Cherne continued: "You have no respect for the thing I am defending and am trying to strengthen. You are a demagogue and a faker and a liar."[35] McCarthy chose not to debate Cherne again.

The Effects of McCarthyism

Freedom House became particularly concerned with Joseph McCarthy in 1951. Cherne prepared a report comparing the tactics of McCarthy and those of the Communists and found a great deal of similarity.[36] Early the following year, with Cherne now chairman of its executive committee, Freedom House denounced the tactics of McCarthy and his supporters: "Their wild exaggerations and inexcusable inaccuracies serve to divide and confuse the country when we should be united in the task of resisting Communist aggression abroad and Communist subversion at home. These methods of defamation have helped the Communists by discrediting the democratic process itself."[37] Based on Cherne's analysis, Freedom House issued a detailed report on McCarthy in 1954. It found close parallels between the approaches used by McCarthy and those of the Communists. Both capitalized on difficulties, confusion, and disaster; both exaggerated illegal or unethical actions of opponents; both employed the "big lie" and with frequent repetition; both selected a portion of the truth, mixed with pure invention; both distorted and misstated quotations from others to prove a point; both believed in dividing one's enemies; both attacked the American military and military figures; and both violated security from restricted files if it served their purposes.[38]

McCarthy's accusations caused untold suffering to innocent people. On the national scene, Cherne believed that McCarthy's wild exaggerations made it possible for real Communists to claim that they were innocent and had been unfairly smeared, thereby increasing the respectability of Communists. Even more damaging were the effects of McCarthyism on legitimate anti-Communists. Subsequent efforts to identify and root out real Communists were widely derided in the media as McCarthyite witch hunts.

In May 1954, McCarthy began hearings on the United States Army and its secretary, Robert Stevens. With a television audience estimated at twenty million Americans over thirty-six days, 187 hours of the hearings were broadcast. McCarthy kept up his attacks, pointing his finger at one person after another, accusing them of misdeeds, and offering little evidence for his charges. When McCarthy attacked a young associate of Joseph N. Welch, chief attorney for the Army, Welch stood up, faced the Senator, and said: "Until this moment, Senator, I think I never really gauged your cruelty or your recklessness. Let us not assassinate this lad further, Senator. You have done enough. Have you no sense of decency, sir, at long last? Have you no sense of decency?" The Army-McCarthy hearings resulted in

McCarthy's censure on December 2, 1954 by the Senate voting 67-22, condemning him for "conduct contrary to Senatorial traditions."

President Truman once proclaimed McCarthy to be the greatest asset the Soviet Union had in America. Cherne believed Truman's assessment to be correct: McCarthy's preposterous, self-serving crusade caused skeptical reactions around the world, and many liberals rejected the reality of a very real Soviet intelligence threat. Many Americans believed that even those Soviet agents who were caught, tried, and convicted had been framed.

Epilogue

- George C. Marshall received the Nobel Peace Prize in 1953 for his work to promote the recovery of Europe during the 1940s.

- After the Senate's censure, Joseph McCarthy drank heavily and was frequently hospitalized. He died on May 2, 1957, at the Naval Medical Center in Bethesda, Maryland. At his family's request, his funeral was held in the Senate chamber.

- When the Republican Senator Margaret Chase Smith was asked to become the chairman of Freedom House, she readily agreed, particularly because of Cherne's membership on the board. She specifically mentioned Cherne's debate with Senator Joseph McCarthy in 1952 as a crucial moment for her.[39]

- As a guest on William F. Buckley's *Firing Line* in 1968, Cherne again stated that McCarthy had received support from Communists in his 1946 election bid for the Senate. Before the show aired, the FBI wrote a memo to Buckley expressing their displeasure with Cherne's statement. Buckley deleted it before the program was broadcast.[40] However, Cherne was delighted to repeat the charges in public again in his testimony before the Senate Select Committee on Intelligence.[41]

- When Cherne was informed that some people, including his friend William Buckley, were trying to rehabilitate Joseph McCarthy, Cherne could not understand it. Until his death, Cherne believed that McCarthy was the single most helpful American to the Communist Party since the end of World War II.[42]

- Ronald Reagan, one of the Hollywood actors Cherne met in 1947, helped oust Communists from the Screen Actors Guild. He and

Cherne stayed in contact over the years. In 1966, he was elected governor of California and in 1980, president of the United States.

- Cherne continued as chairman of Freedom House's executive committee until 1976, and remained on the board until 1994, when he was elected Chairman Emeritus.

Chapter 6

Lobbying for Indochina

Leo never seemed to understand when it was time to bail out. For example, the American Friends of Vietnam, which consisted of forty-some luminaries who consorted to save a struggling new nation from the enemy and hopefully become democratic. As the war became more and more discomforting, the Friends peeled off one by one and disappeared. Until that terrible day in April 1975 when the helicopters were picking the last Americans off the rooftops in Saigon, Leo, Frank Treager and I were staring gloomily at the half-page ad we had put in the *New York Times* that day pleading with the government to do something for a last-minute rescue.

—Jerry Steibel, February 3, 1999

Prologue

After Germany defeated France in 1940, Japan occupied French Indochina. When the United States entered World War II after Japan's attack on Pearl Harbor, the Office of Strategic Services (OSS), the forerunner of the Central Intelligence Agency, supported small groups of underground and exiled nationalists fighting Japanese occupation. Prominent among the anti-Japanese groups backed by the OSS was the Viet Minh, headed by Ho Chi Minh. Recently released documents indicate that the relationship between the OSS and Ho Chi Minh was close. As World War II ended, Ho Chi Minh asked the United States for help in preventing France from reestablishing its colonial empire in Indochina. China and Britain sent military forces respectively into north and south Vietnam to disarm Japanese soldiers stationed in Indochina. Later, France dispatched troops to replace the British and Chinese forces and to reestablish her colonial empire. Craving independence from France after World War II, most nationalists in Indochina joined in league against the French colonists. Initially, these forces, led by the previously American-supported Ho Chi Minh, included a broad array of independent nationalists. But as the conflict dragged on, Ho Chi Minh became troubled by internal opposition; he executed or assassinated 70,000 non-Communist leaders, even though many were equally nationalist and anti-French.

For the United States, the French-Indochinese War posed an agonizing dilemma. If it withheld financial and military support from the French in Indochina, France might retaliate by detaching itself from NATO in Europe, where the United States believed the Soviets were a more important strategic threat. However, if the United States supported the French, it was unlikely that any amount of American aid could turn the tide against the Viet Minh, and the United States would be tarnished with colonialism, which it officially opposed in Asia and Africa. The U.S. government chose to extend limited aid to the French quietly behind the scenes. When the Viet Minh defeated the French at Dienbienphu in 1954, a Geneva Conference was called, attended by the parties directly involved in Indochina. The United States was not a party to these negotiations and did not sign the agreements, which provisionally divided Vietnam in two, with the north dominated by the Viet Minh and the south dominated by non-Communist Vietnamese. The agreements called for an election to unite the country by 1956, and they included a protocol permitting the Vietnamese to travel freely between the two halves for a period of eighteen months. Within days of the Geneva agreement, refugees massed within the zones of North Vietnam still controlled by France. Few observers doubted that the agreement would prompt refugees to leave the Communist zone, but no one expected the stampede that swept southward to the non-Communist portion of the country.

When the trickle turned into a flood, the refugees were transported south by U.S. Navy Task Force 90, called "Operation Passage to Freedom." Among those who assisted these refugees was one Thomas Dooley, who was then serving in the U.S. Navy. Other refugees walked overland from North Vietnam across the seventeenth parallel into South Vietnam. Eventually, 900,000 refugees fled south. Simultaneously, about 125,000 South Vietnamese, Cambodians, and Laotians went to North Vietnam.

In July 1954, South Vietnam had been under French colonial misrule for more than ninety years. The French had done nothing to prepare the country for independence. Indochina additionally had suffered through five years of conflict with the Japanese conquerors and seven years of anti-colonial and anti-Communist civil war. The country was a bleeding wound: devastation, disintegration, dislocation, and war-weariness prevailed. Feudal sects with their own armies battled one another and the new government for supremacy. The remaining French colonists openly conspired with dissidents; inflation was rampant, rice production at a standstill, and the industrial north cut off all trade with the agrarian south. At the crest of these disasters were the refugees. They had to be fed, clothed, housed, and resettled.[1]

Ngo Dinh Diem stepped into this chaos in South Vietnam. Born in 1901, he graduated from the School of Administration in Hanoi. He became province chief in 1930 and two years later Bao Dai, the nominal Vietnamese Emperor, appointed him minister of interior in Annam. When Diem's reforms were blocked, he went into exile. He refused Bao Dai's offer to become premier of Vietnam during the Japanese occupation. After World War II, Diem also refused Ho Chi Minh's offer of a position in his government. Ho Chi Minh arrested Diem in September 1945, but released him in March 1946—a decision Ho Chi Minh later regretted. Diem's brother and nephew were not so lucky: they were killed by the Viet Minh. When the French returned to Vietnam, they offered Diem the same puppet position under their control, but he again refused.[2]

Diem, a Catholic, traveled to Rome via Tokyo to participate in the Holy Year celebration at the Vatican in 1950. While in Tokyo, Diem was discovered by Wesley Fishel, a young professor of Southeast Asian affairs then teaching at Michigan State University. Fishel suggested that Diem visit the United States, which he did in September and October. He met a small group of Americans who were concerned about Vietnam but unaware of the prevailing political and military complexities. Diem left for Europe but returned to the United States in 1951, spending most of his time in Maryknoll seminaries in Lakewood, New Jersey, and Ossining, New York. He lectured at several universities and met a number of prominent Americans, including Cardinal Spellman, Senators Mike Mansfield and John F. Kennedy, and Supreme Court Justice William O. Douglas.

In 1953 Diem went to Paris, staying at a Benedictine monastery. While the French and their Vietnamese allies waged a losing battle against the Viet Minh, Diem met with exiled Vietnamese leaders in Paris, particularly Bao Dai, who was a French puppet. Bao Dai had become emperor of Annam (today the central portion of Vietnam) in 1926 at the age of twelve. He lived most of his playboy life on the French Riviera, and abdicated his throne in 1945 when his empire became extinct. He served as "Supreme" advisor to the Ho Chi Minh government in 1945, but went into exile in 1946. He returned to Vietnam in 1949 as chief of state appointed by the French. Even before the conclusion of the Geneva Conference in 1954, Bao Dai asked Diem to form a government for what would soon become an independent South Vietnam. Diem accepted and one week later left Paris headed for Saigon. On July 7, the day after the Geneva accords were signed, he became South Vietnam's first premier with full political and military powers.[3]

Even before Diem became premier, Colonel Edward G. Lansdale, an undercover American operative working for the Central Intelligence Agency, had arrived in Saigon. Once Diem took office, Lansdale strongly supported him. Through Lansdale, Diem received financial and military assistance from the United States during his critical first few months in power. Lansdale's exploits were so famous that he was the inspiration both for William J. Lederer and Eugene Burdick's *The Ugly American* and Graham Greene's *The Quiet American.*[4]

Cherne Flies to Saigon

When word reached him that a massive flood of refugees was leaving North Vietnam, Cherne believed that the IRC needed to become involved. This matter was raised at the IRC's executive committee in June 1954. The financial outlay for a potential Southeast Asian rescue program was estimated at $550,000. Cherne was directed to go to Vietnam on a fact-finding trip and see if it was possible to launch a successful program. There was opposition to this.[5] IRC's treasurer, Arthur Watson, then president of the IBM World Trade organization and later the U.S. ambassador to France, opposed the potential program, as did two other board members. The IRC had limited resources and it had previously focused its attention on European refugees.[6]

On August 27, Cherne flew to Germany, where he met Watson, who was on a business trip. Cherne tried to convince Watson of the importance of his trip to Vietnam to judge what, if anything, the IRC might do to help the refugees, particularly the political, intellectual, and religious leaders among them. Cherne traveled to Paris where Vietnamese nationalists briefed him about their long and arduous struggle against the French and Ho Chi Minh's betrayal of liberal and left-wing parties. After three days in Paris, Cherne made his way to first to Calcutta, then to Saigon, where he arrived on September 9.[7]

Cherne had tried unsuccessfully to plan his trip with the U.S. ambassador to South Vietnam, Donald Heath, or with Harold Stassen, the perennial Republican presidential candidate, then head of the U.S. aid program in Vietnam. Cherne received no encouragement from Heath or Stassen. Cherne arrived in Saigon without a hotel reservation, in the midst of a monsoon. He sought assistance at the American aid mission. There he met Carter de Paul, Jr., who informed him that there were no hotels in Saigon; De Paul kindly offered to house Cherne as well as introduce him to other

Americans living in the complex. Through de Paul, Cherne met Wesley Fishel, the young professor in Southeast Asian affairs, whom Diem had hired as an advisor on government reorganization.[8] Cherne also met Monsignor Joseph Harnett, the coordinator of the massive Vietnamese relief programs sponsored by the Catholic Relief Services. Cherne and Harnett traveled about Saigon and became friends.[9]

Three days after Cherne arrived in Saigon, he first encountered Diem in a meeting set up by Fishel. At the time of the meeting, Diem was fifty-three years old and had been in office only thirty days. While Cherne was in Saigon, the French officially turned over power to Diem in a moving ceremony, which lowered the French flag and unfurled the flag of the newly formed country of South Vietnam. Twenty-four hours later, the palace was under siege by a combination of Vietnamese and left-over French soldiers. Cherne had difficulty keeping his first appointment with Diem, because mutinous pro-French troops surrounded the palace.

Cherne brought introductions from Christopher Emmet and Peter White, both of whom had known Diem in the United States. Emmet, head of the American Council on Germany, had been obsessed with fascism in Germany in the mid-1930s and saw the urgent need for a free Germany to arise from the ashes of World War II. Peter White met Diem when he was staying in the Marymount monastery in New York. Both Emmet and White were strong Catholics and passionate democrats.

Cherne confessed to Diem that he was not sure that the IRC could help. At the time, the IRC's resources were meager, and the IRC did not then have a presence in Asia. This did not matter to Diem. Cherne was one of the first Americans to consider offering assistance, and Diem thought this an extraordinary development. Diem took it for granted that he would get substantial help from fellow Catholics and the U.S. government. But he was absolutely astonished that the Jewish head of a nonsectarian organization would, on his own initiative, journey to Saigon to see if he could help. In the days that followed, Cherne frequently met with Diem. At first, Cherne could do little but listen as Diem, a compulsive talker, dominated the conversation. However, as Diem was a chain-smoker, Cherne learned to bide his time until Diem inhaled his cigarette, then talk as fast as possible until Diem interrupted. Cherne considered Diem a philosophical nationalist, who had many characteristics of an ascetic: shy, withdrawn, impeccable, and untouchable when it came to women, bribery, and corruption.

Most observers concluded that Diem had no chance of success. He had to contend with far more than just the opposition of the Communists. The French had to leave, but they did not have to do so rapidly. And the

French did not want to relinquish their stranglehold on the Vietnamese economy. In addition, pro-French Vietnamese leaders vied for Diem's power. The sophisticated and politically astute Joseph and Stewart Alsop brothers, then writing columns out of Saigon, were strongly pro-French and anti-Diem. The Alsops agreed that Diem was not corruptible, but they also saw the impossibility of governing Vietnam without making deals. The Alsops believed that Diem did not have a chance of surviving more than a few weeks, let alone heading a viable government. Other news sources agreed. *Newsweek* magazine concluded that South Vietnam was "slipping under Red control at an alarming rate."[10]

By the time Cherne left Saigon, he was infected with Diem's messianic fervor, believing Diem was attracting significant Vietnamese popular support, and therefore had a chance to succeed with American help.

One immediate problem Diem faced was the massive refugee influx from North Vietnam. Three thousand refugees were arriving every day—they numbered more than 900,000 by the time Hanoi closed the borders, resulting in one of the largest refugee movements in history. Of these refugees, 60 percent were Catholic and 40 percent Buddhist. Cherne became convinced that the IRC ought to assist these refugees. On September 13, 1954, Cherne sent a radiogram from Saigon to the Research Institute proclaiming his support for Diem and announcing that the situation was not hopeless. The future, said Cherne, "depends on organizing all resources to resettle refugees, sustain near bankrupt government, give people something to fight for and unite them to resist communism." He ended the radiogram with a flourish: the "West can't afford to lose from now on." The following day Cherne left Saigon.[11]

On Cherne's return trip, he stopped in Manila for two days. There he met Amelito Mutuc, president of the Philippine Jaycees, who had just conducted a survey for their "Operation Brotherhood" aid to the refugees escaping from areas of impending Communist control. This project had been devised by the covert CIA operative, Edward Lansdale, and was supported by the Manila businessman Oscar Arellano, president of the Southeast Asian Jaycees. This project developed into one that "sent Filipino physicians, nurses, and dentists to South Vietnam to offer medical and political support to the Diem regime."[12]

Cherne returned to New York early on the morning of September 20 and a few hours later held a press conference at his office in the Research Institute of America. To the reporters, Cherne offered a gloomy assessment of the problems confronting the government of Premier Ngo Dinh Diem. The government was bankrupt; there were people in power who were not under Diem's control; and the country faced an enormous refugee problem. Cherne argued that the United States "must give more financial and technical assistance and maintain the presence of Americans there as far as the Viet Nam armistice will allow."[13]

Privately, Cherne was not hopeful about Diem's chances of survival. In a letter to William J. Donovan, Cherne reported that the Communists controlled sections of South Vietnam only miles from Saigon, and that in the countryside, there was no clear knowledge of who was in control. Diem controlled neither the South Vietnamese army nor police. As premier, he served at the will of Bao Dai. Cherne was convinced that even South Vietnam would vote heavily Communist if there were an election; but luckily the Geneva accords had put off the election for two years.[14]

There was no time to lose. Cherne went to work launching IRC programs in South Vietnam. Cherne needed a proven leader who could establish the IRC's South Vietnam effort. He chose Joseph Buttinger, who (as mentioned in Chapter 3) had been a leader in the anti-Hitler underground in Austria prior to World War II. From Cherne's perspective, Buttinger was the perfect choice. He spoke fluent French, and his Catholic background should enable him to have good rapport with Diem. However, Buttinger was not eager for the assignment. He had not been a practicing Catholic in years and had no knowledge about Southeast Asia. After the IRC's executive committee approved the creation of a "Freedom Fund for Vietnam" program, Buttinger agreed to visit South Vietnam to see what the IRC could do for the refugees pouring in from North Vietnam. Cherne wrote to Ambassador Heath announcing the Freedom Fund and mentioning that Buttinger would soon arrive in Saigon to help launch it.[15]

Buttinger arrived in Saigon in late October of 1954 to assess the chaotic situation. On December 1, he concluded: "Vietnam is not lost—not by a long shot. It is clear the U.S. was unprepared for the consequences of the Geneva Armistice. It is equally obvious that the government of Premier Diem, appointed just one month prior to the Armistice, was unprepared to meet the exigencies flowing from that agreement and has since been facing constant power conflicts among the nationalist forces in Vietnam as well as opposition by the French. Despite this, the democratic government of Diem is far stronger today than it was thirty days ago." Buttinger believed that the "odds may be against democracy and freedom in Vietnam, but time is on our side. The more stable the situation becomes, the better are freedom's chances for success." But he wrote that the greatest hope lay in the "caliber of devoted men close to the Premier. The position of the Vietnamese anti-Communist and anti-colonial nationalist fighting for his country's independence is difficult. But I assure you that I have no doubts about the political loyalty of those for whom the advent of Diem gave birth to a hope of eventual political independence." Buttinger identified the refugees as the gravest problem. He believed the United States had to take responsibility for their care or lose face, which would be "fatal to U.S. interests in all of Asia. Active assistance to leadership elements among refugees [is] essential to solution of problem."[16]

Buttinger was especially concerned with the fate of 3,000 university and high school students, 200 professors from the University of Hanoi and 500 secondary school teachers. He also pointed out that hundreds of former civil servants, engineers, and small businessmen had fled North Vietnam as well: "The great immediate task is to put this manpower to effective use, to support existing government, to build up broken structures of community life, to train additional personnel. IRC's attempt to help meet this specific problem, therefore, is of greatest urgency now." Buttinger believed that the most effective use of IRC resources would be to work with refugees who had professional backgrounds. He was especially interested in establishing a university in Saigon. He organized a liaison committee of refugee education leaders, and its first working session took place on November 30. They split into four subgroups (writers and journalists, artists, professors, students) for the preparation of specific programs and begin courses. Over 7,000 persons registered for evening courses, because they worked during the day. Of those who registered, 6,000 were turned away. The classrooms were overcrowded, and the professors were overworked. There were few books and no equipment for the science classes. To get the college off the ground, they needed books, tables, chairs, desks, notebooks, typewriters, audio-visual aids, projectors, and mimeograph machines. Buttinger concluded in telegraphese: "Further funds essential immediately to expand our help. We have only a short time to do a monumental task. This is last chance for Vietnam. We must do all we can now."[17]

With Buttinger in Vietnam, Cherne started making the rounds in the United States to try to convince prominent Americans of the urgency of supporting Diem, but he found little encouragement. In Cherne's view, Washington leaders underestimated Diem's enormous potential and integrity. The highest functionary Cherne gained access to was Dorothy Houghton, the deputy director of the Foreign Operations Administration (FOA), and she expressed little interest in Diem.[18] Likewise, Cherne's White House contact had no willingness to in discuss Diem. The White House staff had reviewed the dispatches from Ambassador Heath, who was sym-

pathetic to the goal of a non–Communist South Vietnam, but he had concluded it would be impossible with Diem as leader. Heath urged Washington to oust Diem and replace him with someone who would make the
necessary political deals to build a power base throughout South Vietnam.

By the end of November 1954, Diem had survived four months in
power despite three successive coup attempts by various Vietnamese groups.
One anti-Diem coup leader was General Nguyen Van Hinh, a major power
in the pro-French Vietnamese army and the son of a former premier of
French-controlled Indochina. Hinh was looking for an opportunity to take
over the reins of power from Diem. After the coup failed, Diem convinced
Bao Dai to request a meeting with Hinh in France. After Hinh left, Diem
refused to allow him back into the country. Other conflicts fostered by the
French surrounded him and a major portion of South Vietnam was still
controlled by sects and warlords.

To assure the loyalty of his government, Diem appointed family members to positions of power. He appointed his brother, Ngo Dinh Nhu, "advisor to the president;" placed another brother, Can, in charge of the agrarian
reform and national security efforts in the central region of the country; and
enlisted the influence of a third brother, Thuc, the Catholic bishop of Saigon
and surrounding areas. He appointed his fourth brother, Luyen, the South
Vietnamese ambassador to the United Kingdom. Tran van Chuong, South
Vietnam's ambassador to Washington, was Nhu's father-in-law. These ap-
pointments brought charges of nepotism, but early on they provided the stability necessary to cope with the other problems Diem confronted.

In a move unrelated to Cherne's efforts, the U. S. government decided
to take another look at Vietnam. General J. Lawton Collins, a former army
chief of staff, arrived in Saigon in December to make another assessment.
Collins concluded that the situation was hopeless and that American aid
should be curtailed. The CIA's Edward Lansdale urged the opposite and continued to funnel covert financial support to Diem. Collins's recommendations
were not made public, and Diem's position actually strengthened during this
time. Ambassador Heath believed that continuing aid to the Vietnamese was a
gamble, but that the alternative—chaos, leading to an inevitable Communist
takeover in South Vietnam—was far worse. The United States's announcement of an additional $40 million in economic assistance steadied Diem's
hand further, as did the military assistance and small arms that were shipped
through the U.S. Military Advisory Assistance Group (MAAG).

Buttinger turned over the IRC's funds to Monseigneur Harnett for safe
keeping and returned to New York in late December greatly impressed with
the extraordinary political ability and character of Ngo Dinh Diem. Buttinger

and Cherne convinced the IRC to launch some small programs in South Vietnam. Robert McAlister assumed permanent charge of IRC's Vietnam office in March 1955. It funded the Popular Culture Association, which created the Polytechnic Institute. Also, the IRC helped establish a university in Hue.[19]

With some IRC programs underway in Saigon, Buttinger and Cherne drummed up as much public support for Diem as they could muster in the United States. Cherne submitted his photographs of Vietnam to *Look* magazine, which published them along with an article by Cherne titled "To Win in Indochina We Must Win These People." In the article, Cherne admitted the problems faced by the South Vietnamese, and reported that the refugees needed to be resettled and Saigon needed a university. However, he ended on an optimistic note: "If we do these things, we may still yet save Indochina—and Asia."[20]

Upon the recommendation of Buttinger, Harold Oram, the IRC's fundraiser, was retained by the South Vietnamese government to engage in public relations on its behalf in the United States.[21] Cherne, Buttinger, and Oram formed the American Friends of Vietnam (AFV) for which Angier Biddle Duke sent out a solicitation letter in April 1955. Collectively they cajoled a diverse group of prominent Americans to join the AFV's national committee. Prominent among them were Wesley Fishel and Wolf Ladejinsky, another American in the employ of Diem.

Ladejinsky had been born in the Ukraine, but escaped in 1920 through Rumania and immigrated to the United States. Cherne had first met Ladejinsky in Japan, where he had administered a radical land reform program for Douglas MacArthur after World War II. With this successful land redistribution effort underway in Japan, Ladejinsky then worked in Taiwan and India. These programs proved so successful that they caught the attention of Senator Joseph McCarthy, who proclaimed that all land reform programs were Communist-inspired conspiracies. McCarthy lambasted Ladejinsky, who was dismissed from his position in the Foreign Operations Administration in the State Department. Specifically, he was charged with visiting the Soviet Union in 1939 and belonging to two Communist front organizations. When Ladejinsky heard the charges lodged against him, he quickly proved that he had gone to the Soviet Union at the behest of the U.S. Department of Agriculture and only had been on mailing lists of the two organizations. Ladejinsky was rehired by FOA and sent to Vietnam, where Ngo Dinh Diem gave Ladejinsky the task of creating a land reform program in Vietnam.[22]

In addition to Fishel and Ladejinsky, the national committee consisted of Joseph P. Kennedy, father of the future president; Norman Thomas, one of the founders of the ACLU and the perennial candidate for president on the Socialist Party ticket; U.S. Supreme Court Justice William O. Douglas; Francis Cardinal Spellman, who had met Diem in the United States; J. Bracken Lee, a friend of Senator Joseph McCarthy; John F. Kennedy, who joined because of his anticolonialist views (rather than on account of his Catholicism, as later alleged); General Edward Lansdale, the CIA's head in Vietnam; General William J. Donovan, who had served as U.S. ambassador to Thailand in 1953–1954; and Monsignor Harnett. Also recruited were prominent academics, including top historians Samuel Eliot Morison and Arthur Schlesinger, Jr., both of whom had served as consultants to the Research Institute. The AFV also sought coverage in newspapers and magazines: *Time, Newsweek,* and the *New York Times* all wrote favorable stories about South Vietnam. The AFV later sponsored a visit by Diem to the United States, garnering more favorable publicity for him.[23]

In addition, Oram and Cherne helped raise funds and other support for a newly reconstituted Operation Brotherhood. This continued the work of the Philippine doctors, expanding it to include support from American Jaycees. It also added two new programs: one offering direct assistance to Vietnamese community leaders, and the other offering emergency support for the Polytechnic Institute established by the IRC. Oram issued a press release in March 1955 reporting that the American Jaycees and their President, E. Lamar Buckner, pledged the general support of the 2,700 Jaycees chapters for Operation Brotherhood.

In a letter to Diem, Cherne expressed his preference for private initiatives as opposed to governmental aid programs.[24] Diem appealed for American assistance through Operation Brotherhood. Cherne and Oram enlisted prominent Americans to assist in this project. Richard E. Byrd, Mrs. Kermit Roosevelt, Samuel Goldwyn, Henry Luce, and William J. Donovan joined in supporting Operation Brotherhood. John Foster Dulles, U.S. secretary of state, supported the drive to generate $1 million for Operation Brotherhood as a means to stop Communism in Vietnam. President Eisenhower, informed about Operation Brotherhood, wrote a letter on its behalf and held a White House conference in its support during May 1955.[25] Telegrams soliciting funds were sent to prominent Americans on September 1, 1955.

The attempt to connect specific American Jaycees with projects in Vietnam was launched in the fall of 1955. Despite all the high-profile support and the high volume of activities, Operation Brotherhood never really got off the ground, and the program was discontinued the following year.[26] For most Americans, Vietnam was simply too far away and too little understood. The IRC's final assessment was that it had lost funds on the project, but had gained tremendous visibility. It had another benefit. Through Operation Brotherhood, Cherne met Tom Dooley.

Tom Dooley

From a prominent Catholic family in Saint Louis, Tom Dooley enrolled in the University of Notre Dame in the fall of 1944. After just a few weeks of classes, he enlisted in the Navy and became a medical corpsman. The war ended before he finished his training and he returned to Notre Dame, where he completed five semesters without graduating. He received a special waiver to enroll in the medical school at Saint Louis University, and he barely made it through the course of study. Rather than go into private practice, he chose to rejoin the Navy in 1953. Following the defeat of the French in Indochina, Dooley's ship was ordered to ferry refugees from the North to the South. In September 1954 Dooley was reassigned to collect medical information in a refugee camp in Haiphong and assist in the evacuation of the refugees.

In the midst of frantic confusion in Haiphong, Dooley sent letters off to friends and newspapers about his experiences. One was published in the Navy's *Medical News Letter*, which was brought to the attention of the Navy brass. The Navy identified Dooley as an official morale booster.[27] Dooley's refugee camp in Haiphong became the center of attraction for visiting dignitaries. One visitor was William Lederer, then working on what would become *The Ugly American*. Lederer suggested that Dooley keep a journal, which Dooley did.[28]

Dooley's letters reported atrocities committed by the Viet Minh, particularly against Catholics. Dooley's allegations were widely printed in newspapers in the United States, particularly the Catholic press, and Dooley became a national celebrity. Lansdale read Dooley's letters and concluded that they were just what America needed. Lansdale wrote up an appropriate citation and passed it along to Diem, who conferred an award on Dooley. The U.S. Navy gave Dooley yet another award. His popularity soared in America. By early 1955, he was the most famous American in Indochina.[29]

Lederer helped Dooley compile his letters, which were published in 1956 as a book, *Deliver Us from Evil; the Story of Viet Nam's Flight to Freedom*. It was a blockbuster book that described the atrocities allegedly committed by the Viet Minh. Then Lederer assisted Dooley in making contact with the editors of *Reader's Digest,* who published the book in condensed form in 1957.[30] For most Americans, Dooley's book was their first glimpse of Vietnam. It was more than a compelling chronicle of Dooley's activities; it was a humanitarian view of a Cold War flashpoint. Dooley wrote: "My meager resources in Indochina did not win people's hearts though they helped. What turned the trick were those words, 'This is American aid' and all that those words conveyed. I believe that in the long run such plain help can be the decisive factor in bringing about a victory for all the sacred things we stand for."[31]

At the peak of Dooley's success, rumors circulated about his homosexual relationships. The Navy assigned investigators to follow him clandestinely and interrogate his male acquaintances. After a brief investigation, the Navy quietly discharged him. Within three weeks of his separation from the Navy, Dooley had returned to the United States and met Cherne on board the *Cassandra*, moored in the Hudson River in New York. This was not the first contact between the IRC and Dooley. In November 1954, Dooley wrote to the IRC telling about his work in North Vietnam and requesting assistance. Dooley subsequently received a shipment of clothes and other supplies from the IRC's Operation Brotherhood. Dooley volunteered to help the IRC, but nothing came of his offer at that time.[32]

Shortly after Dooley's first book was published, the American Friends of Vietnam sponsored a symposium on Vietnam, the first ever held in the United States. Dooley was the major speaker. Oram and Cherne saw the star qualities in Dooley: he was handsome, charismatic, and well-spoken. Dooley did have experience with Indochinese refugees and was deeply committed to their welfare. He was anti-Communist with a strong Catholic bent. Finally, he was already famous through the hype surrounding his blockbuster book—and Oram helped him become even more famous. Oram worked with Dooley to mold him into an even more successful promoter. Dooley was an excellent study and proved to be a publicist's dream.[33]

Dooley told Cherne that he wanted to return to Indochina and build a hospital in Laos. With some financial backing from DeWitt Wallace of *Reader's Digest,* Dooley refined his concept. Together Cherne, Oram, and Dooley mapped out the strategy for "Operation Laos," modeled after the original Operation Brotherhood which had sent Philippine medical teams to South Vietnam. Lansdale heard about this new effort and asked the Philippines Jaycees to help Dooley get started in Laos.[34]

This strategy proved successful. With the funds generated, Dooley built his hospital in Muong-sing, Laos, which was not far from the Laotian-Chinese border. When he returned to the United States in mid-1957, he expressed interest in expanding Operation Laos to include other regions of the world. He broached the idea with Oram, Duke, and Cherne, who agreed to support the expanded effort. Dooley had written to Albert Schweitzer, who had expressed interest in the idea. Dooley planned a visit to Schweitzer, the world-renowned humanitarian-philosopher, who lived in Lambaréné, French Equatorial Africa. Dooley believed that the key to the financial success of the plan was to name Schweitzer honorary chairman. Dooley had already purchased airline tickets for his Africa trip, but he fell ill in New York and gave the tickets to Cherne.[35]

Cherne accepted the tickets with alacrity. Schweitzer was one of Cherne's heros; he had even sculpted a bust of Schweitzer in 1955. Cherne readily assumed Dooley's mission and headed for Schweitzer's village in Lambaréné. His companions on this trip were Peter Comanduras—a Baltimore surgeon who Dooley hoped would carry out a substantial part of the medical undertaking of the newly named Medical International Cooperation Organization (MEDICO)—and Erica Anderson, who was to become Schweitzer's photographer. Schweitzer understood English, but he preferred to speak German. Cherne spoke no French or German, so Anderson served as translator between Cherne and Schweitzer. Cherne and Anderson formed an easy friendship mainly because both were compulsive smokers; Schweitzer could not tolerate the idea of smoking so they sneaked outside to smoke. Cherne wandered around during the day observing the activities in the compound. He was deeply impressed. The community was largely staffed by volunteers. The doctors and nurses spent long hours giving medical assistance to hundreds of patients. Cherne was particularly impressed with the leper colony: the sight of volunteer nurses giving care to the lepers amazed him. They washed the lepers' "hands, the feet, the stumps, to treat them with whatever medications were available. It's beautiful," said Cherne.[36]

On the other hand, Cherne was critical of many things he saw. For instance, Schweitzer dished out corporal punishment to his workers. When Adlai Stevenson had visited him a couple of years before and objected to the practice, Schweitzer suggested he close his eyes. Schweitzer was extremely frugal. He wrote his letters in a painstakingly tiny hand to conserve paper. When Schweitzer received long letters, after responding to them, he left the pages outside on a table for antelope to eat. Schweitzer finished work at ten o'clock at night and then came to Cherne's little room. They talked and argued until two or three in the morning. On almost no subject did they agree. Schweitzer said that the worst thing that Europeans had done for Africa was to educate the natives, and he refused to accept the notion that indigenous peoples were his equal. He was a confirmed colonialist; Cherne believed the opposite. Cherne, a secular Jew, disagreed with Schweitzer, the ardent Protestant missionary, on the nature and meaning of Calvinism. Despite their differences, both men loved their conversations and quickly bonded. Cherne had come to Lambaréné for the specific purpose of gaining Schweitzer's agreement to serve as honorary chairman of the proposed MEDICO, and he left four days later with Schweitzer's promise to do so.[37] Dooley visited Schweitzer later and sealed the deal.[38]

Angier Biddle Duke, the president of the IRC, set up the organizational aspects. Fundraising efforts were undertaken, aided very substantially by Dooley's extraordinary abilities. MEDICO, a subsidiary of the IRC, was launched in February 1958. It functioned in various locations in Asia and Africa. Comanduras was the secretary general, residing in the United States, while Dooley was based in Laos. While Dooley was away, Comanduras was responsible for running the organization. Unfortunately, Comanduras was not a skilled administrator. The IRC leaders—including Cherne and Duke—increasingly had difficulties with the operation. Comanduras was enveloped in administrative problems and Dooley submitted excessively large entertainment expenses. Finally, the IRC leaders concluded that MEDICO was a worthy operation, but it was not a refugee undertaking. In 1959, the IRC arranged for CARE to take it over; and so it remains today.[39]

Civil War in Vietnam

During the early months of 1955, the Communists were generally inactive in South Vietnam. The Geneva accords had called for an election to be held throughout Vietnam in 1956. North Vietnam had a larger population than did South Vietnam. In a free and fair election, it was obvious to all that the Communists would win. So the North Vietnamese leaders initially concentrated on rebuilding and reorganizing the North, and waited for the elections to give them power throughout the country. However, neither the South Vietnamese nor the United States had signed the Geneva accords and therefore neither government felt bound to uphold its provisions. So the Diem government, with American backing, refused to participate in the national election. Diem demonstrated his support through the ballot box by scoring an overwhelming election victory against Emperor Bao Dai. Diem then ousted the French-supported emperor, created the Republic of Vietnam, and changed his own title from premier to president.

The North Vietnamese responded by stepping up their military support to the South Vietnamese forces fighting against Diem. Many had been leaders in the war against the French and had then migrated to the North at the request of leaders in Hanoi in 1954. These South Vietnamese had been trained in the North and were now infiltrated back into the South, where they became the core of the Viet Cong—the Communist forces opposing the Diem regime.

Diem successfully fended off the initial Communist guerilla onslaught. By 1957, his government enjoyed some public support among many groups in South Vietnam, for the country had made considerable economic progress. Rice production rose from two million to more than five million tons, and rice exports reached the highest level in Vietnam's history. Rubber production increased annually and earnings increased from $24 million in 1954 to $46 million in 1959. Total exports increased 50 percent from 1954 to 1959, and new light industries emerged: textiles, thread, paper, rubber products, glass, sugar cane refining, cement, and pharmaceuticals. Diem had achieved a decline in imports and an increase in exports, which produced a sharp drop in the trade deficit. Hence, South Vietnam weathered American cuts in foreign assistance, while the living standards in Vietnam improved.[40]

By May 1957, Diem felt comfortable enough with his hold on power to visit the United States. Oram handled Diem's visit to the United States. Cherne and the AFV continued to support the cause of South Vietnam. On September 19, 1958, President Ngo Dinh Diem awarded Cherne the Kim-Khanh, a solid gold medallion that had been given only to two others: Syngman Rhee, president of Korea, and Chiang Kai-shek, president of the Republic of China. In response, the IRC gave Diem the Admiral Richard E. Byrd Memorial Award. Byrd had died just a few months before Diem's visit and had been a strong supporter of the IRC. Diem was the only person ever to receive the award.[41]

Despite Cherne's strong commitment to Diem, problems popped up from the beginning. The first related to Diem's announcement of a voluntary gift of thousands of dollars to the IRC's Hungarian refugees programs in late 1956. As South Vietnam was strapped for funds at the time, these funds could only have derived from U.S. foreign aid funds. This was quickly resolved by the IRC accepting the funds in Vietnamese currency and using them to assist only the IRC's programs in Vietnam. This problem quickly disappeared.[42]

Other problems were more serious. Despite positive economic signs, the political situation in Vietnam was disintegrating. In addition to the Viet Cong, South Vietnamese sects and warlords also opposed Diem. These groups had been funded to fight against the Communists by the French government before their ouster from South Vietnam in 1954. The United States gave its aid directly to Diem, who refused to pass it on to them. Their power weakened as their access to funds declined. In 1957, Diem conquered the warlords and the sects and announced that he intended to execute their leaders. Cherne strongly opposed these actions and sent a telegram to Diem requesting clemency. Diem executed them anyway.[43] While Diem's action strengthened his power in South Vietnam, it also undermined non-Communist forces opposed to the Viet Cong and was a public relations disaster in the United States.

What really concerned Cherne was Diem's increasing authoritarianism. The IRC had supported the development of universities in South Vietnam, where opposition to the Diem regime was blossoming. Diem's police forces jailed professors and students and committed other outrages, undercutting what had been a popular government. The repression and disintegrating political support made it easier for the Viet Cong to gain support in South Vietnam. As Diem expanded his repression, more non-Communists threw their support to the Viet Cong.[44]

Diem's brother Ngo Dinh Nhu convinced the president to take even stronger measures to stamp out internal opposition. Repression, particularly against the Buddhists, unleashed a negative spiral of events in South Vietnam. Nhu was pragmatic and ruthless. He was backed by his ambitious and corrupt wife, Madame Nhu, known as the "Tiger Lady" in the American press. Madame Nhu lived with one of the generals in the Vietnamese army, a fact that was generally understood and regarded as advantageous to Ngo Dinh Nhu. More and more, the government slipped under the control of the Nhus.[45]

This resort to repression increasingly disturbed IRC leaders and the members of the American Friends of Vietnam. Cherne sent cables encouraging Diem to reverse the policies championed by his brother, but to no avail. By the end of 1959, the situation had turned sour. Diem's firmest supporters abandoned hope that his power base could be saved, and all believed that Nhu had to go. When Diem engaged in violent repression of the Buddhists and the democratic opposition, dissenting members of President Diem's cabinet and several members of his own staff urged Cherne to meet with Diem to convince him of the error of his ways. In January 1960, Cherne left for Vietnam with his Research Institute business partner, Carl Hovgard. The ostensible purpose of the trip was to participate in a tiger hunt, an activity that Hovgard had dreamed about. Cherne and Hovgard arrived in Saigon unheralded and went to the Majestic Hotel. Cherne was then escorted to the palace to meet Diem and his aides.[46]

For five days, self-appointed citizen-diplomat Cherne conversed with the president of Vietnam, urging him to change the course of his government. In the midst of these discussions, Cherne and Hovgard were flown to a small town on the edge of the northern Cambodian-southern Laotian border to participate in a tiger hunt. The town was occupied by Vietnamese, but the surrounding mountains were inhabited by the Montagnards—an entirely different ethnic group. The Montagnards, reported Cherne, were a primitive mountain people who wore no clothing or only loincloths. Thirty or forty Montagnards lived communal existences in long houses on stilts.

Cherne and Hovgard rode into the mountains in an open jeep armed with high-powered rifles. At night, a powerful searchlight swung back and forth hunting for tigers. The idea was to look for the reflection of two eyes. The instant the eyes were seen, the hunters were supposed to shoot. Then, the vehicles stopped and the soldiers rushed into the distance to see what had been hit. As neither Cherne nor Hovgard could have told the difference between the eyes of a tiger and the eyes of a wandering Montagnard, they were very relieved that they hit nothing. Cherne noted that the parade of military vehicles rushed through the Montagnard villages at high speed, scaring the cattle and angering the inhabitants. Cherne felt that this demonstrated a ruthless and utterly inhuman approach to the Montagnards and he expressed his disgust to Diem when he returned to Saigon.

Cherne remarked later that he believed that it was a measure of Diem's deep affection that the South Vietnamese president listened to him for five full days. Diem did his best to defend his brother's "misunderstood" actions, but finally, recognizing the severity of the situation, Diem asked Cherne if he would say the same things to his brother. The following day, Cherne accused Nhu to his face of betraying the purposes of Diem's revolution, betraying the hopes for democratic society in Vietnam, eroding and discouraging government officials, and increasing Diem's isolation from the wide range of Vietnamese leaders who had originally supported him. Nhu and Cherne debated each other while Diem and others watched and listened. Nhu disagreed with much that Cherne said. His actions had been misinterpreted. "Let's even assume that your actions are misunderstood," responded Cherne; nevertheless, that was "the way they are seen. And there's one thing that cannot be misunderstood: the outrages which are being committed against a number of the Buddhist monks and others. A simply objective fact. And this is not a Catholic country. This is a country which is fundamentally Buddhist." Nhu responded that, if this was the way close supporters and colleagues of Diem perceived what was happening in South Vietnam, Nhu would alter his political thrust immediately.

Cherne left the five days of meetings believing his mission had been accomplished. By the time Cherne had made his way back from the presidential palace to the Majestic Hotel, a ride of no more than ten minutes, a waiting delegation of thirty Vietnamese and Americans congratulated him on the outcome of this meeting. When Cherne and Hovgard left for the airport the following day, a euphoric delegation gathered to see them off.[47]

During the months that followed, Cherne waited for Diem to make the promised changes. None were forthcoming. When another unhappy episode occurred at the University of Hue, Cherne formally told Diem that the IRC could not continue to participate in its humanitarian programs, since it was evident that no significant change was taking place. The IRC terminated the relationship with Diem. The IRC's orphan programs, children's convalescent center, and its reconstruction efforts undertaken to assist the Montagnards were continued, but with diminished energy. No one was more influenced by these events than Joseph Buttinger, who began a process that eventually led him to reject Diem and the American intervention in Vietnam.

Cherne voted for John F. Kennedy in the presidential campaign of 1960. Cherne believed that Kennedy intended to appoint him ambassador to South Vietnam; but this was not to be.[48] However, the White House was interested in Cherne's views about Vietnam. Shortly after Kennedy was inaugurated, a meeting was arranged between Cherne and Roger Hilsman, who was then in charge of intelligence for the State Department. Cherne still believed that Diem represented the best hope the United States had in Vietnam, but that the situation was hopeless as long as Ngo Dinh Nhu ran the government. Cherne urged the maximum pressure to exile Nhu. Hilsman subsequently supported the military coup against Diem.[49]

As the Viet Cong forces continued to mushroom, President Kennedy escalated America's commitment by sending in two hundred military advisors, members of the new Army Special Forces that Kennedy had championed to fight guerilla wars. At first, the Special Forces' duties were only to train the South Vietnamese in guerilla warfare. Secretly, they launched strikes against the Viet Cong. One of the first reporters to accompany a Special Forces unit into battle was Dickey Chapelle, whom Cherne had hired at the Research Institute in 1956 and who had been apprehended in Hungary by Communists. Chapelle had arrived in Vietnam in May 1961 and promptly accompanied advisors and special forces units into the field. Her story and photographs of American helicopters engaged in combat with the Viet Cong were published by *National Geographic* in November 1962. This was the first widely published evidence that U.S. military forces were waging war in Vietnam.[50]

To gain bipartisan support for his Vietnam policies, Kennedy appointed Henry Cabot Lodge, the Republican vice presidential candidate in

1960, as the U.S. ambassador to Vietnam. Lodge became convinced that the war could not be won with Diem in charge of the government, and he recommended that the United States give the green light to military officers plotting against Diem. Kennedy implicitly gave the go-ahead to overthrow Diem in 1963. But Kennedy and Cherne were appalled when the plotters executed both Diem and Nhu.

In the years that followed, the consequence of executing Diem became apparent as government after government in South Vietnam rose and fell and the Viet Cong position greatly strengthened. Confronted with an imminent Viet Cong victory in South Vietnam, President Lyndon Johnson dispatched massive American ground forces in 1965. At the same time, Johnson requested all voluntary agencies to step up their programs of compassionate help to Vietnam. The IRC's programs in Vietnam focused on children, especially orphans, of which there were an estimated 100,000. Specifically, the IRC participated in the creation of a children's hospital, worked at rehabilitation projects, and operated a children's convalescent center as well as resettling large numbers of families in the United States. The IRC also gave assistance to displaced Montagnards in the Vietnamese highlands.[51]

Cherne inspected the children's medical facilities that the IRC had established in South Vietnam. He paid a courtesy call on General William Westmoreland, who told him about a Special Forces camp recently assaulted in Dong Xoa. With Westmoreland's assistance, Cherne helicoptered to the site and visited a nearby village. While walking around, he found a dazed eleven-year-old boy, wounded in the stomach. Cherne arranged for the child to be flown to a hospital in Saigon. Surprisingly, the boy survived. A piece of jagged metal was removed from the boy's stomach and given to Cherne. For years, Cherne kept the piece of metal on his desk as a reminder of the brutality of war.[52]

Back in the United States, Cherne went on the offensive to support American involvement in Vietnam. On the Barry Gray Show, he debated the American role in Vietnam with William vanden Heuvel, then the President of the IRC. And Cherne wrote articles and frequently gave speeches about America's important responsibilities in Vietnam. In a Freedom House board meeting, Cherne debated his longtime friend Norman Cousins, an ardent opponent of American involvement in Vietnam and the editor of the *Saturday Review*. By all accounts, Cherne ripped into Cousins and "tore him to bits," according to several observers. Cousins resigned from the board and took a few other members with him. Cherne regretted the debate, but Cousins never forgave him. Cousins did permit Cherne to debate the issues surrounding the American involvement in Vietnam with Sanford Gottlieb (the political action director for SANE) and Henry Steele Commager in the *Saturday Review*.[53]

Cherne's support of the war effort did not go unnoticed by those opposed to the war. In 1965, *Ramparts* magazine published "The Vietnam Lobby," written by Robert Scheer and Warren Hinckle, which charged Cherne with being a part of a conspiracy that got the United States into the war in the first place.[54] The heart of this article was a diagram of a dragon surrounded by photographs of those identified as prime movers in this purported conspiracy. The head of the dragon was an unlikely pair: Norman Thomas, the Socialist, and Joseph P. Kennedy, the father of John F. Kennedy. At the dragon's tail was another unlikely pair: Wolf Ladejinsky and Arthur Schlesinger, Jr. In the middle were Tom Dooley and Leo Cherne. Cherne gleefully enlarged the "Vietnam Lobby" dragon illustration and proudly posted it on his wall for all to see.

Many targeted for criticism in the article were identified as members of the American Friends of Vietnam's national committee. Cherne loved to point out that the national committee of the AFV had never met. He had had little or no face-to-face contact with several of the members. For instance, Cherne met Francis Cardinal Spellman only once in passing, when Diem had visited the United States. Likewise, prior to John F. Kennedy's election to the presidency in 1960, Cherne had met him only at a conference luncheon sponsored by the AFV in Washington—and that meeting too was just in passing.[55]

Cherne wrote a measured response to *Ramparts*, which refused to publish it. As Cherne pointed out, the article failed to mention that many connected with the AFV had broken with Diem before President Kennedy escalated American military involvement. By and large, the AFV had been ineffective in its mission. Edward Lansdale, the CIA operative, clearly was far more influential during the early years. His active campaign on behalf of Diem overcame the objections of General Collins, the advisors in the White House, and many decisionmakers in the State Department.

Despite the obvious mistakes in the article, Robert Scheer repeated them again eleven years later in a *New Times* article. In this article, Scheer wrote that Cherne had "a long history of working cozily with various CIA agents like General Lansdale in Vietnam." In fact, Cherne never met Lansdale in Vietnam and only once did he do so in the United States, and that was at a much later date.[56] Likewise, Scheer attacked Joseph Buttinger, reporting that Buttinger met Lansdale on the first day of his arrival in Vietnam and that the two had worked intimately for a year. Buttinger wrote a letter to the editor of the *New Times* stating that he had met Lansdale only once at a private dinner party and at that time he was unaware that Lansdale was a CIA agent. Buttinger had no contact with Lansdale after he returned from Vietnam.[57] Neither Scheer nor the *New Times* bothered to correct their mistakes.

Through Cherne's White House connections, Freedom House sponsored a conference of Asian specialists to consider American postwar policies in Asia. Cherne participated in the conference along with Robert Scalapino and twelve other leading Asianists. The conference report included a paragraph recommending an incremental withdrawal of American forces from Vietnam, a policy later followed by President Nixon. An advisor to President Johnson later reported that the Freedom House report was a major contributor to Johnson's halt in bombing and his call for peace talks with North Vietnam.[58]

Epilogue

- Dickey Chapelle continued to cover American forces in Vietnam. After training at Fort Bragg, she parachuted in with a Special Forces unit. Her stories and photos were published in *Reader's Digest* and many other American magazines. In 1965, while Chapelle was covering a search-and-destroy combat mission, a booby trap exploded a few feet away, killing her instantly.

- Joseph Buttinger's conviction that Vietnam had lost its moral core led to his opposition to American participation in the war. Buttinger, who had no formal education beyond the sixth grade, became the consummate scholar of Vietnamese history, culture, and politics. He published several scholarly books, including *The Small Dragon* and *Vietnam: A Political History*. While conducting research for his books, he amassed the largest private repository of Vietnamese materials in America. The collection was given to Harvard University's Yenching Library after Buttinger's death. In 1972—thirty-three years after Buttinger fled Austria—the Austrian government awarded him its Golden Order of Merit.[59]

- Dooley published two more best sellers: *The Edge of Tomorrow* and *The Night They Burned the Mountain*. He died of cancer in 1961.[60] Cherne believed that Dooley's most important contribution had not been his service as the famed jungle doctor in Laos, but as a writer.[61]

- President Kennedy was disillusioned with the Vietnam War and decided to withdraw a large contingent of American forces. Before this directive was carried out, he was assassinated in Dallas by Lee Harvey Oswald.

- The IRC continued its programs in Vietnam until its fall to the Communists in 1975. Since then, the IRC has been a major resettlement agency for Indochinese refugees in the United States.

Chapter 7

Confronting Genocide

Their skimpy food ration would last about a day, with no assurance that more would get through the choppy seas tomorrow. Medicines and drugs in short supply. A meager and polluted water supply, with the dry season a month or so away. Sanitation? Imagine 16 toilets for 26,000 people. In one week the number of infectious-hepatitis cases—108 of them—had almost doubled. New arrivals sleep on the open beaches under heavy monsoon rains. . . . As I left Pulau Bidong, an island about two and a half hours by fishing boat from the Malaysian resort town of Trenggenau, a Vietnamese refugee said to me: 'Please don't pity us in spite of what you saw here. We're alive, unlike our people who drowned trying to reach land, any land. But when you return to America, please try to make your people understand.'

—Leo Cherne, "Hell Isle,"
New York Times, February 3, 1979

Prologue

As the last American helicopter lifted off from the top of the U.S. embassy in Saigon on April 29, 1975, about 130,000 refugees were in motion, fleeing any way they could. Those who left Indochina in 1975 were brought to military bases in Guam, the Philippines, and the United States, and most were resettled in the United States. For many people remaining in Indochina, the nightmare had just begun.

This was particularly so for Cambodians. The country had gained its independence from France at the same Geneva conference that divided Vietnam. Like South Vietnam, Cambodia was founded as a kingdom, with Prince Sihanouk as its head of state. During the 1960s, Sihanouk concluded that the Communists were going to conquer South Vietnam and clandestinely allowed the North Vietnamese and Viet Cong to station troops in Cambodia. He also permitted sending supplies to them through the Cambodian harbor of Sihanoukville. The North Vietnamese used their bases in Cambodia as staging areas for assaults against South Vietnam. By 1969, the North Vietnamese had established five divisional bases with 50,000 military personnel in Cambodia.

The Khmer Rouge, the indigenous Cambodian Communist forces seeking the overthrow of Sihanouk, consisted of about 2,000 diverse individuals and were militarily insignificant. Ho Chi Minh had withdrawn Cambodian Communist cadres in 1954, and the Khmer Rouge considered this a betrayal. Out of appreciation for Sihanouk's clandestine support for the Communist war effort in South Vietnam, the North Vietnamese did not offer substantial support to the Khmer Rouge.[1]

Sihanouk was overthrown in 1970 by military officers led by General Lon Nol, who tried to rid Cambodia of the North Vietnamese military. The United States openly bombed the North Vietnamese bases in Cambodia, and American military forces were sent into those areas of Cambodia controlled by the Communists. The North Vietnamese retaliated by stepping up support to the Khmer Rouge. Communist forces in Cambodia seeking the overthrow of Lon Nol swelled into an army of nearly 100,000 men.[2]

Cambodian Holocaust

The Khmer Rouge were obsessed with creating the world's first pure Communist society. For starters, Pol Pot, the leader of the Khmer Rouge, planned to evacuate all Cambodian cities and establish an agrarian nation. When the Khmer Rouge occupied Cambodia in 1975, Cambodians, regardless of age, medical condition, or previous occupation, were forced out of all cities and sent to work in rural rice paddies. Most had only minutes to prepare for this trek. To express a clean break with the past, the Khmer Rouge leaders changed the name of their country to Kampuchea.

When the capitol, Phnom Penh, fell to the Khmer Rouge, about twenty international journalists remained in the city. Among the journalists was Sidney Schanberg of the *New York Times*. Schanberg's aide and Cambodian photographer, Dith Pran, had wanted to depart Phnom Penh with his family, but Schanberg requested that he remain. Luckily for Schanberg, Pran honored his request. Pran intervened to save Schanberg from the Khmer Rouge in the days just before the fall of Lon Nol. When the Khmer Rouge interned journalists and other non–Cambodian citizens in the French embassy, Dith Pran was not permitted to remain with them. Like other Cambodians, he was forced to leave Phnom Penh. On May 11, 1975, one month after the fall of Phnom Penh, the journalists were evacuated overland to Thailand. They passed through deserted cities and towns with looted shops. Upon arrival in Thailand, Schanberg wrote a series of articles for the *New York Times* detailing the Cambodian holocaust.

As refugees continued to escape from Cambodia during the ensuing months, Schanberg anxiously sought news of Dith Pran. Hoping that Pran might have escaped, Schanberg contacted the IRC, which had established refugee camps in Thailand, and circulated Pran's photo. Of Dith Pran, Schanberg found no trace, but he did win the Pulitzer Prize in 1976 for his coverage of the Communist takeover in Cambodia.

It was extremely unlikely that Pran would have made it out of Cambodia. The Cambodian refugees fleeing into Thailand reported mass killings by the Khmer Rouge. All Cambodians who had been connected with the previous non-Communist regime—military officers, professors, teachers, doctors, civil servants, governmental administrators at all levels, lawyers, students, technicians, judges, businessmen, religious leaders, and anyone who spoke a foreign language—were summarily killed along with their families. Many more Cambodians died because of rigorous slave labor and the lack of shelter and food. Tens of thousands of Cambodians were reported killed, then hundreds of thousands. Ultimately, the number murdered reached more than one million.

Schanberg interviewed refugees and reported that "Life was totally controlled and the Khmer Rouge did not need a good reason to kill someone; the slightest excuse would do—a boy and a girl holding hands, an unauthorized break from work. 'Anyone they didn't like, they would accuse of being a teacher or a student or a former Lon Nol soldier, and that was the end.'" The rice ration was eventually reduced to one spoonful per day. Cambodians ate "snails, snakes, insects, rats, scorpions, tree bark, leaves, flower blossoms, the trunk of banana plants; sometimes they sucked the skin of a water buffalo." Other refugees reported that in the worst areas of famine, Cambodians dug up the bodies of the newly executed and cooked their flesh.[3]

Despite dramatic reporting on this Cambodia holocaust, Americans were apathetic about events in Southeast Asia. Most American organizations simply felt they could do nothing, so they ignored the situation. An exception was Freedom House. At the time, Cherne served as the chairman of the executive committee. He employed all his eloquence in appealing to Freedom House's board on June 17, 1975 to take action on Cambodia. One month later, Freedom House appealed to the United Nations's High Commission on Human Rights for an inquiry into events in Cambodia, writing in their brief: "It appears to have taken six years to kill nine million human beings in Nazi Germany," but "it appears to have taken one day to inflict catastrophic disaster on more than three million Cambodians." The U.N. Commission took three months to respond negatively.[4]

Another exception to the general American apathy was George Mc-Govern, who had been a leader in the anti-Vietnam War movement. On August 25,1978, he called for an international force to invade Cambodia to expel Pol Pot. McGovern's suggestion was so unexpected that it was covered in newspapers and television reports across America. Cherne had refused to support McGovern when he ran for the presidency in 1972, and had campaigned as vice chairman of Democrats for Nixon. Now Cherne was upset with McGovern's call for an international military force to oust Pol Pot, which was extremely unlikely to happen. Cherne pointed out in a letter published in *New America* that McGovern had failed to speak out about the Cambodian holocaust over the preceding three years and failed even to support resettling refugees from Cambodia, Laos, and Vietnam.[5]

Of course, American newspapers, encouraged by the IRC, Freedom House, and others, covered the plight of the Indochinese refugees. Coverage pressured the U.S. House of Representatives' International Relations Subcommittee to initiate a Congressional inquiry into events in Cambodia. Richard Holbrooke, then assistant secretary of state for East Asian affairs, eloquently deplored the Cambodian atrocities. President Jimmy Carter detailed atrocities committed by the Khmer Rouge and called the Cambodian government "the worst violator of human rights in the world today." Still, no one did much. To many observers, including Leo Cherne, the unwillingness of others to do anything about the Cambodian genocide was a morbid parallel to international blindness to the mass annihilations by Nazi Germany.

While there was lack of willingness to do anything about the horrors in Cambodia, an equal lack of interest hindered support of the refugees who escaped from the killing fields. Congress grudgingly agreed to admit another 14,000 Indochinese refugees into the United States in August 1978, but there was a backlash, especially in the U.S. House of Representatives' Subcommittee for Immigration. Some members of the committee did not believe that the United States had any responsibility or interest in admitting refugees leaving Cambodia or Vietnam three years after their fall to the Communists. More important, the Indochinese refugees did not have the sympathy of the American people, who wanted to forget the war.

Commissioning Citizens

The Khmer Rouge received considerable support from the People's Republic of China, whose leaders opposed the Vietnamese Communists. Shortly after the American forces withdrew from Indochina, the Vietnamese found themselves embroiled both in a hot war with China and a guerrilla war with the Khmer Rouge in Cambodia. The Khmer Rouge in turn occupied portions of disputed areas, proclaiming them Cambodian territory. In response, Vietnam sparked revolts in Cambodia that were put down ruthlessly by the Khmer Rouge. These undeclared wars generated even more refugees.

Shepard C. Lowman, a division chief in the State Department, was particularly concerned about the Indochinese refugees. Since the mass exodus in 1975, thousands of refugees had continued to flee their homelands. They were divided into two categories. The first were the "land people," mainly Laotians and Cambodians. They faced great difficulties escaping from those Communist-controlled countries. Most land people fled into Thailand.

The second group of refugees were the "boat people," who had departed Vietnam in almost anything that floated, hoping to be picked up by ships at sea, or to make it to another country (usually Malaysia) to appeal for asylum. Immediate problems erupted. As the numbers of refugees leaving by boat increased, pirates plundered any valuables that the refugees might have brought with them, and often murdered them to cover their crimes. Many captains of merchant ships transiting the Straits of Malacca and waters near Thailand, Vietnam, Indonesia, and Malaysia, refused to rescue the boat people. Stopping to pick up refugees increased their time at sea and their costs associated with the transit. International Law of the Sea required that there be a humanitarian response. Many joined in the effort to put pressure on ship owners and masters of merchant vessels; as a result, some improvement was experienced.[6]

One estimate was that only one in ten Cambodians, Laotians, and Vietnamese who tried to escape survived the ordeal. The plight of the boat people was documented by Henry Kamm in a series published in the *New York Times*. For these articles, Kamm won a Pulitzer Prize. The citation said that the effect of his articles was to cause the United States "to widen its acceptance of such refugees, as well as induce more humanitarian treatment in the unwilling host countries."[7]

The lucky refugees who survived the harrowing transit and arrived in Thailand or Malaysia were not yet out of crisis. Neither country was economically able to support them. Thailand and Malaysia initially accepted the refugees as a humanitarian gesture under the assumption that they would be promptly resettled in other countries, particularly in the United States. But there was not a lot of support for the refugees in the United States. Congress, reflecting general American apathy, was not supportive of resettling them. As the months passed, the refugee problems in Indochina became critical.

Out of desperation, Lowman called Cherne. The two had met several months before, when Cherne had called the State Department asking for a briefing on refugee crises in Africa, and Lowman had been assigned to do the briefing. Cherne impressed Lowman, who recounted that Cherne was a "very good listener, he didn't interrupt, he asked very good questions, and then Cherne went off to Africa." In the fall of 1977, Lowman briefed Cherne by phone on the crisis in Indochina and asked if Cherne could find some way to help.[8]

Both men concluded that the main issue was the lack of public support in the United States for humane policies for the Indochinese refugees. The IRC had involved prominent Americans in previous crises: the Berlin crisis in 1948–1949; the Hungarian Revolt in 1956; the Zellerbach Commission on the European Refugee Situation in 1957; the Berlin crisis in 1961 before the construction of the Berlin Wall; and the Bangladesh crisis in 1971. Cherne wondered whether an IRC citizens' group might gain attention for the plight of the refugees in Indochina and said he would see what he could do. A week later, Cherne called Lowman with the news that he had launched a Citizens Commission on Indochinese Refugees. William Casey, former undersecretary of state for economic affairs and former chairman of the Securities and Exchange Commission, agreed to co-chair the commission with Cherne. Casey's presence on the commission helped lend it credibility as more than just "a bunch of do-gooders," according to Lowman. Cherne had already contacted a few other luminaries, who had also agreed to serve on the commission: Rabbi Marc Tanenbaum, a distinguished Jewish theologian; Albert Shanker, the president of the American Federation of Teachers; and John Richardson, the former assistant secretary of state for education and cultural affairs. Other prominent Americans would subsequently join, including James Michener, with whom Cherne had kept in touch since the Hungarian crisis; Monsignor John Ahern, director of social development of the Catholic Archdiocese of New York; Father Robert Charlebois, director of Catholic Relief Services; and Elie Wiesel, who headed the U.S. President's Commission on the Holocaust. Bayard Rustin, an African-American who had organized Martin Luther King's march on Washington in 1963 and was the president of the A. Philip Randolph Institute in New York, was also a member. Rustin was also the president of the Social Democrats and had been an IRC board member since 1974. Cherne had met him during the 1950s, probably through Aaron Levenstein, also active in the Social Democrats.[9]

The commission's first mission, launched in February 1978, was spearheaded by two groups. One led by Cherne visited the Vietnamese boat people at Songkhla and the land-people camps in northern Thailand, where thousands of refugees from Cambodia and Laos were sheltered. For some of the commissioners and those reporters accompanying them, it was their first look at a refugee camp. At the first camp, one of the reporters accompanying the commission threw up. Bayard Rustin ducked behind a building and wept. He later wandered away from the group and found himself surrounded by Cambodians who wanted to touch him. Not speaking their language, he decided to sing. Rustin had been a professional singer and a member of a quartet with Paul Robeson, who later became famous for singing "Old Man River" in the Broadway musical *Showboat*. Rustin's singing did much to communicate his feelings to the refugees.[10]

For Cherne, the most moving episode of the mission was at the refugee camp at Nong Khai, where several thousand Laotian refugees and their Buddhist leaders conducted a ceremony in which a white string was placed around the commissioners' wrists to symbolize their reverence. Tradition required that the strings remain on until they fell off on their own. As a sign of respect, many commissioners kept faith with the tradition.[11]

The second group, led by Casey, investigated the situation in Hong Kong, the Philippines, Singapore, and Indonesia. This group had intended to visit Malaysia, a largely Islamic country, but the government refused to permit the commission to enter the country unless Rabbi Marc Tanenbaum were excluded. The commissioners voted unanimously not to accept this condition, and proceeded to Indonesia. To the press, Rustin pointed out that Rabbi Tanenbaum had greatly assisted Moslem refugees in the Bangladesh crisis and trumpeted: "We did not come out here on behalf of human rights to accept the violation of the human rights of one of our group."[12]

After completing their investigations, the two groups met in Bangkok, compared experiences, and conducted a press conference. A transcript of each group's report was distributed to the press. The main concern was the immediate problem of providing havens of first asylum and assuring assistance to the countries bearing the brunt of the tidal wave of refugees. Also addressed was the refusal of sea captains to respond to signals of distress, as required by maritime law. The press conference received extensive coverage in Asia and the United States.[13]

A tangible success of the commission was a side-trip by Warren Meeker to Taiwan, where leaders promised to establish a reception center and contribute half a million dollars to IRC's Asian refugee activities. Other accrued effects were in the realm of consciousness raising. Commission members met in Washington to brief State Department officials, congressmen, Vice-President Walter Mondale, and National Security Advisor Zbigniew Brzezinski.[14] Within a month after the commission's findings had been reported in the press, the White House took steps to formulate a new refugee program for the United States.[15]

The entire commission also testified before the House Judiciary Committee, which held jurisdiction over immigration. Monsignor Ahern spoke out forcefully about the American ability to absorb more refugees. While the hearing was underway, several congressmen demanded to know what commitments other countries had made to resettle Indochinese refugees. Rustin interrupted the proceedings, completely out of order, and reported that he had just come back from Indochina, where he had visited the refugee camps. He believed that if America could not help refugees, then America was never going to solve any of its other social problems. Rustin believed it was possible to do both. According to Shep Lowman, the very fact that Rustin spoke up with great eloquence significantly influenced the ultimate outcome.[16]

Cherne and Rustin remained highly active in the days following their testimony. Both met with AFL-CIO leaders and asked for assistance. Both made major personal pleas to the AFL-CIO Executive Council. Rustin targeted George Meany and Cherne spoke to Lane Kirkland. In less than twenty-four hours, Meany, Kirkland, and other labor leaders threw their total strength behind the admission of more refugees in March 1978. It was this critical support that pressured the Democratic Congress and the Democratic president to reexamine their policies on the Indochinese refugees. Cherne's belief was that the subsequent interest on the part of Carter administration officials to meet with commission members was mainly due to labor's support.[17]

Cherne and Rustin also promoted their views through the media. Cherne detailed the atrocities committed by the Khmer Rouge in an article for *World View* titled "Cambodia—Auschwitz of Asia," which was published in 1978.[18] Meanwhile, Rustin secured the signatures of eighty-five African-American leaders for a manifesto in support of helping Indochinese refugees. Signatories included Vernon Jordan of the Urban League, Ralph Abernathy of the Southern Christian Leadership Conference, Julian Bond, a former congressman from Georgia, Roy Wilkins, former executive director of the NAACP, and Coretta Scott King and Martin Luther King, Sr. This manifesto was published in a full-page announcement in the *New York Times* and other newspapers.[19] Although it was an advertisement, many newspapers picked up the story in their news and editorial departments. *The Wall Street Journal* complimented the commission on gaining the support of the AFL-CIO and African-American leaders. These actions, said *The Wall Street Journal*, "played a significant part in finally forming an administration policy. The government now says it intends to use parole authority to admit more of the refugees, and to support legislation to make the treatment of refugees more liberal and flexible."[20]

The commission's second 1978 mission took members to Malaysia's island of Pulau Bidong, which had been an unsettled, rocky wasteland on which a makeshift refugee camp had been constructed of cardboard, plywood, plastic sheeting, and palm fronds. On this island, 26,000 men, women, and children lived on the equivalent of two city blocks. Water and food had to be ferried from the mainland. The United Nations and the Malaysian Red Crescent Society supplied each refugee with twenty-four ounces of rice, a can of beans, a tin of sardines, eight ounces of chicken stew, and some dry crackers every three days. There was a severe lack of sanitation and sewage disposal. Upon Cherne's return, he wrote his Op Ed piece for the *New York Times*, titled "Hell Isle."[21]

Vietnam's armed forces, backed by the Soviet Union, invaded Cambodia in January 1979. Within days they occupied Phnom Penh and installed Heng Samrin as the new premier of Cambodia. Pol Pot and the Khmer Rouge retreated to the jungle and commenced a guerrilla war against the 200,000 Vietnamese occupation troops. The invasion and the subsequent fighting caused yet another increase in the flow of refugees from Cambodia into Thailand. The flow of boat people from Vietnam increased exponentially. The refugee crisis worsened. The International Rescue Committee quickly expanded its medical work in Thailand. IRC medical teams consisting of 58 doctors, nurses, paramedics, and lab assistants sprang into action along the Thai-Cambodian border. About 80,000 Cambodian refugees were confined to overcrowded camps, and an estimated 400,000 sick, wounded, and hungry Cambodians massed along the border area. At Sa Kaeo, where 40,000 Cambodian refugees were concentrated, the IRC set up a blood bank and oxygen equipment and installed six hundred hospital beds. A medical team of seventeen doctors, nurses, and paramedics from the San Francisco Bay area was stationed at Kao I Dang, a camp for 30,000 Cambodian refugees that rapidly expanded as many more refugees poured out of Cambodia. IRC staff ran the hospital in the camp at Nong Khai, which held more than 45,000 refugees from Laos.[22] By 1979, the IRC maintained sixty-five doctors, nurses, and paramedics, supported by refugees trained on the job. This number expanded to 105 by April 1980. IRC staff were supplemented by rotating volunteers from the New York Hospital-Cornell Medical Center.[23] The IRC became the coordinating group assisting the U.S. embassy and representing all the voluntary agencies engaged in resettling refugees in Thailand.

The commission's third mission in October 1979 again focused on the refugees in Thailand. Commissioners visited Sa Kaeo refugee camp in Thailand, where Rustin was appalled by the "stench of death."[24] The commission's report concluded that "the Vietnamese government, with the concurrence and perhaps the encouragement of the Soviet Union, has adopted a conscious policy of withholding adequate relief from the Cambodian people," a finding corroborated the day it was issued by a *New York Times* article that stated: "The International Commission of the Red Cross has issued a warning to the pro-Vietnamese government in Phnom Penh that it may not indefinitely continue its deliveries of relief materials to local authorities who do not distribute the supplies." While 33,000 tons of food and medical supplies had been delivered to the Cambodian port of Kompong Som, the Vietnamese refused to distribute food to areas controlled by the Khmer Rouge, and they did not want Westerners delivering food and medical aid at all in Cambodia. As the Khmer Rouge were particularly strong and active along the Cambodian-Thai border, the Vietnamese had no interest in permitting food and supplies to enter this area. The commission report concluded that: "The survival of the Cambodian people is at stake and so, too, is the conscience of all nations and of people who care."[25]

The visibility of the Citizens Commission had another important spin-off. In late 1979 Joseph Papp, a major Broadway producer, and Leo Cherne organized a "Theater Committee for Cambodian Relief" to raise funds from actors and theater audiences. In early December 1979, a 35-minute presentation ceremony was held in New York's theater district: Papp served as the master of ceremonies; the actor Michael Moriarty read a statement about IRC activities in Cambodia; five Cambodian refugees expressed their thanks to the IRC. Liv Ullmann, who gave Cherne the check for the collected funds, was starring in a Broadway musical, "I Remember Mama," at the time.[26] After presenting Cherne with the check, Ullmann recalls, she told him, "'If you need me for anything, please call on me.' Several days later I received a call from him, asking me to go to Thailand to visit refugee camps. Not knowing exactly where Thailand was, I asked, 'How long will it last?' He responded, 'The rest of your life.' I was just ending the play then and a few weeks later I was on my way to Thailand."[27]

On December 18, 1979, Cherne testified before the House Foreign Affairs Subcommittee on Asian and Pacific Affairs. He reported that United Nations statistics indicated that only a fraction of the food delivered to Cambodia was actually being distributed—only 447 tons of the 22,619 tons of food that had reached Cambodia in November had been given to Cambodians. Cherne said that 60 percent of the Cambodian population was not accessible to the supply routes allowed by the Vietnamese-controlled Phnom Penh government. In Cherne's testimony, he said that the commission had been told that there had been "some improvement" in food distribution but he doubted that it had been very substantial. He said that only fourteen officials of the major international relief agencies had been permitted to evaluate the distribution of relief supplies in Cambodia. Cherne and Rabbi Marc Tanenbaum called for the United States to organize an emergency international conference on Cambodian relief.

The only course of action Congress took was to pass a nonbinding resolution asking President Carter to work with Secretary General Kurt Waldheim of the United Nations and with leaders of concerned countries to convene such a conference.[28] Clearly, something more had to be done if the Cambodian refugee problem was to be solved.

March for Survival

By early 1980, an estimated 140,000 Cambodian refugees lived in deplorable conditions in Thailand. An estimated 740,000 refugees within a short distance of the border were enduring even more disastrous circumstances, and their situation was rapidly deteriorating.[29] Some slipped across the border. One medical volunteer reported, "The cases come every day. Most get better but too many die. For those who get well, there is great joy all around, playing and joking and happy scenes of departure when they leave. You hope it will be those that stay in your memory, but it is the ones that break your heart that stay most vivid. Like the grandfather who buried all but one of his children and grandchildren in Cambodia, and brought in his last sick grandson. A day later, the little child just faded away. Then, a teenage girl carried in her little brother stricken with meningitis. As we tried to save him through the night, she stood by, touching him, sponging him off and weeping. When he died, she quietly left, leaving her brother on the floor wrapped in an old blanket."[30]

After the Vietnamese invasion of Cambodia, Médecins Sans Frontières (MSF or Doctors Without Borders) had tried to obtain visas to send food and medical supplies across the Thai-Cambodian border to the refugees. At the time, MSF was a relatively unknown French group that specialized in emergency medical relief. The organization was founded in 1971 and its volunteers worked mainly in Africa and Central America. MSF set up a medical relief program in South Vietnam before it fell to the Communists. After the fall in 1975, MSF leaders visited Thailand and the IRC staff took them to refugee camps along the Thai border with Cambodia. Wanting a presence in Thailand, MSF made arrangements with the IRC to send medical teams to work in IRC's Thai refugee camps. For some time, Claude Malhuret, the MSF leader in Thailand and one of the cofounders of the organization, had been on the IRC payroll. Their relief work steadily multiplied and expanded during the following years. By 1979, the MSF had about a hundred medical personnel in Thailand.

But the real refugee crisis was in Cambodia, and the Vietnamese forces refused MSF's application to send supplies overland from Thailand. The Vietnamese feared that the supplies would end up in the Khmer Rouge's hands. Out of frustration, MSF leaders decided to launch a "March for Survival" to give visibility to the plight of the Cambodian refugees. They planned to march to the border with symbolic medical supplies and food, and attempt to open a land route to feed the refugees. A few weeks before Christmas 1979, Claude Malhuret visited Leo Cherne in New York to invite IRC's participation in the march. Cherne immediately saw the potential significance of the march and readily volunteered to send an international contingent.[31]

The March put the Thai government in an awkward position. While it desired increased aid for the refugees, it also wanted them resettled in other countries. The Thai premier finally approved the March as a humanitarian gesture provided that the marchers agreed not to cross the border without the permission of the Cambodian government, which was extremely unlikely. The Vietnamese-controlled government in Phnom Penh condemned the March as a "very vile action" designated to interfere in Cambodia's internal affairs.[32] Vietnamese troops in Cambodia attempted to drive the Khmer Rouge into Thailand. Some speculated that the Vietnamese drive was connected with the March for Survival.[33]

Cherne wanted to use the March for Survival to gain visibility for the holocaust in Cambodia and to assist the refugees who had escaped to Thailand. He concluded that the best way to gain visibility was to bring in celebrities to guarantee that American and European media would cover the march. Eighteen persons came under the auspices of the IRC; among them were the folk singer Joan Baez and the actress Liv Ullmann.[34] In addition, the group was joined by international representatives from other countries, including Winston Churchill III, a member of the British parliament, and Aleksandr Ginsburg, a leading Soviet dissident.

The international contingent of the March for Survival arrived in early February 1980.[35] Among the first was Joan Baez, the American folk singer who had strongly opposed American involvement in the Vietnam

War. In March 1979 she started an informal group called Humanitas, which was concerned with human rights violations in Indochina. Baez raised $50,000 to place advertisements in leading newspapers appealing to Hanoi to stop human rights abuses in Vietnam. Those advertisements had been signed by other former antiwar activists, such as Daniel Berrigan and Allen Ginsberg. This letter provoked extensive denunciation by many of Baez's former peace-activist friends and even one Soviet official.[36]

Before Baez gave a concert on behalf of Indochinese refugees in New York's Central Park, she called the IRC, requesting that some Vietnamese join her on stage during the concert. Several IRC staff were Vietnamese and were delighted to attend the concert. Subsequently, Baez went to Thailand and visited IRC programs.[37] When the March for Survival started to take shape, Cherne invited her to join the international contingent. She readily agreed.

When Baez deplaned in Bangkok, she walked off arm-in-arm with Cherne, who had accompanied her on the flight from the United States. Having been alerted to her arrival, reporters had assembled, and she conducted an impromptu news conference. She proclaimed to the reporters that she was naturally concerned about possible dangers of approaching the border, particularly as heavy fighting between the Vietnamese and the Khmer Rouge had been reported in the area, but she wanted to draw attention to hunger as a major world issue. She reported that the Cambodian refugee issue had "almost completely dropped out of sight of middle America." This press conference, as well as Baez's participation in the March for Survival, was videotaped and made into a documentary titled "Music Alone Is Not Enough," produced by Georges T. Paruvanani.[38]

Aleksandr Ginsburg had spent seven years in a Soviet prison and then was expelled from the Soviet Union without his family. He made repeated attempts to gain his family's release. Finally, just before the trip, the Soviets freed them. Ginsburg met his family briefly before proceeding to Thailand. Unfortunately, his baggage did not make it. He bought a Hawaiian shirt in the hotel shop and wore it the entire time he was in Thailand.

Ginsburg and the other international representatives went in several cars to the border area. When the cars stopped at a Shell station to gas up, Aleksandr Ginsburg got out of one car and Eli Wiesel another. This was their first meeting. They embraced, and became fast friends.

On February 5, about 120 members of the March visited the Sa Kaeo refugee camp. Bayard Rustin noted that there had been amazing improvement in the camps since he had last been there the previous October. However, the camps stilled needed help. While visiting its makeshift hospital, a French doctor appealed for blood donations: "We are very short here, please help us." Ullmann said, "I am a big coward, I've never given blood." As Ullmann gave blood, the camera shutters snapped. In all, forty marchers donated blood. Baez sang "Oh, Freedom," "Ain't Nobody Going to Turn Me Around," and "The Farmer's Song" for the refugees.[39]

On the following day, February 6, the European and American entourage marched to the Klong Luek Bridge leading from Thailand into Cambodia. Unfortunately, the march was delayed by squabbles between the French and American organizers. The IRC group had been waiting since 9 A.M. for the larger contingent of Médecins Sans Frontières, which finally arrived at 1 P.M. The French were upset that the press was paying too much attention to the celebrities in the IRC delegation and neglecting their cause.[40]

The marchers then trekked to the border, accompanied by an equal number of reporters and twenty trucks filled with medicine and food. Some marchers carried banners; one read: "Please allow us to help the people of Cambodia." The main group of marchers approached the old one-lane bridge. When the marchers finally arrived at the border, Vietnamese troops had barricaded the road with barbed wire to prevent their entry into Cambodia. This was all for the best, as the bridge was unlikely to have held the weight of even one truck. By agreement with the Thai authorities, the leaders of the March halted some distance from the bridge.[41]

Some representatives of the marchers did approach the border. Claude Malhuret, MSF's leader, appealed "to those who've been standing on the other side of the border" to allow entry of twenty truckloads of relief supplies and a medical team to help "survivors of a too-long tragedy." Using a bullhorn, Cherne shouted: "Today, the 6th of February 1980, we have come here, men and women from all parts of the world, having left behind our quarrels, differences of opinion, with only one single aim: to help the Cambodian people." He begged the guards "to permit those trucks filled with foods, those medicines, those teams of doctors who ask only and simply permission to bring assistance to the survivors of a too-long tragedy." Stone-faced, pith-helmeted guards on the Cambodian side offered no verbal response, but some snapped photos of the marchers.[42]

The March leaders returned to the main body, sat down on the sun-scorched road and meditated. Then Bayard Rustin took the bullhorn and proclaimed, "I will sing a song that I sang for 15 years with Martin Luther King, with the words somewhat different." To the tune of "We Shall Overcome," Rustin sang his new lyrics: "We Shall Overcome, Children will be fed, mothers will be fed, and all will be fed some day. Yes, we will remember. Yes we will remember now." Rustin's moving performance was followed by the chanting of four Buddhist monks.[43]

Elie Wiesel then recited the Kaddish, the Jewish prayer for the dead, for his father who had died thirty-six years before in the Buchenwald concentration camp in Germany. In his ten-member prayer group was Bayard Rustin, a Quaker, who announced, while looking at Cherne, that he was more Jewish than some Jews. Wiesel equated the Cambodian tragedy with the German murder of Jews. Citing his own experiences in Buchenwald and Auschwitz, he later told reporters: "I came here because nobody came when I was there." And: "One thing that is worse for the victim than hunger, fear, torture, even humiliation, is the feeling of abandonment, the feeling that nobody cares, the feeling that you don't count." Wiesel continued: "Perhaps we cannot change the world, but I do not want the world to change me." He wondered, "What would have happened in 1939 if international organizations had come to the German border like this?" He believed that Hitler would have expelled the German Jews rather than exterminate them in the death camps.[44]

Joan Baez reported that the March for Survival was not there "to prejudge the situation but just to pose the questions of why Kampuchea does not let in more doctors and more food." Aleksandr Ginsburg compared Kampuchea with the Soviet Union's gulag, but said Soviet citizens did not have the same international support that the March for Survival offered Cambodians.[45] Rustin heralded the March as a success: "We wanted to come here knowing full well that they were not going to let us come across and that we were not going to be able to get food and doctors in, but we wanted to make a stab at calling the world's attention to two things: That people are starving and that the government will not permit people to bring doctors and food."[46]

Not everyone was happy with the March. While the marchers marched near Cambodia, Stanley Mooneyham, president of World Vision International, was in the process of distributing relief supplies in the Cambodian city of Siem Reap. He exclaimed that he thought the marchers looked "ludicrous." The *Bangkok Post* called it "simultaneously silly and dangerous." The editor believed that there had already been enough publicity given to "the plight of the Kampuchean refugees." The only worthwhile benefit from the March, the editor said, was the concert given by Joan Baez to generate financial contributions for the Thai Red Cross.[47] In fact, the Thai Red Cross received the twenty truckloads of food and medicine that IRC and MSF had tried to take into Cambodia.[48]

Despite criticism, the March for Survival did focus international attention on Cambodia.[49] Most participants were extremely active upon their return home. Joan Baez wrote a letter to the *New York Times* complaining about the Vietnamese response to their efforts.[50] Liv Ullmann headed an all-star program of performers, including Rock Hudson, Phyllis Newman, Burl Ives, and Lana Turner, in a benefit concert under U.N. auspices in Oslo, Norway. Ullmann persuaded Knut Kloster of Klosters Rederi, which owned the Norwegian-Caribbean Line, to offer records of the concert for sale on cruise ships.[51] American policy toward the refugees changed, and many impartial observers credited Cherne's orchestration of the March for the shift.

With funding in place, the IRC actively assisted the refugees in Southeast Asia and helped resettle them in the United States. During the four-year period from 1975 to 1979, the IRC had resettled only 35,000 Indochinese refugees. Beginning in 1980, the IRC averaged 2,000 refugees per month. To meet their needs, the IRC expanded the number of resettlement offices around the United States.[52]

Despite generous support by the United States during 1980 and 1981, "compassion fatigue" again set in. A growing discussion of the distinction between economic and political refugees. Many nations were not interested in accepting refugees who left their homelands seeking better jobs. More than 90,000 Cambodian refugees remained in Thai camps for two and a half years. In the spring of 1982, the Citizens Commission recommended that the United States accept 100,000 more Indochinese refugees. In addition, it exhorted the United States to appeal to all nations to renew commitments to resettle the refugees.[53]

In the fall of 1982, the *Bangkok Post* reported "Without continuing help from the world community, we cannot adequately care for the Indochinese refugees." The resettlement rates were down in all countries, most especially the United States. Aid money dwindled. The article continued, "Foreigners speak openly of what they say is an exhaustion of the compassion once felt by their citizens for refugees. We in Thailand are grateful for the help we have received in dealing with the refugee problem. But if it is true that this help is going to continue to drop, then Thailand will have to seek other ways to solve its refugee problems." Thailand's national security council was deeply concerned about the world's diminished interest in the Indochinese refugees. Thailand had continued to accept refugees from Laos, Vietnam, and Cambodia with the understanding that other nations would eventually relieve it of the burden by accepting refugees for resettlement. Thailand was alarmed by the drop in resettle-

Left: Eleven-year-old Leo Cherne at camp, Catskills, summer of 1923.

Below: Leo Cherne, right, with mother, Dora, and brother, Jack, 1923.

Bottom: Cousin Meyer, brother Jack, Leo Cherne (middle, facing camera), and father, Max Cherne, circa 1928.

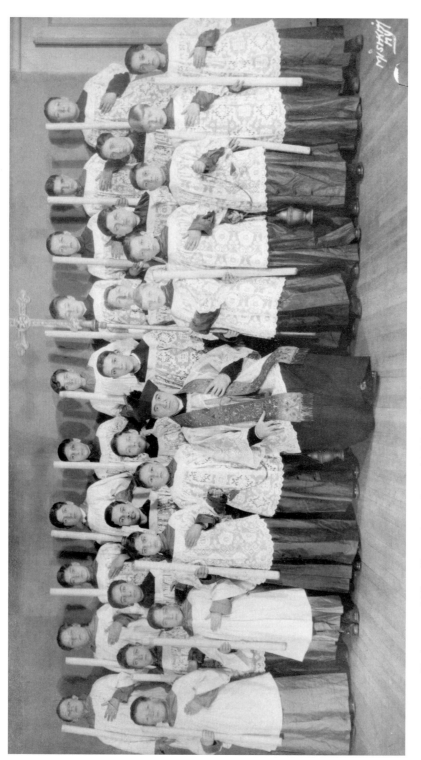

Twelve-year-old Leo Cherne (second row, third from the left) in the Metropolitan Opera Children's Chorus, circa 1924.

Above: Leo Cherne as a young man. Below: Teenage Leo Cherne engraving linoleum block in 1935.

EMERY ROTH & SONS ARCHITECTS

Top: Artist's rendition of the Research Institute Building, part of the Rockefeller Center at 589 Avenue of the Americas.

Left: Professional photo of Leo Cherne about 1940 used by the Research Institute of America.

Top: Leo Cherne's best seller, *Adjusting Your Business to War*, first published in 1939, received little attention. The second edition published the following year sold more than 17,000 copies after it was attacked in Congress.

Right: Leo Cherne served as a commentator for WOR radio during and after World War II.

Leo Cherne in his war correspondent's uniform, 1945.

Leo Cherne dressed in his military correspondent's uniform when he visited Europe in 1945. (Photo: Anthony Stevenson)

Leo Cherne at the controls of his airplane during the late 1940s.

Leo Cherne at the airport near Grossinger's, with Eleanor Roosevelt (middle) and a companion, circa 1950. Cherne's airplane is in the background.

Above: Leo Cherne with Carl Hovgard at the Research Institute of America late 1940s.
Below: Cherne with Leon Henderson at press conference at Avenue of the Americas at
Research Institute of America in 1946.

Above: Leo Cherne, President Eisenhower, and Berlin Mayor Ernst Reuter in the White House in 1953. Below: Pfizer executive giving Terramycin to Leo Cherne (right) and Angier Biddle Duke (left) at Idlewild Airport (subsequently named Kennedy Airport) in October 1956.

Above: In October 1956, Leo Cherne went to Hungary and took many photographs, including this one of Freedom Fighters burning Communist propaganda.   Below: Leo Cherne rode in Marcel Faust's car with red cross flag draped on the front while in Hungary in 1956.

Left: One of the leaders of the 1956 Hungarian uprising photographed by Leo Cherne. She died four days later fighting Soviet troops.

Below: Front page of RIA Review, headlining Dickey Chapelle's capture in Hungary.

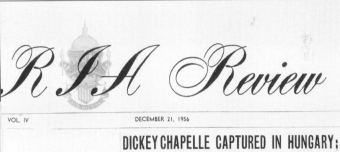

RIA Review

VOL. IV   DECEMBER 21, 1956   NO. 1

DICKEY CHAPELLE CAPTURED IN HUNGARY; PRESS CLUB REQUESTS OFFICIAL SEARCH

Chapelle on the Hungarian Border

Sometime after night-fall on December 5, Mrs. Dickey Chapelle, RIA Public Information Director, was, according to an eye-witness, captured in Hungary. Despite the urgent efforts of the Hungarian desk of the State Department and the American Embassy in Vienna, Dickey's whereabouts since sun-up on December 6 cannot be traced. The Overseas Press Club, of which Dickey is a member, has added its voice to our own and appealed to Secretary of State Dulles to take every possible action to locate her.

The project which took Dickey to Vienna on November 15, was a photo-story for Life Magazine on the refugees who were beginning to stream across the Hungarian frontier.

The Institute arranged a leave of absence for her in order to enable her, as a free-lance photographer, to perform this vital function.

SCOOP!

As this issue of Review was going to press, the Institute received a batch of exciting photographs taken by Dickey. Some of these pictures were used by Life Magazine.

On page 4 we have reproduced a few. Included also is one of Dickey herself, standing near a group of border guards.

Last Communication

In her last direct communication with the Institute, Dickey wrote from Vienna on December 2, of the tremendous immediate need for expediting the flow of refugees. "There simply aren't enough relief experts camps, buses, truck and policing for the 100,000 refugees."

Word of Dickey's capture somewhere less than ten miles inside the Hungarian border came as a shock.

Above: Leo Cherne on the Ed Sullivan Show, November 4, 1956.   Below: Leo Cherne with jazz musician Dizzy Gillespie.

Leo Cherne with Albert Schweitzer in Lambaréné, French Equatorial Africa (today Gabon), in 1957. (Photo: Erica C. Anderson)

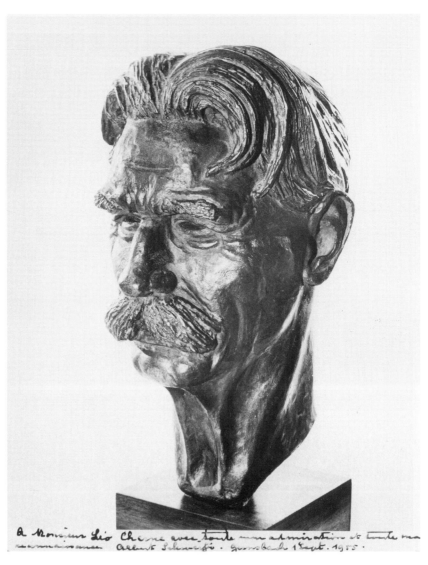

Leo Cherne sent Albert Schweitzer several photographs of his sculpture of Schweitzer in 1955. Schweitzer later returned one photo with the inscription at the bottom.

On September 19, 1958, President Ngo Dinh Diem awarded Cherne the Kim-Khanh, a solid gold medallion that had been given to only two others: Syngman Rhee, president of Korea, and Chiang Kai-shek, president of the Republic of China.

Above: Leo Cherne with then Senator John F. Kennedy at an American Friends of Vietnam conference in Washington, D.C., 1958. (Photo: Leslie A. Toth)   Below: Leo Cherne with Barry Goldwater, circa 1960. (Photo: Brooks Edler)

Leo Cherne sculpting from life Undersecretary of the U.N. Ralph Bunche in 1960.

Leo Cherne with President Lyndon Johnson and Cherne's sculpture of Lyndon Johnson, 1966.

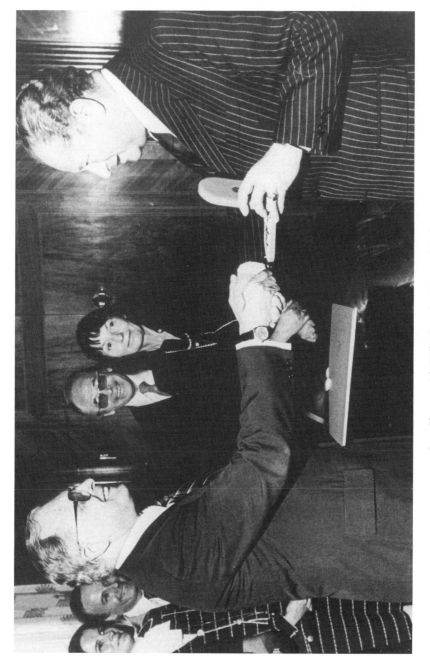

Leo Cherne with Willie Brandt, Mayor of Berlin.

Cherne's busts of Kennedy and Churchill at the Churchill Memorial Museum in Fulton, Missouri.

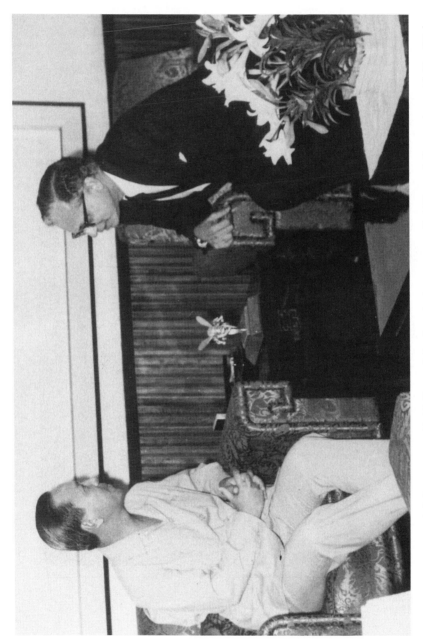

In January 1960, Cherne left for Vietnam with his Research Institute business partner, Carl Hovgard, for meetings with Ngo Dinh Diem.

Leo Cherne gives an award to William J. Casey at the Bankers and Brokers function, November 1, 1971, the Waldorf-Astoria Hotel. (Photo: Camera Arts Studio)

Cherne meeting with President Ford in the White House in 1976.

Leo Cherne (left) and John Richardson (middle) with Henry Kissinger, spring of 1977, State Department luncheon.

Cherne (far left), Robert DeVecchi, and Bayard Rustin at a refugee camp in Cambodia, circa 1978.

Leo Cherne and Nelson Rockefeller, whom Leo first met while they served on the President's Foreign Intelligence Advisory Board (PFIAB) in 1973. Rockefeller later became Vice President under President Ford.

Leo Cherne being sworn in as Vice Chairman of PFIAB, with Vice President George Bush and Leo's second wife Phyliss Brown.

Leo Cherne with President Reagan, circa 1984.

Leo Cherne at the Research Institute of America office on Avenue of the Americas in the early 1980s.

Leo Cherne, 1986. (Photo: Pach Brothers)

ment. That year, 175,000 refugees flooded into Thailand, which could simply not accept more. Thailand threatened to close the border to more refugees.[54]

The commission once again took on this new challenge. President Reagan authorized the admission of up to 64,000 new Indochinese refugees to the United States. Even so, the Citizens Commission on Indochinese Refugees was deeply distressed at the ominous trends: decreasing responsibility and concern on the part of many countries and a sense of increasing self-protection on the part of many countries and the countries of first asylum. "Caught in the crosscurrents, the refugees fleeing Vietnam, Cambodia, and Laos look to us for some recognition of their desperate plight."[55]

Commissioning Effects

The Citizens Commission on Indochina Refugees survived until 1987, when it concluded its tenth and final mission to Southeast Asia. When the commission was launched, many observers predicted wholesale forced repatriation of the Indochinese refugees. This did not happen, and the commission undoubtedly played a part in averting this disaster.[56] Hence, the most tangible impact of the commission was on the nations of Thailand and Malaysia. The Citizens Commission explored firsthand the growing plight of those fleeing the three Indochinese countries and regularly gave hope to the leaders of the countries of first asylum that the refugees had not been forgotten.[57] In Malaysia, the IRC was the only non-Malaysian organization permitted to provide medical assistance to refugees concentrating there.[58]

Although the commission had not been created as an official lobby group, its specific accomplishments of the commission were impressive. Vice President Mondale traveled to Bangkok and promised Thailand $2 million to develop a plan to raise "tens of millions of dollars" and help resettle the refugees. Senator Edward Kennedy introduced legislation in Congress, and President Carter agreed to increase the monthly quota of Indochinese refugees from a few hundred to 6,000 per month. He also increased aid for the refugees from $200 million to $350 million. The passing of the Refugees Act of 1980, which authorized the admission of 50,000 refugees per year, was clearly related to the work of the commission.[59]

The powerful advocacy of the commission was widely acknowledged to have been a major factor in convincing the United States to adopt a generous and ongoing commitment to the resettlement of Indochinese refugees. Its recommendations were adopted as government policy virtually in their entirety: among them the admission of greater numbers of refugees to the United States and other countries, a special resettlement program for Cambodians, the rescue of boat people in distress by merchants and Navy vessels, and the formulation of a long-term refugee policy.[60] IRC offices processed a large portion of the 280,000 refugees that were resettled in the United States. While much of the work was accomplished by individual commission members and the IRC staff connected with it, credit for the commission and its effect upon American policy rested with Leo Cherne, who orchestrated the selection of its members and the events that gained publicity for it.

When Cherne initially spoke out against the Communist regimes in Indochina, he was in the minority and was frequently criticized for his positions. He was almost alone when he demanded forcefully that America assist the refugees. He wrote articles in the *Washington Star* and other publications, and most were sharply rebutted by others. Yet he refused to remain silent. The idea of a citizens commission was not original. But it was an excellent tool for Cherne in awakening public interest, and through the commission he succeeded in changing American policy.

Cherne's interest in the commission transcended the important mission of saving Indochinese refugees. In his words: "While the commission's work sharply focused its urgency and effort on the refugees from Indochina, the results already brightened the prospects for continued haven in the U.S. for those who flee dictatorships in Latin America, the Soviet Union and wherever else the most elemental human rights remain denied."[61]

Perhaps the most important lesson related to the notion of citizen involvement in governmental policy. To one participant, the commission and the March operated on "gall." Well-informed, determined American citizens can affect governmental policy "profoundly and promptly —provided they are willing to extend themselves."[62]

Epilogue

- William Casey took a less prominent role in the commission during 1979, mainly due to his political activities. He had become Ronald Reagan's campaign manager. Reagan was elected president in November 1980 and he appointed Casey director of Central Intelligence.

- Richard Holbrooke, the assistant secretary of state for East Asian affairs, who denounced the Cambodian atrocities in 1977, joined the IRC's board. He subsequently served in several government positions, including ambassador to Germany and assistant secretary for European and Canadian affairs. He also served as President Clinton's special envoy on Yugoslavia. In 1999, he was appointed the U.S. ambassador to the United Nations.

- Against all odds, Sydney Schanberg's aide Dith Pran made it out of Cambodia on October 3, 1979. He teamed up with Schanberg to publish the story of his experience in an article in the *New York Times Magazine*. This story was made into a film titled *The Killing Fields*. When the film premiered on October 30, 1984, Schanberg held a benefit for the IRC. With the assistance of Liv Ullmann, six hundred tickets were sold, generating $57,000 for the IRC.[63] Dith Pran subsequently joined the board of the IRC.[64]

- Liv Ullmann joined the IRC's board and organized fund-raising events for its programs. She dedicated her book *Choices* to "Leo Cherne, the Chairman of the International Rescue Committee, who introduced me to the IRC and thus opened the door to everything that happened to me afterward. It is dedicated not only with admiration to a very gifted human being—but even more with love to a dear friend." Building on her experience with the IRC, Ullmann went on to work for UNICEF as a goodwill ambassador.[65] Ullmann and Cherne remained close friends throughout his life. Ullmann currently serves as the IRC's vice chairman international.

- Bayard Rustin remained on the IRC board and continued as a member of the Citizens Commission for Indochinese Refugees. When Casey resigned from the commission, Rustin moved up to co-chair it with Cherne. Rustin took part in the commission's tenth and final trip to Southeast Asia in 1987. He died shortly thereafter.

- The Vietnamese withdrew from Cambodia in 1989, and elections were held in 1993. Pressure on the Khmer Rouge continued until 1998, when most remaining units surrendered. Before they did so, leaders of the Khmer Rouge executed Pol Pot and a few other leaders.

- Elie Wiesel won the Nobel Peace Prize in 1986. At the time he was an IRC vice president. He nominated the IRC for the award in 1989.

He referred to Cherne as "one of the most fervent humanists" and summed up his contribution to refugee relief as "irreplaceable."[66]

- Médecins Sans Frontières continues to assist refugees. In October 1999, the organization received the Nobel Peace Prize.

Chapter 8

Sculpting the World

Of necessity, a portrait of a President reflects a personal view of the man. The roots of this man are sunk deep in the soil of mid-America. He knows the rigors of the land. He shared the hopes, the disappointments, the courage of those whose lives and fortunes are governed by cloud, wind, sun and water. I hope I have captured something of weathered flesh and eyes narrowed in their protective encounter with the elements, bright and bitter. Perhaps you will find, as I did, in the deeply etched grooves of the face, the furrows in the brow, some of a lifetime's imprint of care and concern, of hope and frustration, of disappointment contained, high purpose strengthened.

—Leo Cherne, describing his bust of
Lyndon Johnson, February 23, 1966.

Prologue

After singing at the Metropolitan Opera as a child, Cherne rebelled against classical music for a time. He talked his parents into allowing him to attend a jazz school on 125th Street that taught popular music for twenty-five cents a lesson. During this time, his parents also arranged for him to take piano lessons. To Cherne, these sessions were "a pain in the ass." He failed to practice and never became an accomplished pianist. But he did have enough knowledge and ability to compose. So at the age of fifteen, he wrote popular music. He particularly enjoyed harmony. The following year he fell in love with Julia Lopez, who lived on the same block, about 100 yards from his building. She was a superb musician, and they teamed up: he composed the scores and lyrics, and she transcribed them into proper form. Cherne submitted one of his compositions to a song-writing contest sponsored by a New York newspaper. The winning songs were to be announced in Madison Square Garden and played by popular orchestras. Cherne was heartbroken when his composition did not win.[1]

Not deterred, Cherne decided to sell his music to publishing houses, then located mainly in the area known as Tin Pan Alley in midtown Manhattan. Accompanied by Julia on the piano, Cherne sang his compositions for potential publishers. At one of the publishing companies, he was asked to leave his song, "My Cabin Down South," for further consideration. Three weeks later, the music was returned. A few months later, he was shocked to find that his song had been published under the title "Black and Bluely" with different lyrics, but with virtually no change in the music itself. It subsequently became a classic of American jazz. He made no further efforts to sell his music, although he continued composing.

While attending New York Law School several years later, Cherne wrote a musical comedy with Henry Denker, a satire on the Seabury investigation and Jimmy Walker scandals.[2] After law school, Denker and Cherne collaborated on an antiwar play titled, *Father Forgive Me.* It was warmly received by the then new Brook Theater, especially by a young director named Elia Kazan. Unfortunately, it was edged out of a competition by another antiwar play called *Bury the Dead,* written by Irwin Shaw.[3]

Cherne pursued his interest in music into the late 1930s. He had an organ keyboard built into his desk at the Research Institute.[4] He continued to compose music and enjoyed singing his compositions as his wife Julia accompanied him on the piano. Eventually, he wrote about a hundred compositions, ranging from ballads to symphonies.[5] Shortly after *The New Yorker* profile of the Research Institute titled "Cassandra, Inc." mentioned that Cherne composed popular music, he was visited by a representative of Horace Hight, a big-band leader with a national weekly radio show. After looking over several songs, Hight expressed interest in recording one, "I'll Never Forget." Hight was scheduled to debut the piece on his radio program Sunday evening, December 7, 1941. Having heard the news of Pearl Harbor earlier in the day, Cherne rushed to the office to listen to reports from Hawaii. While he was deeply concerned about those events, he also feared that his composition might be interrupted by a Pearl Harbor bulletin. Fortunately, it wasn't, and the song was a hit. As a result, the song was recorded by seven other prominent recording stars, including the King Sisters, Freddie Martin, Glenn Gray; and a Canadian group arranged it for full orchestra.[6] It made the Hit Parade and sold over forty thousand copies.[7] Cherne made more money on that one song than he did on his best-selling book, *M-Day.*[8]

During World War II, Cherne put his musical pursuits on hold. His work at the institute consumed increasing attention, and he thought it "undignified for an economist, an industrial mobilization planner to be writing love songs."[9] Painting, however, was somehow more appropriate. After watching the movie, "The Moon and Sixpence," Cherne remarked to Aaron Levenstein that if the impressionist painter Paul Gauguin could launch a successful painting career after a prosaic business life, there was no reason why he could not do the same. Levenstein gave Cherne some oil paints and Cherne completed about a half dozen landscapes and still lifes, which he hung on the wall of his office at the Institute. Many other Institute staff were also engaged in artistic endeavors. They decided to hold an exhibition of their works at the Institute. A memo was sent out to the three hundred Institute staff members in New York, soliciting their works. The exhibit was held on a vacant floor of their building. More than one hundred staff members brought in paintings, etchings, sculptures, pastels, photography, needlework, and every conceivable art form. Cherne's paintings gained visibility, but he turned down a $400 offer for one of his canvases.[10]

After the war, Cherne continued to paint. He even attended an art school on Ninth Street in Greenwich Village once a week for a year. One of his classmates was Joseph Campbell, the American scholar who had proposed the theory that all myths and epics were cultural manifestations of the universal human need to explain social, cosmological, and spiritual realities. Cherne found Campbell to be a "simply extraordinary" person. Although Cherne continued to draw and paint throughout this period, his artistic work did not satisfy him. He felt his paintings were technically competent, but artistically "quite dreadful." He believed that if he continued painting for a number of years, he would have been as good as President Eisenhower; but, Cherne did not think much of Eisenhower's paintings. He finally concluded that he would never be satisfied with his own paintings.[11] He shifted to sketching and again attended class twice a week during the late 1940s, but this did not satisfy him either.[12]

From Patient to Sculptor

On Cherne's return trip from South Vietnam in 1954, he became ill in Hawaii. He stayed an extra day simply because he was too exhausted to continue his flight back. Back in New York, he made an appointment to see his doctor, Irving Graef, who took one look at Cherne and sent him immediately to Lenox Hill Hospital. Graef was concerned that Cherne had had a heart attack. Cherne was subjected to numerous tests during the next six days. All were negative: Cherne was suffering from exhaustion caused by his stress-filled life. Graef urged him to relax, work less intensely, enjoy his leisure time, and find a hobby far removed from his professional work.[13]

Cherne assessed his artistic talents: he saw no hope for his painting and drawing, but he rekindled an earlier interest in sculpting. His parents had sold plaster busts of Bach, Brahms, and Berlioz in their store. Years later Cherne thought this memory might have been the reason for his choice of art form.[14] When Cherne was fifteen, he sculpted a head with the mouth open, to be used as an ashtray.[15] He completed three or four other items, all of which he later considered terrible. He put sculpting aside and didn't return to it until the 1930s.[16] During the winter of 1943, the Research Institute staff spent many nights and early mornings at Publisher's Printing waiting for jobs to be completed. They whiled away these hours by taking blocks of printer's wood and whittling them into an assortment of figures. From this grew the Institute's sculpture bug. Cherne caught it and began sculpting again.[17] He entered a stone torso into the Institute's employee art exhibition. He had done a torso because he could not do "anything as complex as arms, hands, legs, let alone a head." Cherne found the torso "satisfying," but for unknown reasons, he stopped sculpting.[18] After his illness in 1954, he decided to resume this lost passion.

Albert Schweitzer

Early in 1955, Cherne converted the servant's room in his apartment into a studio and began sculpting again. Diverging from his earlier efforts, Cherne decided to sculpt a bust. This was much more difficult than his previous work, and he wanted to see what he could do with this new challenge. He chose Albert Schweitzer as the subject of his first sculpture. It was not an accidental choice. He had read Schweitzer's biography and was impressed. Schweitzer, a renowned theologian, philosopher, and physician, had written a monograph on Johann Sebastian Bach and had co-authored a critical edition of Bach's organ works. Cherne admired the extraordinary devotion of a man like Albert Schweitzer, who could have selected any one of three careers—theologian, organist, or doctor—but chose to separate himself from the easy life in Alsace and became a Protestant missionary in Lambaréné, French Equatorial Africa (today Gabon). There he cleared the jungle, built hospital structures, and set up a leper colony. Schweitzer's renunciation of the world to do good works in Africa inspired reporters, who in turn made Schweitzer famous throughout the world.[19] In postwar America, Schweitzer was a very popular figure. He became even more legendary when he won the Nobel Peace Prize in 1952.

Admiration was not the only reason for Cherne's selection of this great man as a subject. Guilt played a part. Norman Cousins, editor of the *Saturday Review* and Cherne's longtime professional acquaintance, had arranged an invitation for him to address the 1947 Goethe Festival in Aspen, Colorado. Cherne later admitted that at the time he was "young, arrogant, busy," too "busy to participate in this festival." Schweitzer, on the other hand, found the time to travel all the way from Africa for his first visit to the United States to participate in the Goethe Festival. Cherne felt guilty afterward and at this later date decided that, to atone for his arrogance, he would sculpt a portrait bust of Albert Schweitzer.[20] At the time Cherne sculpted Schweitzer, they had not met.

Cherne had no formal instruction in sculpting. He acquired twenty photographs of Schweitzer and with his fingers he molded a clay bust. When it came to Schweitzer's hair, Cherne used a comb. For five months, Cherne labored on the work, occasionally spending as many as thirty hours in his studio on weekends. When he was finished, in August 1955, he proudly showed the work to his friends, one of whom was an editor at Abrams art books. The publisher, impressed by the result, recommended that two of his friends see it. Cherne was astounded at his reaction, but said he would be "thrilled" for others to view his work. Virginia Pollock and Lafred Wolkenberg of Alva Studios examined it and were duly impressed. Wolkenberg had just pioneered a new method of creating sculpture reproductions of extraordinary fidelity using material he called Alvastone. He and Pollock only reproduced works from major museums of the world, so they wondered if Cherne would allow Leonard Carmichael, a curator of the Smithsonian Institution, to examine Cherne's piece. Cherne was pleased. Upon seeing the head, Carmichael requested a bronze copy for the Smithsonian's permanent collection. With his daughter, Cherne unveiled it on October 12, 1955. He then gave a reproduction to the Overseas Press Club on October 25 in "recognition of the fact that foreign correspondents first brought Dr. Schweitzer to the attention of the American people." Cherne later reported that there "was no one more surprised than I that the completed work was received seriously. Nor could anyone have been happier."[21]

Even before the unveiling ceremonies, Cherne sent out a fundraising letter on behalf of Schweitzer's efforts in Africa. Cherne sent Schweitzer the collected contributions on September 21, 1955, reporting about his trip to Vietnam the year before. The letter included photos of Cherne's sculpture. Schweitzer responded by saying that the bust embodied him as he was ten years earlier when he was still in possession of his "full vigor." He continued: "And you have truly succeeded in embodying the spirit of my thought in bronze. I am completely astounded that anyone could have done such a work without knowing me." Schweitzer also declared that the sculpture was "so real you can see the uncompleted manuscripts in my head." He asked that four copies be sent to his grandchildren in Switzerland, which Cherne was delighted to do.[22] When Tom Dooley asked Cherne to visit Schweitzer in Lambaréné in 1957, Cherne was delighted to accept. After the visit, Cherne and Schweitzer kept up a correspondence until Schweitzer's death.

Sculpting the bust of Schweitzer led Cherne to a sculpture teacher, Clara Fasano, who taught at the New School of Arts. She came to Cherne's home every Saturday morning and remained for two or three hours, teaching him the tools and techniques of sculpting.[23] Cherne began sharing a studio with playwright Sidney Kingsley overlooking Central Park.[24]

Lincoln

As a rule, Cherne never executed a piece of sculpture if good likenesses of that subject already existed. The exception was his second sculpture. While examining Stefan Lorant's book containing all the major photographs of Abraham Lincoln, Cherne was struck by a photo in its closing pages. It was taken on April 10, 1865, hours after news had reached the White House about General Robert E. Lee's surrender at Appomattox Court House in Virginia. In his diary, the photographer Alexander Gardiner described Lincoln as terribly depressed and fatigued. Three times during the photo session, Lincoln recited the assassination lines from Macbeth. Four days later, Lincoln was assassinated. The photographer took the glass plates back to his studio. When he removed the last plate from the developing bag, the glass plate was cracked diagonally across the entire head. Lorant included that photograph in his book and it haunted Cherne; he could not get it out of his mind. For Cherne, it captured Lincoln's desolation and depression. Working solely from that one photograph, Cherne tried to capture Lincoln three dimensionally.[25]

When the Lincoln bust was finished, Alva Museum Replicas showed it to the curators of the Lincoln Museum in Washington. They immediately wanted it. Senator George Aiken of Vermont unveiled the sculpture, which the museum titled "The Lincoln of the Final Sacrifice." Cherne sent copies of the bust to many prominent people, including Lincoln's foremost biographer Carl Sandburg, who proclaimed it a "superbly keen sculpture," which was "the best representative plastic art shaping of Lincoln that I have met." Cherne also gave a copy to President Eisenhower, who placed it in the Cabinet Room at the White House, where he thought it would be "admired by the members of the Administration and the many visitors we have in the White House." Eisenhower was so taken with this sculpture that he decided to present reproductions to various leaders of other countries. On the eve of his trip to India, he decided to give one to Nehru, only he did not want to give away his own copy. So he called the curator of the Lincoln Museum and requisitioned their copy. The curator, somewhat embarrassed, called Cherne and requested another one, which Cherne happily supplied. When Eisenhower left the presidency, he took the Lincoln bust from the Cabinet Room and placed it in his Presidential Library.[26]

When John F. Kennedy moved into the White House, he directed his aide Fred Dutton to acquire three sculptures: a bust of President James Monroe, Jo Davidson's Roosevelt, and Cherne's Lincoln. Kennedy placed the Lincoln sculpture on a pedestal directly opposite his seat in the Cabinet Room so that when he sat at the Cabinet table he could look at Lincoln directly opposite him. After Kennedy was assassinated, the Lincoln sculpture ended up at the Kennedy Presidential Library. The Lincoln sculpture has been in the White House during all the presidencies through Ronald Reagan except for Carter's. In each case, at the end of the president's term or death, the sculpture was removed for display in his official library and Cherne supplied another copy.[27]

President Kennedy followed Eisenhower's penchant for giving away reproductions of Cherne's bust of Lincoln. Copies ended up in Africa, Asia, and Latin America. The Lincoln bust ended up in two rather unusual places. The U.S. State Department received a request from the government of Guatemala for a bronze cast of Cherne's Lincoln. They placed it on a pedestal at one end of the Reforma Boulevard in Guatemala City. The second unusual location for the Lincoln bust was underwater. When the nuclear powered submarine *Abraham Lincoln* was commissioned, the first captain asked for a special copy of the Lincoln bust for placement in the officers' quarters. Due to the limited space on the submarine, a small bronze head was produced especially for it.[28]

Boris Pasternak and Others

By 1959, Cherne's Schweitzer and Lincoln busts were two of the best-selling sculptures in America, and Cherne gained national visibility in major magazines, such as *Life* and *Look*. When asked why he sculpted, Cherne responded, "I still find sculpture relaxing."[29]

The bust of Lincoln was one of two works that Cherne created using a single photograph. The other was his portrait of the Soviet dissident writer Boris Pasternak.[30] Unable to publish his work in the Soviet Union, Pasternak had smuggled out his book *Dr. Zhivago* to an Italian publisher. By November 1957, it had been published in twenty-four languages. The following year Pasternak received the Nobel Prize for Literature, an award he was forced by Soviet authorities to turn down. Cherne saw a photograph of Pasternak on the cover of the American edition of *Dr. Zhivago*. The photo fascinated Cherne, who immediately began work on a portrait sculpture. When finished in August 1959, Cherne sent Pasternak photographs of the completed work. Pasternak responded graciously that the likeness was "flattering." The spirit of his image had been "marvelously caught in a nice, subduing manner." Cherne expressed his intent to mail Pasternak a small reproduction. Pasternak requested that Cherne not send the bust, because the Soviet police would confiscate it. So, when Eisenhower planned his trip to the Soviet Union in 1960, Cherne made arrangements to join the group with the purpose of presenting Pasternak with the sculpture. Cherne received a letter in broken English from Pasternak pleading with Cherne not to visit him: "Don't try to see me if you come to Russia. You will yourself have heard, I suppose, of the difficulties and embarrassments meetings with me usually involve." Within months, Pasternak was accused of currency violations flowing from the royalties generated by the Italian publication of *Dr. Zhivago*. Cherne abandoned his plans to give Pasternak the sculpture. As it turned out, Eisenhower did not go to the Soviet Union either. Khrushchev canceled the visit after an American pilot, F. Gary Powers, was shot down over the Soviet Union while flying a U-2 spy plane.[31] Pasternak died in 1960 and never saw the sculpture.[32]

Cherne's bust of Pasternak has been appreciated by many, including Christopher Barnes, Pasternak's biographer, who told Cherne that his bust was "strikingly good" and much better than several portraits of Pasternak he had seen that had been done from life. Barnes requested permission to use a photograph of the bust in his massive biography.[33]

During the late 1950s and early 1960s Cherne completed several other works, including a representation of Sigmund Freud, a reproduction of which is at the Yenching Library at Harvard University;[34] a bust of Eleanor Roosevelt, who Cherne befriended during the 1940s; a portrait of undersecretary of the United Nations Ralph Bunche, which was unveiled at the University of California at Los Angeles;[35] a bust of Jean Sibelius, commissioned by the government of Finland on the occasion of Sibelius's ninetieth birthday;[36] and a sculpture of General William J. Donovan, then the IRC chairman emeritus.[37]

During the late 1950s, Cherne completed a languishing nude sculpture of Karen Salzmann, the wife of IRC president Richard Salzmann. Later, Cherne photographed the undraped figure of Marilyn Monroe, whom he met through the Kennedys on several occasions. Monroe saw Cherne's Lincoln bust and asked Cherne if he would consider doing a sculpture of her. Her beauty and look of sexual innocence fascinated him. He photographed her in the nude at the Carlyle Hotel in New York in 1961. Cherne began working on a clay sculpture. When Monroe died in 1962, he was about three-fourths of the way finished. He destroyed the clay model, which he later regretted.[38]

Cherne's two most famous sculptures were of Winston Churchill and John F. Kennedy. Cherne had always been impressed with Winston Churchill, although they never met. Cherne decided to sculpt his image when President Kennedy made the decision to confer American citizenship on the distinguished Briton. The White House called Cherne and requested a sculpture of Churchill for the White House ceremony, which Churchill was not able to attend. Cherne sent Churchill a photograph of the sculpture. Churchill admired the bust and requested the original plaster model of the sculpture for his collection. When he received it, Churchill complimented him "on the remarkable way in which you have achieved this work of art."[39]

Cherne sent Robert F. Kennedy a copy of the Winston Churchill bust in September 1963. Less than three months later, President John F. Kennedy was assassinated. Cherne had known the President since 1955. When Kennedy was elected president, Cherne sent him a copy of his Lincoln. When John F. Kennedy admired Cherne's bust of Churchill, Cherne sent him one.[40]

After John F. Kennedy's assassination, the city of Berlin commissioned Cherne to sculpt Kennedy. The mayor of Berlin, Willy Brandt, intended to place the work at the location in Berlin where Kennedy had made his famous "Ich bin ein Berliner" speech in 1961. Cherne worked for five months on the bust. He considered it the most difficult sculpture he had undertaken. He tried to reflect the private man more than the public figure. Cherne attempted to go behind Kennedy's public wit, control, and look of detachment to a hidden man who was sensitive, introspective, and shy. The sculpture was unveiled in Berlin's newly constructed symphony hall by the American civil rights leader Martin Luther King, Jr., in August 1964. A second bust was given as a gift to the U.S. government and was placed in front of the United States pavilion at the New York World's Fair in Flushing

Meadow, Queens, in May 1964, where two years before, Kennedy had participated in the groundbreaking ceremonies.[41]

Cherne sculpted only two people from life. One was Robert Frost, who Cherne thought was one of the ten brightest men in America.[42] When Cherne revealed his sculpture to the poet, he asked Frost what he thought of it; Frost refused to respond to Cherne's question. This was not an indication of Frost's disapproval. It was just in his artistic creed that only the creator's judgment mattered.[43] The other person whom Cherne sculpted from life was Lyndon Johnson.

The Ending of Sculpting

When Lyndon Johnson became president, his chief of staff, Marvin Watson, requested a bust of Lincoln to replace the one removed by Kennedy's estate. Dick Salzmann, IRC's president, brought it to the White House. Two weeks later, Cherne received another letter from Watson. Johnson wanted to know what would be involved in Cherne's creating a similar portrait. Johnson was not known for his patience with artists. He had given Peter Hurd, a celebrated painter, just forty-five minutes to paint his portrait. When Johnson took a look at the painting, he swept it out of his office and never wanted to see it again. But Cherne had known Johnson when he had been in the House of Representatives and the Senate; they had worked well together. So Cherne agreed to sculpt Johnson in the White House. As his tools and metal sculpture stand were heavy and the sculpture, made of plastilene, was soft and fragile, he built a wooden box on wheels with holes that went through the wooden base of the armature on which the sculpture was mounted, matching holes in the bottom of the box allowing the sculpture to be bolted down. He placed a handle on the box so he could wheel it around. The only way he could safely transport the box to Washington was by car. Unfortunately, Johnson was not always able to plan more than a day in advance for a posing session. Cherne would usually receive a phone call in the evening inviting him to see Johnson the next day for a one-hour session. When he received a call, Cherne had to cancel whatever was on his agenda for the evening and following day, load his car, and drive to Washington. On one occasion, the White House called at midnight. Cherne arrived in Washington at 4 A.M. for an 8 A.M. appointment.[44]

When Cherne arrived at the White House, he set up his stand and sculpture in the little office next to the Oval Office, called the "Think Tank." It served as the president's private office furnished with three television sets, some memorabilia, and an easy chair. Johnson rarely said anything during the sessions. Already deeply worried about events in Vietnam and the reaction of prominent Americans, the president was sullen and hostile. Cherne believed that Johnson read each casualty report and watched all the television coverage on his three sets in the Think Tank.[45]

Johnson was a tall man, and there was no way Cherne could sculpt his head while looking up at him. Finally, Cherne asked Johnson to sit in the easy chair. Johnson did as he was told, but this meant that the president was now below Cherne's line of sight, and he could not sculpt Johnson's head by looking down at him. Cherne lowered the sculpture and worked on his knees. Positioning Johnson in the easy chair proved to be fortunate, because every now and then the president dozed off, allowing Cherne a moment of relief.[46]

After several sessions, Johnson finally asked: "Would you stop a minute?" These were among the first words Johnson had addressed to Cherne since he had begun the sculpting sessions. Cherne halted. Johnson came around and looked at the sculpture. He asked Cherne: "Do you think that's the way I look?" "Yes, Mr. President," Cherne responded. Johnson grabbed Cherne by the jacket and pulled him through the Oval Office to the secretary's office. He asked his secretary: "Would you get this man one of those pictures of me by Norman Rockwell?" When the portrait was delivered Johnson announced: "That's the way I look." In Rockwell's portrait, Johnson was a folksy, benign, soft character; Cherne saw none of those qualities in Johnson in 1965. Cherne took the sculpture home and spent that next weekend trying to combine his views with those of Rockwell. He failed; and finally he destroyed the sculpture.[47]

A week or two passed. Cherne talked himself into starting again on the sculpture using photographs of Johnson, but his subsequent work never equaled the strength of his original sculpture. When the White House next requested another session with Johnson, Cherne walked into the Oval Office only to find Johnson reading Cherne's debate with the renowned American historian Henry Steele Commager and Sanford Gottlieb, the Political Action Director of SANE, in the pages of the *Saturday Review*. Cherne supported American policy in Vietnam, Commager opposed it. Johnson made no comment on the article, and simply asked Cherne: "When do we start?"[48]

After fourteen sessions with Johnson, Cherne was satisfied with the sculpture. He finally said, "Mr. President, I'm finished." Johnson looked at it and asked his photographer, Yoichi Okamoto, who was almost always with him, "Okie, come here, take a look at this, will you? Is this a finished piece of sculpture?" The photographer responded: "Mr. President, I think it is an excellent piece of sculpture, it's an excellent portrait of you." Johnson asked Marvin Watson to come in the room and inquired: "Marvin, be honest with me, does this look like me?" Watson looked at the sculpture and replied, "Mr. President I think it's a very faithful, strong portrait of you." Johnson then said, "Well, if you say it's finished, it's finished." Johnson threw his hands up, stalked out of the room, and never said "Thank you" or "Goodbye."[49]

That was the end of Cherne's White House sculpture sessions, but not the end of his connections with Johnson. Freedom House gave out a Freedom Award annually to the person it felt best symbolized the urgent issues of the day. The recipient usually received a plaque. In 1966, Freedom House chose to give out Cherne's bronze of Johnson with a plaque on the base bearing the Freedom Award inscription. The recipient was President Johnson. The ceremony, held in the ballroom at the Hotel Waldorf Astoria in New York, was filled with dignitaries. Douglas Dillon unveiled the sculpture, and Cherne spoke briefly about what he had tried to capture in the likeness. He stated that in the "President's face lies mirrored something of the anguish of a time and place in history. Familiar with man's inhumanity to man and a community's reluctance to permit fundamental change, this man moved a nation across a new political frontier toward more complete freedom for all men." He closed his speech with "I will treasure always this opportunity to express my admiration and respect for one to whom public service is the highest order of human endeavor." No sooner had he finished his speech than Johnson, sitting to the right of the podium, tugged Cherne's jacket sleeve and said: "That was damned good. Can I have a copy of that?" Cherne gave Johnson the copy of his speech.[50]

Weeks later, Roscoe Drummond, a well-known columnist, invited Cherne to the Gridiron Club dinner in Washington. Afterwards, everyone headed for the cocktail parties hosted by *Time*, *Newsweek*, and other magazines. Cherne went to one party, but knew few of the people there. He left quietly after a polite interval. As he waited for the elevator, the doors opened and out walked President Johnson flanked by three Secret Service agents. Johnson grabbed Cherne by his lapels and said: "Cherne, that was a goddamned good speech you did. A lot better than your sculpture." Cherne responded feebly, "Mr. President, I've been speaking a lot longer than I've been sculpting." Johnson proceeded into the party, and Cherne left the hotel.[51]

Johnson did not hesitate, however, to ask Cherne for more copies of the Lincoln bust, which he gave out to foreign dignitaries. He gave one to

Houphouet Boigny, the president of the Ivory Coast, and wrote to Cherne reporting that, "This gift greatly pleased the President and I wanted you to know how appreciative I am of your generosity." Despite his appreciation for Cherne's generosity, Johnson was never able to bring himself to thank Cherne for the pro-bono work on his own portrait sculpture. Two years after Cherne completed the Johnson bust, however, he received a letter from John P. Roche, special consultant to President Johnson, saying. "the President thinks extraordinarily well of the bust you did of him and plans to have it in the Johnson Institute in Texas."[52]

Sculpting into History

Although Cherne liked several of his sculptures, he never considered himself a great sculptor. He was genuinely astounded when his first portrait bust gained the fame that it did. Much of the visibility of his work arose from the fact that he was not a professional sculptor. Whatever the reason for the visibility, Cherne knew how to exploit opportunities. He made sure that his sculptures ended up in high-profile museums or public arenas such as the White House. He encouraged presidents to give out his sculptures to foreign dignitaries. He made sure that the unveiling ceremonies received good publicity. He gave out reproductions to family, friends, and professional contacts. Even before the Schweitzer had been unveiled in the Smithsonian, Cherne had sent copies to Max Rabb, Sherman Adams, and President Eisenhower. Other political leaders who received copies were his longtime friend Leon Henderson, Hubert Humphrey, Congressman John Bradamas and Senators Barry Goldwater, Adlai Stevenson, Nelson Rockefeller, Patrick Moynihan, and James Buckley. Cherne sent sculptures to all presidents and some former presidents. Internationally, he sent the Dalai Lama and Ngo Dinh Diem busts of Lincoln. He sent them to his friends in television, the press, and publishing, among them Clare Booth Luce, Roscoe Drummond, and Edward R. Murrow. He also sent them to a wide spectrum of others, including Norman Vincent Peale, Carl Sandburg, Wolf Ladejinsky, and the sculptor Jacques Lipchitz, whom Cherne had befriended.[53] In addition, organizations and businesses gave out his sculptures to other prominent personages.

Two gifts were particularly poignant. The first was to Yoichi Okamoto, the presidential photographer who told Johnson that he liked Cherne's sculpture. But it is interesting to note that Okamoto received a bust of Lincoln, not one of Johnson. The second intriguing gift was to Irving Graef,

Cherne's physician, who had encouraged Cherne to take up a hobby in 1954. Cherne sent him the sculpture of Sigmund Freud.[54] After the Johnson ordeal, Cherne never completed another sculpture. He simply no longer enjoyed it. What had begun as a rewarding and relaxing hobby had become yet another complex, pressure-filled component of his life.

Epilogue

• Although Cherne gave up composing music and writing lyrics in 1941, he enjoyed music throughout his life. While working, he invariably listened to the music of Beethoven, Mozart, Haydn, Bach, Wagner, Tchaikovsky, Richard Strauss, Debussy, and Ravel. He frequently attended concerts.[55]

• Cherne believed that his problem with painting was that he used his right hand. He had been left-handed and his elementary school teacher had required him to write right-handed. He never got over it. Cherne sculpted with his left hand.

• Cherne's bust of Major General William J. Donovan is located in the lobby of the Central Intelligence Agency Headquarters Building in Langley, Virginia.

Chapter 9

Ransoming Prisoners

We sailed on a fifteen-knot breeze across the straits all night, seeing the lights of many large and small boats blinking off in the distance all along the way. The following afternoon we entered Mariel harbor about twenty-five nautical miles west of Havana. There, immigration and military officials came aboard a few hours later and told us that we could take on thirty to forty refugees from the Peruvian embassy, and two or three family members. They told us to anchor out in the harbor amid the approximately eight or nine hundred other vessels of varying descriptions, and to await further information.

—Anthony Drexel Duke, 1980[1]

Prologue

Havana was the first foreign city Cherne ever visited. In 1927, at the age of fifteen, he had enlisted as an ordinary seaman on a tramp steamer transporting cargo and passengers between New York and the Caribbean. Thirty years later, he still remembered his first glimpse of Havana: the stark white buildings in the bright sunshine, and the incredible heat in summer. There were thousands of prostitutes thronging the seaport in doorways, streets, and hallways. He recalled the adventure of being on his own, wandering through the streets of a foreign city. No one he met spoke English; he spoke no Spanish. It was his first exposure to alcohol, which resulted in his being carried aboard by crew mates after just a couple of hours at a bar situated within yards of where the ship was docked.[2]

Cherne visited Havana's Chinatown before he had visited the Chinatown in New York. He was surprised to find that it was populated almost entirely by men, who had made their way from China with the presumed hope of finding their way to the United States. The ships that Cherne sailed on carried cargo and passengers; one such "cargoe" consisted of Chinese immigrants bound for New York. They barely survived in a filthy, tiny area at the stern of the ship, just above the waterline. Cherne never knew whether the Chinese were entering the United States legally.[3]

Cherne had a lifelong love affair with Havana. When he and his wife went on a belated honeymoon, it was to Havana. Later, he convinced the Research Institute staff to vacation together in Cuba.[4] He also studied Cuban politics. Cherne disliked Gerardo Machado, who became president of Cuba in 1925. He was a dictator, and his authoritarian regime suffered frequent revolts. Cherne observed one such insurrection and immediately cabled United Press (which at that time had no correspondent in Cuba), volunteering his services as a foreign correspondent during the failed coup attempt. Seven years later, Machado was deposed by a popular revolt and fled to the United States. Fulgencio Batista participated in the coup deposing Machado in 1933. Batista actively supported others until he was elected president himself in 1940.[5]

Batista was a revolutionary who greatly strengthened the Cuban economy and opened up the political process. Batista built a modern army with American support. He encouraged and strengthened the power of the sugar cane growers, who generated the world's largest crop. Domestically, his popular government harnessed broad support, including that of the Cuban Communist Party. Internationally, he encouraged foreign investment and American businessmen flooded into Cuba. Unfortunately, among those who took advantage of this open invitation were some of the most powerful figures in American organized crime. When Batista's term ended in 1944, he chose not to run again. During the next eight years, Cuba lost the momentum. Batista concluded that only he could properly govern Cuba. He ran and was elected president for a second time in 1952. This time, the aging Batista employed repression and violence to enforce his will. At first, it had some positive economic effects, and Cuba's economy spurted ahead, but Batista's growing corruption alarmed many businessmen. Organized crime thrived in Cuba, most of it controlled from the United States criminal syndicates. The now unpopular and undemocratic Batista was reelected in 1956 in a fraudulent election. Into this volatile mixture burst Fidel Castro.[6]

Fidel Castro

Fidel Castro opposed Batista right after the 1952 election. Along with a band of idealistic comrades, Castro failed in an assault against an army barracks in Santiago on July 26, 1953. He was captured and imprisoned. After his release in 1955, he journeyed to Mexico and organized a wider, anti-

Batista revolutionary movement. The following year, Castro and a few followers returned to Cuba and initiated a guerilla war in the Sierra Maestra Mountains. They called their group the July 26th Movement in honor of Castro's failed attempt in 1953. Castro was charismatic and attracted not only Cuban supporters, but American newspaper and magazine reporters as well, including Herbert Mathews of the *New York Times,* and photographer and writer Dickey Chapelle, who interviewed Castro in the mountains and published several articles, including one for *Reader's Digest.* Since Batista was corrupt and undemocratic, Cherne and many other Americans cheered Castro's guerilla war against Batista.[7] Castro defeated the well-equipped Cuban army on January 4, 1959, and one month later, Cherne flew to Havana at the behest of the IRC to offer assistance to the Castro government.[8]

Cherne did not immediately carry out his assignment; he first headed for Veradero Beach to sun himself, which proved fortunate. Cherne ran into Bill Fitelson, a longtime IRC board member, who was also trying to ascertain what was underway in Cuba. Fitelson told Cherne about Bill Morgan, who had been an American soldier during the Korean War. After the war, Morgan found himself in a boring job in Texas. The fighting in Cuba looked like an exciting adventure, so Morgan joined a group of two thousand partisans fighting in the Escambrey mountains. The Second Army Front, as it was called, was led by Eloy Gutierrez Manoyo, a bartender by trade, who was anti–Batista but not a Communist. Because Morgan had military experience, he became Manoyo's chief of staff and was responsible for military intelligence. Fitelson believed that Morgan would give Cherne an inside picture of what was underway in Cuba.[9]

Cherne sought out Morgan in Havana. Morgan had never heard of Cherne, but nevertheless invited him to his hotel room.[10] Cherne told Morgan that he was in Cuba on behalf of the IRC. As Morgan had no idea what the IRC was, Cherne gave him an IRC brochure that happened to feature a picture of General Donovan, then the honorary IRC chairman. Knowing that Donovan had headed the OSS during World War II, Morgan assumed that Cherne worked for the CIA. Cherne did not bother to correct Morgan's mistaken impression. Morgan was further delighted when Cherne asked to tape the conversation—yet more evidence for Morgan that Cherne was working for American intelligence. Morgan told Cherne that Fidel Castro's brother, Raul Castro, was surrounded with Communists. Raul Castro had no appreciation for the non-Communist Manoyo and, during the war, tried to have Manoyo assassinated. The assassin was captured and implicated Raul Castro. As Raul Castro marched from Santiago toward Havana, he placed Communist cadres in charge of each city he conquered. In Havana, Raul Castro's forces seized government buildings, weapons depots, and military installations. Shortly after Fidel Castro took Havana, the non-Communist but anti-Batista Second Army Front was immediately demobilized. Manoyo went back to tending a bar. Morgan believed that the new government was controlled by Communists.[11] That some of Castro's supporters had Communist ties was obvious, but Morgan identified the names of leading Communists close to Castro. Cherne was surprised with Morgan's openness and comprehensiveness.[12]

Morgan introduced Cherne to one of Castro's secretaries, who promised to arrange a meeting between Cherne and Castro. Cherne believed that the information Morgan passed on to him could be devastating to Castro, and thus, was dangerous information to have. Cherne made notes and asked a friend to carry them back to the United States in case something happened to him. He wondered if the meeting with Morgan had been monitored by Castro operatives and also considered the possibility that he was being set up. Rather than wait around for a meeting with Castro worrying about his own safety, Cherne left Cuba four days after he had arrived. He handed over the tapes to an unidentified intelligence official, who was surprised that Cherne had acquired information that the CIA's Cuban agents had failed to obtain.[13]

Morgan and Manoyo shortly thereafter flew from Cuba to Miami, where they told the press about the Communist infiltration in Cuba. Then they flew back to Havana. Morgan returned to the Escambrey mountains to lead a guerilla war against Castro. The uprising was quickly crushed; Morgan was captured and executed. All those he had identified as Communists ended up in positions of power in Castro's Cuba. Those he identified as anti-Communist were removed from influential posts and some were jailed. Many ended up as refugees in the United States.[14]

On May 3, 1959, a CBS-TV News Special claimed that Cuba was now under a dictatorship, that it was "rapidly becoming a Communist beachhead in the Caribbean." The Cuban government claimed this was untrue and demanded the opportunity to answer the charges. CBS agreed to air a program titled "Is Cuba Going Red?" on May 17. CBS selected Cherne as one of the two debaters who agreed that Cuba was heading toward a Communist dictatorship. Cherne publicly attacked Castro as a Communist and his regime as totalitarian. He reported on television that the Communists had taken over the Cuban revolution. The pro-Castro Cubans on the program and the *Times of Havana* quickly denied Cherne's charges.[15]

Bay of Pigs

While asserting liberal democratic beliefs, Castro converted Cuba into a totalitarian state. Some citizens were shot; tens of thousands were jailed. Refugees began streaming out of Cuba. Those who had been Batista supporters had good reason to fear Castro. Others were anti-Batista Cubans who also opposed Castro's revolutionary excesses. As doubt about Castro's intentions increased, the U. S. government opened the door to admit Cuban refugees without administrative difficulty. In September 1959, the IRC formally offered to support the exiles. This was another defining moment for the IRC. Previously, it had operations underway in Europe and Southeast Asia, but never in the Americas. By mid-1960, forty thousand Cuban exiles lived in Florida. Cherne announced a fundraising drive to generate $1 million to assist them.

The August 1960 issue of *Reader's Digest* announced "These Victims of Castro's Tyranny Need Your Help" and encouraged readers to contribute to the IRC's program. Along with Leonard Bernstein, Samuel Eliot Morison, Arthur Schlesinger, Frank Tanenbaum, David Dubinsky, and others, Cherne signed an "Open Letter" to the people of Cuba, alerting them to the Communist penetration.[16] These and other fundraising activities generated at total of $180,000 during the first six months.[17]

The Cuban government immediately denounced the refugees as traitors and condemned the IRC effort to assist them. Despite the criticism, the IRC inaugurated a Miami office, thus becoming the first national agency to develop Cuban refugee assistance programs. Toward the same end, the IRC further established programs in New York, New Orleans, Los Angeles, and Madrid.[18] Cherne pressed the U.S. government also to offer services and support for the Cuban refugees. Six months after the IRC had launched its program, the federal assistance was offered.[19]

During the last year of the Eisenhower administration, the CIA trained and supported a brigade of 1,500 Cuban refugees to fight Castro. Cuban intelligence were well aware of these preparations. On January 4, 1961, the Cuban Foreign Minister Raul Roa delivered a speech before the U. N. Security Council charging that Cuba was in "imminent danger of a U.S. invasion." In his address, Roa charged that the IRC, headed by Leo Cherne, handled "a million dollar fund for the anti-Communist fighters in Cuba."[20] The IRC issued a press release pointing out that Roa, who had condemned Soviet suppression of the Hungarian freedom fighters in 1956, was now supporting Castro, who was importing Soviet tanks to suppress dissent in Cuba. The IRC had indeed invested in the refugees, but not for purposes of overthrowing the Castro government. Its funds were used solely to resettle Cuban refugees in the United States.[21]

When John F. Kennedy was inaugurated as president in January 1961, he was informed of the CIA-backed plan to invade Cuba with the brigade of Cuban refugees. The CIA believed that the invasion would incite a popular uprising against Castro. Kennedy agreed to permit the invasion to proceed, but at the last minute withdrew most of the promised American air support for the invasion, fearing a political backlash if American involvement were discovered. Unfortunately for the brigade, no popular uprising materialized after it landed at the Bay of Pigs in Cuba. Forewarned of the invasion, Castro's military forces were on alert and rushed to the beach. Without American air cover over the beachhead, Cuban jets were able to strafe the beach and chase off the invasion transports in Cochinos Bay. Within days, the lightly armed brigade was destroyed by Cuban tanks, and 1,241 CIA-trained soldiers surrendered on April 19, 1961.[22]

One month later, Castro expressed his willingness to release the prisoners, provided that the United States paid a ransom of $28 million in credits. Believing that acceptance of Castro's terms would imply that the United States had been responsible for the invasion, Kennedy refused the offer, but he did encourage a private group to negotiate with Castro and collect money for the prisoners. Cherne was upset with Kennedy for not immediately settling with Castro. While the notion of paying a ransom was disagreeable, Cherne believed that the United States had gotten the prisoners into Castro's jail, and had the responsibility to get them out, at the earliest possible time.

Eleanor Roosevelt, Milton Eisenhower, and the labor leader Walter Reuther announced their plans to organize "Tractors for Freedom" to raise the funds necessary to free the imprisoned Cubans. New York Senator Jacob Javits and New York Mayor Robert Wagner joined in the call. Cherne chaired the organization's New York committee and William J. vanden Heuvel, already a longtime IRC board member, became its executive vice president. While negotiations were underway, the New York committee sent out a direct mail appeal to 140,000 potential contributors, who sent back the paltry total of $34,000.[23] When it became clear that the United States government was unwilling to give him funds or credits, Castro stalled on the negotiations. In June 1961, Castro refused the committee's "final" offer, and "Tractors for Freedom" was disbanded. Contributors were offered a choice between having their contribution returned or giving it to the IRC Cuban refugee assistance.[24]

Negotiations dragged on until mid-1962, when Castro finally agreed to a $62 million ransom package composed of medicines, tractors, and other humanitarian supplies. Robert Kennedy approached General Lucius Clay and asked him to raise the money from private sources. Clay called his old friend Leo Cherne and asked him to help raise the new funds necessary to purchase the supplies. Cherne agreed. Cherne hit the road to convince Americans of the need to free the prisoners. He gave speeches, wrote articles, addressed the nation through the "Barry Gray Show" and other programs, and offered press conferences. He believed that Castro's ransom offer was a major propaganda blunder, generating great sympathy for the prisoners. Thirty leading newspapers in Central and South America supported the ransom-raising effort and asked their readers to contribute. Eventually, the funds were raised. The prisoners were freed in December 1962, more than a year and a half after the failed invasion and Castro's first offer to release them for ransom.[25]

After the Bay of Pigs invasion, Castro announced that he was indeed a Communist: he had previously concealed his affiliation lest he lose popular support while he grabbed the reins of totalitarian power.[26] He removed the trappings of liberal democracy and jailed thousands of dissidents. Cherne estimated that Castro jailed about 200,000 political prisoners for varying lengths of time.[27] When these political prisoners were released, they along with many others tried to flee Cuba. Castro tried to prevent Cubans from leaving, yet they left in every imaginable way: some hijacked airliners and small planes; some traveled through other countries; others stowed away on ships and planes; and some risked their lives by crossing the hazardous open sea between Cuba and the United States in small boats or rafts. They were welcomed by the U. S. government officials who believed that the refugees provided a propaganda victory for the United States, as well as depriving Castro of Cuba's most educated groups—doctors, lawyers, educators.[28]

An estimated 41,600 Cuban refugees were registered by 1961. The IRC cared for almost 9,000 of them. By 1962, the IRC alone had expended about $400,000 on the Cuban refugees. The following year, 162,000 Cuban refugees were registered in Miami alone.[29] By 1965, 325,000 Cubans had fled their country with all but 35,000 eventually winning asylum in the United States.[30]

This flow of refugees from Cuba to the United States increased when Castro suddenly reversed his policy of blocking refugee departures and announced that anyone wishing to leave Cuba was free to do so. President Johnson responded by announcing at the Statue of Liberty on October 3, 1965, that those Cubans who sought refuge in the United States would find it: "The dedication of America to our traditions as an asylum for the oppressed will be upheld." An agreement was reached with Castro, providing for two plane loads of refugees to arrive in the United States each day. In December 1965 the airlift commenced and continued until 1971. When the airlift stopped, thousands of Cubans braved ocean currents, trying to reach the United States in small boats and rafts. In all, many hundreds of thousands of Cuban refugees entered the United States, and tens of thousands of others settled in Spain and Mexico. The IRC, under Cherne's chairmanship, played a major role in processing and resettling a large number of these refugees.[31]

Mariel

But even this was not enough to stem the tide of those Cubans wishing to flee. With the Cuban economy in a downward tailspin, Castro announced in 1979 that hard times were ahead. A handful of Cubans crashed through the fence around the Peruvian embassy in Havana and requested asylum. When the Peruvians refused to hand them over to the Cuban government, Castro removed the police surrounding the embassy, and some eleven thousand Cubans squeezed into the compound. Even though the compound had no sanitation, food, or shelter, the asylum-seekers refused to leave. To help alleviate the problem, the United States announced that it would accept 3,500 of the squatters, if Castro would permit them to leave. Castro agreed and announced that other Cubans who wanted to join their families in the United States could do so. Americans could pick up these relatives in the Cuban port of Mariel. Neither Castro nor the American government anticipated the effect. Thousands of Cubans headed for Mariel. When the size of the potential exodus became apparent, a thousand American boats of every description headed for Cuba to pick them up. More than 125,000 Cubans left the island and made their way to the United States before Castro closed the port to prevent even more would-be refugees from flocking to Mariel.[32]

Many Cuban Mariel refugees had relatives in the United States. Those who did not were placed in processing camps. The IRC, along with many other relief organizations, processed and resettled them. On June 18, 1980, President Carter thanked Cherne and the IRC for its efforts on behalf of the Cuban refugees.[33]

Cuban exiles have continued to come to the United States, where an estimated 2.4 million now reside. The IRC resettled approximately 100,000 of them. Like the earlier European and Southeast Asian refugee waves, Cuban exiles have repaid America many times over for the initial helping hand. Refugees have enriched American life from the arts to politics to business.

Epilogue

- Even though the Communist empire in Eastern Europe crumbled as did the Soviet Union, Castro has continued to hang on to power in Cuba.

- General Lucius Clay, who had helped raise the funds for the release of the Cuban Brigade, was honored by the IRC for his lifetime of work in 1969. Congratulating Clay were Presidents Eisenhower, Johnson, and Nixon.

- Eleanor Roosevelt, Cherne's friend since 1946, who had established a committee to ransom the Cuban Brigade after the Bay of Pigs, died in 1962, before the prisoners were released.

Chapter 10

Guiding Intelligence

Leo Cherne is hereby awarded the Director's Medal on 5 March 1998 in recognition of his invaluable contributions to the mission of the Central Intelligence Agency during a period of time extending over several decades. Mr. Cherne's contribution, first as a member of PFIAB, later its chairman, and always as a strong support to the men and women of the CIA, have been a source of great strength to this institution. During the 1970s, 1980s and early 1990s he was a tireless mentor to CIA's work on internal economic matters including the issues of technology competitiveness, third world economic stability and threats to the global financial system. His commitment to the mission of our Agency in these and other areas of concern, during and after the Cold War, helped make the Central Intelligence Agency a more effective provider of analysis and information to policy decisionmakers in the national security arena.

—Central Intelligence Agency Citation,
March 5, 1998

Prologue

Leo Cherne was not an admirer of Richard Nixon. Before Nixon became vice president, Cherne and Roy Wilkins had debated him on the radio program "On the Hot Seat." After the program, Cherne was invited to join Nixon at Wilkins's Manhattan apartment. The three spent several hours discussing many things, all in a collegial manner. The Nixon that emerged in the course of that discussion was friendly, warm, thoughtful, and open-minded. Both Wilkins and Cherne were surprised, but neither man changed his views about Nixon.[1]

Cherne voted for Kennedy in the 1960 Nixon-Kennedy election in which Nixon was defeated, but he and Cherne remained in communication.[2] When Nixon ran again for the presidency in 1968, Cherne publicly supported the presidential election campaign of his opponent Hubert Humphrey. Cherne's lack of support did not deter the successful President Nixon from requesting a Lincoln bust for the White House. Cherne willingly sent it.

157

Nixon liked it so much that he requested reproductions to give to visiting dignitaries. When Pat Nixon went on trips, Nixon requested more reproductions of the Lincoln so that she could give them to foreign leaders. Cherne was invited to the White House so that Nixon could thank him for the Lincoln sculptures. The conversation was cordial and lengthy.[3]

Cherne also sent a reproduction of his sculpture of Churchill to Nixon, who responded: "When I received your bronze bust of Lincoln last year, I was certain that you could never surpass that marvelous piece of sculpture. However, when the bust of Winston Churchill arrived, you proved that I was wrong!"[4] When Cherne was ill and went into the hospital, Nixon phoned him and wished him well. Again, Cherne visited Nixon in the White House for a lengthy conversation that ranged from personal matters to international politics. Cherne expressed support for Nixon's foreign policy successes and was surprised to see a more sympathetic side of Nixon. Nixon asked Cherne to sculpt him, laughingly stating that he wanted to make sure that Cherne sculpted his nose just right. Cherne avoided making any commitment.[5]

Like most Americans, Cherne was not prepared for the Watergate scandals, and he was extremely upset by Nixon's behavior. He felt personally offended when Nixon made several speeches declaring his innocence from the Oval Office, with Cherne's Lincoln bust prominently visible on the table directly behind him.[6] Cherne remarked that the scandal's great unnoticed impact was that it made many staff people who had no involvement in Watergate ashamed of being identified with the White House, when previously it had been a source of great pride, and for some, the pinnacle of their careers.[7]

William Casey

One person who did like Nixon was Bill Casey, Cherne's longtime professional and personal friend.

In 1938 Cherne, in the early phase of his leadership at the Research Institute of America, had hired Casey, a recent graduate from Saint John's Law School. Cherne, sensing great potential, worked with Casey to improve his writing abilities and then gave Casey responsibility for editing the Institute's taxation publications. When Cherne worked on the Industrial Mobilization Plan, Casey worked with him. In June 1943, Casey joined the Navy, yearning for action. Fearing that he would end up sitting at a desk shuffling paper in Washington, Casey arranged a meeting with an aide to

General William J. Donovan, then the head of the Office of Strategic Services (OSS). As a result of this meeting, Casey joined the OSS, and Donovan became the most influential man in his life. By December 1944, Casey was the Chief of the OSS Secretariat in the European Theater of Operation—a huge responsibility.[8]

After the war, Casey returned to the Institute at an annual salary of $12,000, far above the average salary of the day. By the time Casey had settled back into the routine of the Institute, his salary was doubled. The Cherne and Casey families became close and often vacationed together at the beach.[9] In 1948, Casey took a leave of absence from the Institute to serve as general counsel to the Marshall Plan in Paris. Casey found the experience valuable; however, he had expected to become director of the Marshall Plan after the departure of W. Averell Harriman. When it became clear Harriman had no intention of leaving that post soon, Casey returned to the Institute, six months after he left.[10]

Casey was strongly anti-Communist. Unlike Cherne, but like his mentor General Donovan, Casey was an ardent Joseph McCarthy supporter. He believed America needed McCarthy to flush out the Communists. At Cherne's urging, Casey joined the board of the International Rescue Committee, and through Casey, Cherne met Donovan, who also became active in IRC programs. Casey wanted the IRC to become more proactive as a political instrument in the unfolding Cold War. When the IRC failed to follow this path, Casey quit the board and assisted in the creation of the American Friends for Russian Freedom, which intended to oppose Communism in the Soviet Union more aggressively. This group proved unsuccessful.[11]

Despite what Cherne considered a close personal and professional friendship, Casey set up a rival business in 1950 that competed with the Research Institute of America—and Casey enticed several of the Institute's senior employees to join him. Ultimately called the Institute for Business Planning, Casey's new outfit produced several good business publications, but lost a fortune. Casey sold the firm to R. P. Ettinger at Prentice Hall, the same executive who had fired Carl Hovgard, cofounder with Cherne of the Research Institute, in 1935. Casey remained editor-in-chief, receiving 50 percent of the profits from the new arrangement, which worked out extremely well for him. He quickly became a millionaire.[12]

For about ten years, Cherne and Casey had limited contact. Eventually, they repaired their friendship, and Casey rejoined the IRC board. In 1968, Casey joined Nixon's presidential campaign, working particularly on tax reform initiatives. In late summer, in the thick of the campaign, Casey took time out to rush with Cherne to Communist-ruled Czechoslovakia. Earlier in the year, the Czech leader Alexander Dubček had promised his countrymen "socialism with a human face." In what was called the "Prague Spring," Dubček tried to distance Czechoslovakia from Moscow. This resulted in an invasion of his country by Warsaw Pact forces led by the Soviet Union on August 20, 1968. Dubček was arrested and flown to Moscow.

Shortly after the Soviet invasion, Cherne, hoping to repeat his successful Hungarian experience, flew with Casey to Munich, then Nuremberg, and finally Vienna, trying to find a way into Czechoslovakia. In Vienna they rented a car and driver and headed to Bratislava. The Czech border guards allowed them through, but four miles into the country, they were blocked by fifteen Soviet tanks. When approached by a Soviet officer, Cherne demanded to be taken to the officer's superior. This stratagem had worked well in Communist-controlled East Berlin in 1953; but it did not work in Czechoslovakia in 1968. While Cherne was arguing with the Soviet officer, Casey calmly remained in the car reading an Allen Drury novel. Cherne leaned into the car and demanded, "Can you tell me how you can sit there reading while all this is going on?" Casey smiled thinly and retorted, "Do you know anything useful I might be doing?" After a two-hour interrogation, Cherne and Casey were sent back to Austria.[13]

Casey returned to the Nixon for President Campaign. After Nixon's inauguration, Casey was appointed first to the U.S. Export-Import Bank, and later chairman of the Securities and Exchange Commission. Casey encouraged Nixon to appoint Cherne a member of the U.S. Advisory Commission on International Educational and Cultural Affairs in 1969. For a short period, Cherne served as the commission's acting chairman and was a major player in the work of a group led by Frank Stanton, chairman of CBS, which had been created to review and reorganize all overseas public diplomacy activities, including the United States Information Agency, the Voice of America, and the Fulbright and other international exchange programs.

During the 1972 election campaign, Cherne switched sides and became vice chairman of Democrats for Nixon. This did not imply any change in his personal opinions about Richard Nixon. Although he had been supportive of Nixon's foreign policy achievements during his first term, Cherne's active campaigning for Nixon was simply an expression of opposition to what he thought were the soft-on-communism foreign policy positions of the Democratic candidate for president, Senator George McGovern. Nixon won in a landslide. The reelected President Nixon appointed Casey, his campaign chairman, to the newly created post of undersecretary of state for economic affairs in February 1973. After Casey's confirmation by the Senate, Nixon appointed Cherne to the President's Foreign Intelligence Advisory Board.

President's Foreign Intelligence Advisory Board

President Eisenhower established a Board of Consultants on Foreign Intelligence Activities in 1956. It was created at the recommendation of the Hoover Commission on the Reorganization of the Government. Its purpose was to offer the president independent, objective, and expert advice on the effectiveness of the conduct of U.S. foreign intelligence. It was also created to head off an attempt by Senator Mike Mansfield to create a Joint Congressional Committee on Intelligence.[14]

Appointed to the board were prominent Americans who tried to perform their part-time function in an unbiased, objective manner. Independent of the intelligence community and free from any day-to-day management or operational responsibilities, the board rendered its advice directly to President Eisenhower. When Kennedy was elected, Eisenhower did not discuss the importance of the board, and Kennedy considered eliminating it. But after the Bay of Pigs fiasco, Kennedy reconstituted the board and renamed it the President's Foreign Intelligence Advisory Board (PFIAB). Kennedy later claimed that PFIAB was one of his most useful advisory boards.[15]

Over the years, PFIAB members met with leaders of intelligence agencies, examined reports, and visited intelligence installations to identify deficiencies in the collection, analysis, and reporting of intelligence. The board tried to eliminate unnecessary duplication and functional overlaps. Its recommendations influenced the composition and structure of the intelligence community, the development of major intelligence systems, and the degree of collection and analytic emphasis. In carrying out its mandate, board members had access to all the information related to foreign intelligence that they needed to fulfill their vital advisory role.[16]

When he was appointed to PFIAB, Cherne had no background in government service or foreign intelligence. His appointment was made at the urging of Casey, in return for Cherne's participation in Democrats for Nixon. Whatever the reason, Cherne was an excellent choice. In the fall of 1973, economic intelligence was not a high priority within the intelligence community. But the October Yom Kippur War in the Middle East, coupled with the shock in the United States over the Arab oil embargo, moved economic intelligence to the forefront of PFIAB's agenda. Few people in the

United States were better qualified than Cherne to assist in economic analysis and to understand the importance of economic data.[17] He had been collecting economic intelligence at the Research Institute of America since the 1930s. Cherne was once again in the right place at the right time.

Cherne came onto the Board knowing some of its members. For years, he had known Edward Teller, the father of the H-bomb. In 1959, the IRC had given Teller the "William J. Donovan Memorial Award," which was Cherne's bronze bust of Donovan. Teller often offered Cherne advice. Cherne also knew Clare Boothe Luce, the former U.S. ambassador to Italy and congresswoman from Connecticut. Luce was the first woman appointed to PFIAB. Cherne and Luce had communicated during the 1940s and had co-authored three publications on Hungary. Other members of the board were new to him, for example, Nelson Rockefeller, who regarded his membership on the board as the single most important service he had ever performed for the U.S. government. Cherne and Rockefeller became close friends.[18]

Lionel Olmer, a U.S. Navy commander with a specialty in cryptology and Soviet naval communications, was the PFIAB staff member assigned to introduce Cherne to the work of the board. According to Olmer, Cherne was like "a kid in a candy store." Cherne wanted to know about everything, so Olmer made available to him dozens of secret studies on all manner of subjects, people, and places. Olmer communicated with Cherne daily, passing on the latest news and offering suggestions for further study. Cherne soaked up the vast amount of information and still wanted more. He had a compulsion to know more than anyone else about every economic matter that came before PFIAB and possessed an insatiable curiosity about the more exotic aspects of the intelligence system.[19]

After several weeks, Olmer recommended that Cherne write up his findings as a way of drawing attention to the importance of economic intelligence. For seven days Cherne dictated his report, which ended as a forty-page document. Olmer believed that the result was an artful, literate, but verbose critique of several intelligence agencies' programs. With some trepidation as to how Cherne would respond, Olmer told him that the report had great content, but that its style was off base considering its audience: it lacked the appropriate "bureaucratese" essential for government reports. Much to Olmer's surprise, Cherne was open to frank criticism, although Cherne cringed when Olmer red-lined some of his favorite expressions. They worked over the weekend, and in the end, Cherne mastered governmentese while losing nothing of what he believed was really important for the president of the United States to understand.

According to Olmer, Cherne's revised report was a huge success: it changed the future course of economic intelligence collection, analysis, and reporting. Equally important, it drew the attention of senior government policymakers to the enormous significance of economic intelligence and the array of resources that could be directed to answering their needs.[20]

Cherne's specific expertise was economic intelligence; but he participated actively in all PFIAB's activities. Throughout the late 1960s and early 1970s, the Soviet Union was building up its military forces. Several observers had begun to express dissatisfaction with the National Intelligence Estimates, particularly those related to the military power of the Soviet Union. PFIAB chairman, Admiral George W. Anderson, a retired four-star admiral and chief of naval operations at the time of the Cuban missile crisis, and PFIAB board member John S. Foster, a former deputy secretary of defense for development, research and engineering, suggested the development of an outside competitive analysis using the same information as that available to the CIA. President Nixon did not support the recommendation, mainly because the director of the CIA, William Colby, opposed it. When Ford became president, Anderson restated his concerns and recommended that the competitive analysis be conducted through the National Security Council. Colby demurred. When George Bush took over from Colby, things changed. Bush was receptive to PFIAB's proposal.

PFIAB established "Team B" as an experiment in competitive analysis. The idea was to use nongovernment experts on the Soviet Union to second-guess the CIA's estimates of Soviet intentions and capabilities. The PFIAB Board and staff involved were: Edward Teller, William Baker, Edwin Land, Robert Galvin (chairman of Motorola), Bill Casey, and Lionel Olmer. Many more private sector experts were recruited to this project, and they reported their findings to PFIAB.

The "Team B" conclusions projected a more powerful and dangerous Soviet threat than the intelligence establishment had reported to the president. Perhaps the most significant conclusion was that the accuracy and power of Soviet strategic missiles could potentially overwhelm U.S. missile forces and thereby negate the fundamental premise of America's nuclear deterrent: that enough would be left, even after a first-strike, to retaliate and destroy the Soviet Union.[21]

At this time, the nation as well as the intelligence community were in disarray. The Watergate scandal had engulfed the Nixon administration. Congressional investigations uncovered a variety of unsavory practices, upsetting many Americans, including Cherne. President Nixon resigned in

August 1974, and Gerald R. Ford became president. Ford selected for his vice president Nelson Rockefeller, a member of PFIAB.

Coming on top of the Watergate scandals, the American defeat in Vietnam led to public cynicism and distrust of the government. Watergate also led to increased scrutiny of the American intelligence community, which was tangentially connected through Nixon's effort to blame the CIA to cover his misdeeds. Most Congressmen were unfamiliar with the American intelligence operations. Like all large bureaucracies, the intelligence community had made its share of mistakes; though unlike other large bureaucracies, the intelligence community's mistakes had been hidden. When Congressional committees examined and critiqued intelligence practices, mistakes were exposed. Senator Frank Church's committee focused on intelligence abuses. Otis Pike's House Select Committee on Intelligence examined and reported on intelligence failure in the Middle East. President Ford attempted to head off these investigations by creating a blue-ribbon commission chaired by Vice President Nelson Rockefeller. One member of the Rockefeller Commission was the ex-Governor of California, Ronald Reagan.[22]

Shortly after Gerald Ford became president, several White House staff members solicited Cherne's advice. During this difficult period for the intelligence community, President Ford appointed Cherne chairman of PFIAB. At the time, Cherne was a registered Democrat, and he asked why he had been appointed chair. Ford's response was: "I worked with you and watched you for some time, and I reached the conclusion that you would be the one most likely to tell me what I might not wish to hear."[23] As chairman, Cherne continued to meet with the White House aides concerned with intelligence, and he met several times with the president. Through these meetings, Cherne shaped the board agenda. PFIAB met on the first Thursday and Friday of every other month, with ad hoc committee meetings as required. Intelligence agency leaders, Cabinet officers, and others were invited to attend as necessary.

On the same day that Cherne became chairman of PFIAB, President Ford expanded the board from ten members to seventeen. PFIAB increased in importance when, as a result of the Rockefeller Commission report, it was given responsibility for policing the intelligence community.[24] Most PFIAB members contributed actively during meetings and offered advice outside of meetings as their schedules permitted. Cherne saw PFIAB as his primary job. He estimated that he worked the equivalent of 94 days on PFIAB business during the first half of 1976.[25]

By all accounts, Cherne was an excellent chairman. He possessed great skill in running the meetings of this board composed of individuals of great distinction. Cherne skillfully organized presentations of complicated and diverse material outside his own area of expertise, then involved members and staff in their areas of expertise or responsibility. Cherne did not himself pontificate, but led the meeting to ensure that PFIAB's busy agenda was met. He had the ability to listen and comment without hurting feelings or egos. Edward Bennett Williams, one of the top lawyers in Washington, said at the end of the first one-and-a-half day meeting Cherne chaired: "That's the best meeting I've ever been to in my life."[26]

Although the "Team B" work had been launched by the previous PFIAB chairman, Admiral George W. Anderson, its work became public during the time that Cherne chaired the board. This publicity upset the new director of the Central Intelligence Agency, George Bush.[27] Subsequently the concept of a competitive analysis was discontinued. However, the "Team B" concept reemerged in 1986, when Senator Jesse Helms raised the issue in the Senate for a competitive analysis focused upon the Soviet Union. Helms's views were adopted by a Senate resolution, but PFIAB did not conduct further competitive analyses.[28]

In the days before George Bush left the position of director of the Central Intelligence Agency, he wrote to Cherne reporting that the year 1976 had been a good one for the U.S. foreign intelligence community. The CIA and other intelligence agencies introduced innovations and restored confidence in the integrity of their foreign intelligence function. Bush believed that PFIAB under Cherne's leadership had contributed significantly to these changes. Handwritten at the bottom of Bush's note to Cherne was, "I hope our paths cross in the future."[29]

Intelligence Oversight Board

The committees exploring intelligence-gathering submitted their reports in 1975. They publicly aired charges of abuses going back twenty-five years. Whether true or not, the allegations resulted in widespread distrust of the entire intelligence community. President Ford responded to these investigations by issuing Executive Order 11905 on February 17, 1976. This order restructured the intelligence community, established guidelines for the intelligence agencies, and created a three-person Intelligence Oversight Board (IOB). For the IOB, Ford selected Robert D. Murphy as chairman and Leo Cherne and Stephen Ailes as the other two members.

The IOB reported directly to the president. The Executive Order creating the IOB required all elements of the intelligence community to report to the IOB, at least once quarterly, concerning any activities that raised a question of legality or propriety. The Board averaged one formal meeting every three or four weeks. Between meetings, Board members were in frequent communication among themselves and with staff. The IOB also received annual reports from the heads of departments and agencies comprising the intelligence community, as well as allegations regarding intelligence agency improprieties, from other employees of intelligence agencies and from members of the public.

PFIAB's Death and Rebirth

Cherne raised money for Gerald Ford's presidential election campaign and was unhappy when Ford lost to Jimmy Carter in November 1976. Carter examined the role, function, and composition of PFIAB, and concluded that the National Security Council system and the intelligence community had been restructured to effectively review and assess foreign intelligence activities. He was concerned about "Team B," championed by PFIAB, which, he was told, had caused tension in the intelligence community. Carter was also concerned about the ensuing leaks to the press about PFIAB activities. Cherne had supported Ford's reelection campaign and did not expect to remain chairman of PFIAB; but he was stunned by Carter's decision to eliminate the board without discussion or forewarning. Cherne first heard about Carter's decision in a news bulletin. He quickly phoned the other members to inform them personally. Carter retained the Intelligence Oversight Board, but Cherne was discharged as a member.[30]

Cherne disagreed with many of Carter's foreign policy positions and decisions. When Carter offered to recreate PFIAB with Cherne serving as chair, Cherne declined. During the next presidential elections in 1980, Cherne became vice chairman of "Democrats for Reagan." Bill Casey served as Reagan's campaign manager.

After the elections, President Reagan appointed Casey to the position of Director of the Central Intelligence Agency. Cherne spoke on Casey's behalf at the Senate confirmation hearing.[31] President Reagan reconstituted PFIAB on October 20, 1981 with Executive Order No. 12331, which charged PFIAB with assessing "the quality, quantity, and adequacy of intelligence collection, of analysis and estimates, of counterintelligence, and other intelligence activities." He appointed as chairman of PFIAB Anne Armstrong, former U.S. ambassador to the United Kingdom and the former co-chairman of the Reagan campaign. Cherne was appointed vice chairman, and nineteen other members were added to form the reconstituted board. Cherne served Armstrong loyally, but both believed that a group of twenty-one individuals was simply too large for effective functioning. When Armstrong had difficulty working with several members of the board, Cherne supported the removal of eleven members. This was done, but four new members were added, bringing the Board's total to fourteen.[32]

Cherne served on the board until he resigned in 1990. His second term on PFIAB brought just as many accolades as did his first. Clare Boothe Luce reported that Cherne had "tremendous intellectual and spiritual integrity. [He is] absolutely selfless in extending himself for things for which there is neither celebrity nor money." She continued, "He really is the quintessential public servant, if ever I saw one."[33] President George Bush wrote to Cherne: "As Vice Chairman, your wisdom and experience have helped guide the national intelligence effort, as well as improved the quality of its product and planning for future objectives."[34]

Coverting Networks

In 1976, John M. Crewdson wrote an article about Cherne for the *New York Times* claiming that the International Rescue Committee had received funds from the CIA via the Norman Foundation, previously known as the Aaron E. Norman Fund. The source of Crewdson's information was Frank Weil, the director of the Norman Foundation, which had been identified in 1967 as a conduit for CIA financing of a number of domestic organizations, principally the National Student Association. In fact, the IRC had received a total of $15,000 from the Norman Fund from 1962 to 1964 for hiring one doctor to assist Angolan refugees. When interviewed by Crewdson, Cherne denied that he or anyone else at the IRC was aware that the funds received from the Norman Fund had been given by the CIA and he claimed that the funds were used solely to hire a doctor to work with refugees. The following day Weil called Crewdson to report that he had checked the records of the foundation, and concluded that the monies given to the IRC during the 1960s had not come from the CIA. Crewdson printed a retraction of his story the following day. The IRC requested a statement from George Bush, then the director of the CIA, about allegations of CIA funding. Bush sent letters stating that the IRC had never requested or been given funds directly or indirectly from the CIA.[35] Since Bush wrote the letters in 1976, no evidence has surfaced indicating anything to the contrary.

However, in 1980, Arthur O. Sulzberger reported that Cherne, whose name had been raised as a possible candidate for membership on the Board for International Broadcasting, had "reportedly received $15,000 in C.I.A. money in the mid-1960s." While Carter had broached the possible appointment of Cherne to this Board, Cherne had turned it down weeks before Sulzberger published his article. Cherne immediately called Sulzberger, who claimed that he had not put the statement in his article and that a copy editor had done so. He apologized and printed a retraction. Senators Moynihan, Javits, and Pell were upset enough by the article, and its use by other Senators, to speak out on the Senate floor on behalf of Cherne's and the IRC's reputation.[36]

In December 1982, Robert Scheer, who had published unflattering articles about Cherne in 1965 and 1976, published a third article about Cherne, this time in *Playboy Magazine.* Cherne responded by drafting a letter to the editor citing all the so-called facts that he considered to be "completely false, malicious, or both." Scheer had dug up and regurgitated his previously published material about Cherne's activities in Vietnam during the 1950s, and had added more distortions about Cherne's activities in PFIAB. Specifically, Scheer charged Cherne with creating PFIAB's recommendation for the "Team B" competitive analysis. In fact, "Team B" (as previously discussed) was a creation of the previous chairman, Admiral George W. Anderson.[37] Cherne decided not to send the letter: it would just give Scheer and *Playboy* more visibility.

In 1995, critic Eric Thomas Chester proclaimed that the International Rescue Committee was in fact part of the CIA's "covert network."[38] Charges that the IRC had maintained illegitimate connections with the CIA and other intelligence services had been made before. The IRC had an image problem. General Donovan had been closely connected with the IRC. Casey, who headed the CIA, was an off-and-on board member. Cherne was a member, vice chairman, and chairman of PFIAB, and also served on the Intelligence Oversight Board. Cherne believed in the importance of intelligence gathering and would likely have helped the CIA had he been asked. He voluntarily briefed intelligence officers after some of his trips, for example, in the aftermath of the Hungarian Revolution in 1956 and after his return from Cuba in 1960. But, this was nothing unusual. Many Americans who traveled abroad voluntarily passed on information to U.S. intelligence agencies. Like many other Americans, Cherne considered it his patriotic duty to do so and would have been delighted if his information had been helpful. However, he was not briefed by intelligence officers before he went on trips and he did not serve as an agent to collect information, drop off packages, or pass on information to foreign agents. No evidence has surfaced indicating that Cherne received any funds directly or indirectly from any intelligence agency other than his per diem from PFIAB and the IOB. Cherne felt strongly about his work with these two groups and was honored to have helped improve the United State's ability to collect information about the economic capabilities and intentions of other nations. Mixing the IRC, Freedom House, or other such organizations with the intelligence community would not have made any sense, nor would it have made any difference.[39]

Directing Medals

During the mid-1980s, David Cohen, director for operations of the Central Intelligence Agency, worked with Cherne in his role as vice chairman for PFIAB. Cherne mentored many CIA officers engaged in economic intelligence and technology. When Cohen left Washington, he lost contact with Cherne. Ten years later, while in New York, Cohen decided to get in touch with Cherne. A few phone calls later, Cohen had an appointment to see him. Cherne, although ailing, was delighted to see Cohen. After several meetings, Cherne agreed to meet with new CIA officers.

Cohen circulated the invitation to CIA employees and several willingly flew up from Langley, Virginia, to meet with Cherne. Cherne spoke about the people he had known and the importance of economic intelligence. Despite his ill health, the agents were captivated. Cohen approached the CIA director, George Tenet, about recognizing Cherne's contributions to America and the CIA. Tenet had not known Cherne, but he listened and checked the records.

On March 5, 1998, George Tenet flew up from Washington, and in Cherne's home, awarded him the Director's Medal for his work on economic competitiveness, third-world economic stability, and threats to the global financial system. This award has been given rarely to non-CIA employees. While Cherne had received many awards and prestigious honors, he was proud to receive the Director's Medal and it meant a great deal to him in his final months of life.[40]

Epilogue

- Alexander Dubček, who had been arrested by the Soviets in 1968 after the Prague Spring, survived to witness the removal of Soviet troops from Czechoslovakia in 1989.

- Bill Casey and Leo Cherne remained friends until Casey's death in 1987 ended their forty-eight-year relationship.

- Lionel Olmer was appointed by President Reagan and confirmed by the Senate to the position of undersecretary of commerce.

- When the Berlin Wall fell in 1989 and the Soviet Union imploded a few years later, Cherne's long campaign against Communism ended. He was delighted with these events and satisfied that his forty years of work contributed to this triumph; nevertheless, Cherne continued his campaigning for political refugees throughout the world.

Chapter 11

The Falling Curtain

In addition to being a humanitarian, Leo has been an economist, political scientist, sculptor, and advisor to presidents for over 40 years. His extraordinary service to his country and to mankind are inspiring and deserving of recognition from his fellow citizens. . . . Although he has never held elected office, Leo Cherne has had more influence on governmental policy than many members in Congress. Since the late 1930s, Leo Cherne has stepped forward and with brilliance, energy, and moral passion to help this nation overcome countless challenges.

—Citation for the Presidential Medal of Freedom, given to
Leo Cherne by President Ronald Reagan, 1984

Throughout most of his adult life, Cherne worked full-time at the Research Institute of America. The Institute was a privately owned corporation, with Carl Hovgard the majority stockholder, and Cherne plus another employee minority stockholders. In 1964, the owners sold the Institute to the Lawyers Cooperative Publishing Company in Buffalo. Cherne became vice chairman of the Lawyers Cooperative Board of Directors, and the following year, chairman.[1] This role permitted Cherne's active participation in the International Rescue Committee, Freedom House, and the President's Foreign Intelligence Advisory Board, with a bit of time left over for his other interests. The Lawyers Cooperative eventually sold the Research Institute to Thompson International. Cherne's relationship with the Institute ended in 1990, after 54 years of service.[2]

Awarding Medals

By the early 1980s, Cherne's life had reached a peak. His office walls had for decades been covered with awards and photographs testifying to his extraordinary achievements. They included many decorations from foreign governments. Friends and colleagues thought Cherne deserved public recognition from the United States—specifically, that he should be awarded the Presidential Medal of Freedom.

President Truman had initiated the Medal of Freedom, which was awarded for meritorious war-connected acts or services. General Lucius Clay had first proposed this distinction for Cherne to President Eisenhower, citing Cherne's postwar work in Europe, Japan, and Hungary. Clay's proposal did not succeed, but sporadic attempts were made to place Cherne's name in nomination. President Kennedy replaced Truman's award with the Presidential Medal of Freedom, the nation's highest civilian honor given in the United States. It was awarded for meritorious contributions to security or national interest, world peace, or cultural or other significant public or private endeavors.[3]

When Ronald Reagan was elected president, renewed efforts were made to obtain the Medal of Freedom for Cherne, but the campaign was blocked by Michael K. Deaver, Reagan's Deputy Chief of Staff in the White House, who believed the award should go to individuals who had greater visibility and public recognition than did Cherne.[4] Then fate intervened. Fred Demech, a naval lieutenant commander who was assigned to the White House and who had known Cherne when he was appointed to PFIAB, was asked to write President Reagan's speech for the IRC's fiftieth anniversary celebration, scheduled for November 15, 1983. Demech wrote into Reagan's speech the following announcement: Cherne's "extraordinary service to his country and to mankind are inspiring and deserving of recognition from his fellow citizens. It is with great pleasure that I announce tonight that I am awarding the Presidential Medal of Freedom, our nation's highest civilian award, to Leo Cherne. Congratulations, Leo, on a well-deserved honor." Unable to attend the ceremony, Reagan videotaped his speech, which had been cleared by his staff. It was played for an enthusiastic audience at the IRC's fiftieth anniversary ceremony at the Waldorf in New York. When the list of recipients for the Presidential Medal of Freedom was drawn up in February 1984, Demech made sure that Cherne's name was on the list. Deaver again objected. Demech pointed out that President Reagan had already announced that Cherne would receive the award. Deaver was furious with Demech, but could do nothing.[5] On March 26, 1984, President Reagan delightedly conferred upon Cherne the Medal of Freedom in the White House; some of the others who received the same honor on that day were Reverend Norman Vincent Peale, Louis L'Amour, and James Cagney.

Predicting the Future

Before the concept of "futurist" was born, Cherne was one. For over fifty years he publicly projected what would happen—economically, politically, and socially—during the upcoming year. His first speech to forecast the future was given at the Sales Executive Club of New York in 1940. The club had been started by Thomas Watson, Sr., the founder of IBM, in 1932. Watson required all his top sales executives to belong. His idea, at the height of the Depression, was to get the economy rolling again by starting a selling crusade. The club focused on improving salesmen's methods and morale. The club published newsletters, held seminars, and invited big-name speakers for its events. Over the years five presidents, Wendell Willkie, Henry Ford II, Bob Hope, Eddie Cantor, Alan King, Norman Vincent Peale, and Ann Landers addressed the club.[6]

Cherne was one of the club's speakers in January 1940. His talk was such a success that the club invited him back. This continued annually for the next fifty years. His speeches were often given in the grand ballroom at the Waldorf-Astoria, which would be packed with thousands of executives. Cherne used these occasions to predict what was going to happen during the upcoming year. His presentations started with his predictions of the previous year, which he graded for accuracy. He usually gave himself a grade of 90 percent or higher and few participants disagreed with his self-assessment. Then he proceeded into what he projected for the upcoming year. His speeches were widely attended by a broad segment of America's political and business leaders.[7] In addition, newspaper and magazine reporters often covered his predictions.

Cherne's fiftieth "Consecutive and Final First-of-the-Year Forecast Luncheon Program" was titled: "Millennium: A Reach into the Future," and was attended by more than 2,000 executives in the ballroom at the Waldorf. The program co-chairs included Alan Greenspan, Henry A. Kissinger, Happy Rockefeller, and Liv Ullmann. Malcolm Forbes, Jr., and Nelson A. Rockefeller, Jr., gave special introductions.[8] Kissinger uttered admiring accolades: "What courage it has taken each year for fifty years to polish your crystal ball before a roomful of the country's brightest and best-informed leaders. Surely the entire world pauses early each January to learn from you what is expected of it!"[9]

Retiring Chairman

Cherne prodded the IRC to seize new opportunities for assisting refugees. He advocated for new programs during the 1980s and early 1990s. For instance, he encouraged the IRC to become involved in Africa; after programs were launched, he traveled to inspect them.

Cherne was also deeply worried by the plight of the Afghan refugees. Tens of thousands had fled the country when the Soviets invaded Afghanistan in 1979. Throughout the 1980s, more refugees poured into Pakistan. During the Cold War, the United States supported the refugees and those groups who opposed the Soviet forces in Afghanistan. When the Soviet Union agreed to withdraw its forces from Afghanistan ten years later, about 3.5 million Afghan refugees lived in Pakistan. With Soviet forces no longer in Afghanistan, Cherne was worried that the United States would give significantly reduced attention to their refugees in Pakistan. The U.N. High Commissioner for Refugees (UNHCR) at the time, Saddrudin Aga Khan, issued statements to this effect, urging continued attention to the refugee situation.

During an IRC Board trip to Pakistan led by Olmer, which included meetings with the president of Pakistan and with the UNHCR, these matters were discussed. On return to the United States, Cherne urged that a Citizens Commission be created to sustain a worldwide focus on the Afghan refugees, notwithstanding the apparent end of military conflict. As a result of the commission's work, the IRC was the first foreign operation to assist Afghan refugees.

The IRC's Citizens Commission had unintended positive consequences for the IRC. While trying to select commissioners, Olmer met Sadako Ogata, then the director of the Institute of International Relations at Sophia University in Tokyo. She previously represented Japan on the United Nations Commission on Human Rights, and in 1990 was selected as the independent expert of the United Nations Commission on Human Rights on the human rights situation in Myanmar. She declined Olmer's invitation to join the commission when the General Assembly elected her to the position of United Nations High Commissioner for Refugees. However, she worked closely with the IRC for the following ten years on many refugee matters including those connected with Yugoslavia. In 2001, after her retirement as UNHCR, she became an IRC board member.

By 1990, IRC programs operated on five continents and was the largest nonsectarian, nongovernmental refugee operation in the world. Much of IRC's success can be attributed to Cherne's work. It was not just his promotional activities or his fundraising prowess. This phenomenal success derived from the board and staff he recruited, encouraged, and mentored. John Whitehead, who Cherne brought on to the IRC's board after the Hungarian uprising in 1956, had risen to the top of the investment banking profession and then served as deputy secretary of state. He was the obvious choice to succeed Cherne when the infirmities of age made him realize in 1991 that it was time to step down.

Tributes flowed in from Presidents Nixon, Ford, Carter, Reagan, and Bush and from many others. In his tribute to Cherne, Henry Kissinger remarked that it had always "meant a great deal to me to know there was a Leo Cherne in this world, always ready with advice, always ready to give his time and his compassion in difficult circumstances." He continued: "Anybody can project the familiar into the future. But the greatest role of a leader is to take a people from where they are to where they have never been. That is a journey that requires faith and dedication and we honor Leo Cherne, above all, for the faith and dedication he has always shown in our journey towards a world in which the just can be free and the weak, secure."[10] Characteristically, it didn't occur to Cherne, in his new role as chairman emeritus, to stop working. Flashes of the old eloquence, the old brilliance, the old fire, still continued to inspire, move, and persuade his board, staff, and colleagues.

Emerging Refugee Emergencies

Throughout most of its history, the IRC has had limited private funds, and has been forced to rely heavily on U.S. government funds and those of the U.N. High Commissioner for Refugees. In refugee emergencies, sometimes hours and days were lost while funding was sought. Yet refugee emergencies required quick and effective responses. Mobilizing at the first sign of a serious refugee problem saves lives and enhances the ability of the refugees to survive in the long term. Failure to take quick and effective action in such crises often results in social turmoil and political instability within the country to which refugees have fled, and sometimes the strife spreads to neighboring countries, exacerbating unstable and chaotic situations.

When Yugoslavia imploded in 1991, the IRC was one of the first agencies to respond; quickly it was heavily committed, assisting tens of thousands of Bosnian, Serbian, and Croatian refugees, who struggled for survival in the heart of Europe. Hence, when Kurds fled into northern Iraq after the Gulf War, the IRC had no reserves to assist the refugees who were fleeing Iraqi military forces. Still, the IRC sent a team to help and was the first voluntary organization to arrive to help these refugees.

IRC Board members Lionel Olmer and Jim Strickler went to Turkey and northern Iraq to review the IRC's efforts. The person running IRC's program was doing wonderful work alongside the U.S. and other NATO military forces that were engaged for almost the first time in a major humanitarian effort. The trouble with the IRC's effort was that it lacked money, communications equipment, shovels, and supplies. Eventually, the IRC was able to provide shelter and bring medical, public health, and sanitation specialists into the situation, professionals drawn from the IRC's worldwide pool of refugee emergency experts and volunteers. But the time lost early in the crisis meant that many Kurds died or became ill due to exposure and the lack of water, food, and proper sanitation.[11]

While in Turkey, Olmer phoned Cherne, who was delighted with the on-the-spot report and was only saddened by the fact that he could not be there with them. On the return trip, Olmer and Strickler discussed what the IRC could do in the future to be better prepared for emergencies. Olmer suggested that the IRC pre-position kits of supplies for future emergencies. This led to the thought that U.S. companies might be cajoled into donating an emergency radio system to the IRC. While this would be useful, better still, they concluded, would be an emergency rescue fund that could meet whatever the next critical situation required.[12]

Upon his return to the United States, Olmer asked Cherne if he would mount a major effort to help deliver the IRC from its dependence on governmental funding sources by putting together a fund to be used only in emergencies. Cherne approved the concept, as did the IRC board. Cherne agreed to begin contacting individuals in hopes of establishing a $1 million fund—which everyone thought was very ambitious.[13]

With a $1 million corpus, the emergency fund was expected to generate an annual income of $50,000, enabling the IRC to take immediate action in one or two emergency situations should they arise. Decisions to draw on the fund were to be made by the IRC Executive Committee, which must declare that a refugee emergency had arisen. The fund's principal could be invaded only by a decision of the IRC board, and only when the severity of the emergency required such action. The principal would be then replenished as expeditiously as possible following any withdrawal.[14]

Cherne was delighted to help raise money for the fund, which was named in his honor, "The Leo Cherne Emergency Refugee Fund." The IRC board and staff worked out the details. Cherne approached Peter Drucker, who agreed to chair the fund. Drucker had worked as a volunteer with the International Relief Association during the late 1930s. Drucker had worked at the Research Institute as a consulting editor to their associate member's program from 1950 to 1953.[15] Drucker and Cherne had stayed in touch and Cherne had involved Drucker in IRC activities. Much to everyone's surprise, the fund exceeded $1 million within six months and doubled again a few years later.[16] This was the crucial first step toward financial stability as well as an assured capability for rapid and effective response to refugee emergencies. When refugees fled Kosovo a few months after Cherne's death, the Leo Cherne Emergency Fund helped them survive.

Dying and Remembering

Although Cherne was active in many Jewish groups, he was not an obser-
vant Jew. Cherne had not had a Bar Mitzvah ceremony. He was not a Zion-
ist, much to the chagrin of some of his Jewish friends. Yet, Cherne reflected
the best values and traditions of Judaism in his forceful and successful public life. Said Lionel Olmer: "Although he was not a religious man in a con-
ventional sense, as he came closer to the end of his life, he seemed more
drawn to the meaning of his Jewish heritage and its traditions."[17]

Following in his parents' footsteps, Cherne rarely was seen in a synagogue, but he always considered himself a Jew. He celebrated Jewish holi-
days, and he particularly enjoyed Passover, which marks the deliverance of
Jews from Egypt and slavery. Passover celebrated freedom. According to his
friend Henry Denker, Cherne "always took special pleasure in that part of
the service where it is recalled the various works by which God brought
forth the Jews out of slavery, inflicting the plagues to force Pharaoh to let
the Jews go free, sparing the first-born of each Jewish family, parting the
Red Sea, providing manna to sustain the Jews in the desert, bringing the
Jews to Mount Sinai, giving us the Ten Commandments, and finally bringing us to the Holy Land."[18]

Cherne died at 9:30 A.M. on January 12, 1999. He had chosen to be
buried in a Jewish cemetery on the easternmost reaches of Long Island. As
prescribed by Jewish tradition, Cherne was buried the day following his
death. The service had been scheduled for 11:00 A.M. but it had to be delayed due to the bad weather. The service began at 11:30 and lasted about
half an hour. "The Rabbi's sermon was brief and crisp, but it captured
Cherne's commitment to the cause of freedom in behalf of refugees," reported Olmer.[19]

The burial site was in a brand new cemetery a forty-five-minute
drive from the temple. His grave site was located on a small hill difficult to
climb due to the ice on the ground and the bitter cold wind. Cherne's
casket was draped with an American flag in honor of his many years of
service to the U.S. government. An honor guard folded the flag and presented it to his daughter. The few words required for the dead under Jewish law were spoken by the Rabbi, and Cherne's body was lowered into
the grave wrapped in a shroud enclosed in a plain pine box. According to
custom, each of the mourners threw a handful of dirt into the grave onto
the casket.[20]

A Memorial Service took place in New York City on February 3,
1999. About 350 people from all walks of life attended. Speakers included

Henry A. Kissinger, Liv Ullmann, Henry Denker, and many other prominent Americans. Many more wanted to attend, but the space in the hall was limited.

To John Richardson, who had known Cherne since the Hungarian Revolution in 1956, Cherne epitomized the American dream. Cherne possessed "extraordinary skills as a team builder, organizational leader, public speaker, public relations expert, and sculptor." As important, Richardson revered him for his "unlimited commitment to the causes he believed in," admired him "for his penetrating political analysis," and "loved him for his capacity for unlimited friendship, can-do spirit, human foibles, boyish enthusiasms, unvarnished patriotism, devotion to freedom, and for his warmth and charm."[21]

Lionel Olmer, Cherne's friend since 1973, recalled that Cherne "was the soul of the IRC. He gave it a philosophy and mission, a raison d'etre, rather than analytically sound business objectives, and this motivated its volunteers to an extraordinary degree. The people he was attracted to and who were attracted to him knew that he stood for 'values' such as freedom and dignity more than anything else, and they, particularly the youngsters, held him in awe. Leo was not one to be locked into formal job descriptions and annual performance reviews. He knew—and they knew—what was expected, and most would do anything to earn his praise. Leo was admired around the world for what he had done with his life and what he had done for others." For Olmer, "Leo was an inspirational leader, who knew what was right and did it, and whose personality and image made others follow him, convinced of their humanitarian purposes and of the transcendent value of what they were doing."[22]

Elie Wiesel said in his tribute that Cherne "gave homes to the homeless and hopes to the hopeless." Senator Daniel Patrick Moynihan concluded in the *Congressional Record*, "I think it is safe to say Leo Cherne's life helped to redeem the 20th century."[23]

Notes

Introduction

1. Leo Cherne, Oral History, 413.

2. Cherne was most willing to discuss the "Green Book Affair," which involved the disappearance of a PFIAB's staff member's coded notes on conversations about economic matters with U.S. Embassy officials in Europe. This book's disappearance was promptly reported to the appropriate agencies and an investigation ensued. No known negative consequences resulted from the loss. Cherne saved a large number of documents and tape recordings about this event. After reviewing them, I have concluded that the story leads nowhere and therefore have omitted further discussion of it.

3. Dale van Atta, "Leo Cherne's Magnificent Obsession," *Reader's Digest* (May 1986): 119–122.

Chapter 1. Setting the Stage

1. H. G. Wells, *The Future in America; a Search after Realities* (London: Chapman & Hall, 1906), 185–190; quote 187; Howard M. Sachar, *A History of the Jews in America* (New York: Alfred A. Knopf, 1992), 116–139.

2. H. G. Wells, *The Future in America*, 185–190, 196; Harold Evans, *The American Century* (New York: Alfred A. Knopf, 1998), 84, 89.

3. H. G. Wells, *The Future in America*, 206; Harold Evans, *The American Century* (New York: Alfred A. Knopf, 1998), 89, 91.

4. Kishinev has a confusing history. It was annexed by Czarist Russia in the mid-nineteenth century. At the time of Max Chernetsky's birth it was a part of Russia. After World War I, it became a part of Romania. The Molotov-Ribbentrop Pact between the Soviet Union and Germany gave Bessarabia to the Soviet Union, which took it in 1940. During World War II Bessarabia was re-occupied by Romania, then reconquered by the Soviet Union. In 1991 Kishinev became the capital of the independent Moldova Republic.

5. *Current Biography* (New York: H. W. Wilson Co., 1940), 164–165.

6. Leo Cherne, Oral History, 2; Jack Cherne, telephone interview with Andrew F. Smith, December 9, 1999.

7. Leo Cherne, "Leo Cherne's Autobiography Birth to 1938," mimeographed undated paper, 1.

8. George R. Leighton, "Cassandra, Inc.," *The New Yorker* 16 (October 5, 1940): 23; Leo Cherne, Oral History, 3–4, 19. According to Cherne's application for a security clearance filed in 1988, he was born Leopold Chernetsky. He occasionally used the middle initial "M.", which did not stand for anything. His family legally changed their name to "Cherne" in August 1929. See Leo Cherne, "Security Investigation Data for Sensitive Position," February 1, 1988.

9. Leo Cherne, "[Draft—4/19/90]" photocopied paper.

10. Leo Cherne, Oral History, 13.

11. Leo Cherne, Oral History, 32–33.

12. George R. Leighton, "Cassandra, Inc.," 23; Leo Cherne, Oral History, 3–4, 19.

13. "Max Cherne Wins Medal Awarded First Prize in Paris," *Rehoboth News* 4 (March 1931): 1.

14. Leo Cherne, Oral History, 2, 7; Leo Cherne, "Leo Cherne's Autobiography Birth to 1938," 2; Leo Cherne, "[Draft—4/19/90]" 1.

15. Leo Cherne, Oral History, 31–32, 69.

16. Leo Cherne, Oral History, 8–9; Leo Cherne, "Leo Cherne's Autobiography Birth to 1938," 3; Leo Cherne interview with Andrew F. Smith, New York, June 10, 1998.

17. Leo Cherne, Oral History, 24–25.

18. Leo Cherne, interview with Dale Van Atta, New York, December 14, 1984.

19. Leo Cherne, interview with Dale Van Atta, New York, December 14, 1984.

20. Leo Cherne, Oral History, 15, 28–30; Details concerning the portrait (of Albert Schweitzer), undated, 2.

21. Leo Cherne, Oral History, 32, 39.

22. Morris High School record for Leo Cherne; Cherne, "Leo Cherne's Autobiography Birth to 1938," 4; Booth Tarkington, *Seventeen: a Tale of Youth and Summer Time and the Baxter Family, Especially William* (New York: Harper, 1916).

23. Leo Cherne, Oral History, 15, 36.

24. Leo Cherne, Oral History, 46–48, 54; Henry Denker interview with Dale Van Atta, New York, February 1, 1985.

25. Leo Cherne, Oral History, 46–48, 54; Henry Denker interview with Dale Van Atta, New York, February 1, 1985.

26. *New York Times*, September 14–October 30, 1928; Leo Cherne, "Reflections of an ex-M. O. President," clipping in Leo Cherne's high school scrap book,

written about 1930; Leo Cherne, Oral History, 40–42; Henry Denker, Memorial Service.

27. Leo Cherne, "Reflections of an ex-M. O. President"; Leo Cherne, Oral History, 40–42; Henry Denker, Memorial Service.

28. The name was legally changed on August 9, 1929. Since Leo was a minor at that time he assumed the name change at the same time. Jack Cherne, e-mail January 5, 2000.

29. Leo Cherne, Oral History, 43; Henry Denker, Memorial Service.

30. Henry Denker, Memorial Service.

31. "Fete Speaker," *Washington Post,* clipping dated December 1936, in Leo Cherne's high school scrap book.

32. Leo Cherne, copy of letter to unidentified person dated April 3, 1932; Leo Cherne, Oral History, 64–65, 68, 113, 163, 165.

33. Leo Cherne, Oral History, 64–65, 68, 113, 163, 165.

34. Leo Cherne, Oral History, 112.

35. Leo Cherne, untitled autobiography dated September 1, 1943, 2; Leo Cherne, Oral History, 113–116.

36. Leo Cherne, Oral History, 117–118; Leo Cherne, interview with Dale Van Atta, New York, December 14, 1984; Leo Cherne, photocopy of book outline draft, April 19, 1990, 3.

37. Leo Cherne, Oral History, 117–118; Leo Cherne, interview with Dale Van Atta, New York, December 14, 1984; Leo Cherne, photocopy of book outline draft, April 19, 1990, 3.

38. Leo Cherne, untitled autobiography dated September 1, 1943, 5; Leo Cherne, Oral History, 118–120; Leo Cherne, Photocopy of Book Outline Draft, April 19, 1990, 6.

39. Leo Cherne, untitled autobiography dated September 1, 1943, 5.

40. Leo Cherne, Oral History, 60, 128, 161, 167; Leo Cherne, untitled autobiography dated September 1, 1943, 7; Irving Stone, "The Research Institute Biography," carbon copy undated, 17.

41. Leo Cherne, Oral History, 157–158, 160.

42. Leo Cherne, Oral History, 124–125. Although Cherne never graduated from New York University, he received their distinguished alumnus award in 1974. To clarify Cherne's attendance at NYU, I phoned the university archivist, who, unfortunately, could not locate Cherne's records.

43. Leo Cherne, Oral History, 125–126.

44. Leo Cherne, untitled autobiography dated September 1, 1943, 7; Leo Cherne, Oral History, 119, 126–28; Henry Denker, Memorial Service.

45. Leo Cherne, Oral History, 128; Leo Cherne, untitled autobiography dated September 1, 1943, 7; Irving Stone, "The Research Institute Biography," 17; Leo Cherne, Oral History, 161, 167.

46. Leo Cherne, untitled autobiography dated September 1, 1943, 9; Leo Cherne, Oral History, 158; Henry Denker, Memorial Service.

47. Leo Cherne, Oral History, 127, 131–133.

48. Leo Cherne, Oral History, 148.

49. Leo Cherne, Oral History, 157–158, 160.

50. Leo Cherne, Oral History, 134–136, 148.

51. Leo Cherne, Oral History, 134–136, 146–148; Cherne interview with Andrew F. Smith, New York, June 17, 1998.

52. Aaron Levenstein in collaboration with William Agar, *Freedom's Advocate: A Twenty-five Year Chronicle* (New York: The Viking Chronicle, 1965); Aaron Levenstein, *Escape to Freedom: The Story of the International Rescue Committee* (Westport, Conn.: Greenwood Press, 1983).

53. Henry Denker, Memorial Service.

Chapter 2. Researching America

1. George R. Leighton, "Cassandra, Inc.," *The New Yorker* 16 (October 5, 1940): 23.

2. Leo Cherne, untitled autobiography dated September 1, 1943, 10–11; Leo Cherne, Oral History, 149–150, 336–339.

3. Leo Cherne, untitled autobiography, 10–11; Leo Cherne, Oral History, 149–150, 336–339.

4. Irving Stone, "The Research Institute Biography," carbon copy undated, p.14; Leo Cherne, Oral History, 341–342.

5. George R. Leighton, "Cassandra, Inc.," 23; John Kobler, "The Rover Boys, 1941," *The Saturday Evening Post* (October 11, 1941): 12–13, 98, 101, 103; Leo Cherne, untitled autobiography, 12; Irving Stone, "The Research Institute Biography," 10, 19; Leo Cherne, Oral History, 343–345, 419.

6. George R. Leighton, "Cassandra, Inc.," 23; John Kobler, "The Rover Boys, 1941," 12–13, 98, 101, 103; Irving Stone, "The Research Institute Biography," 10, 19; Leo Cherne, Oral History, 343–345.

7. Leo Cherne, Oral History, 348–349.

8. George R. Leighton, "Cassandra, Inc.," 23; John Kobler, "The Rover Boys, 1941," 12–13, 98, 101, 103; Leo Cherne, untitled autobiography, 13–14; Irving Stone, "The Research Institute Biography," 10, 19; Leo Cherne, Oral History, 343–345.

9. Leo Cherne, untitled autobiography, 17–18; Irving Stone, "The Research Institute Biography," 22; Leo Cherne, Oral History, 348–349.

10. George R. Leighton, "Cassandra, Inc.," 23; *Current Biography* (New York: H. W. Wilson Co., 1940), 165.

11. *The Progressive*, May 29, 1937, RIA History file, Box 5, Cherne Archive, Special Collections and Archives of Boston University's Mugar Memorial Library.

12. Leo Cherne, Oral History, 358–359. The *Business and Legislative Report* was not the first newsletter geared for inside information for businessmen. *Kiplinger's* began in 1921, and several others were launched thereafter.

13. Irving Stone, "The Research Institute Biography," 31–33; George R. Leighton, "Cassandra, Inc.," 25; Dixon Wecter, "How Much News in the News Letter?" *Atlantic Monthly* 175 (March 1945): 49.

14. Leo Cherne, Oral History, 189, 193, 359–360, 366–367.

15. Leo Cherne, Oral History, 189, 193, 359–361.

16. Leo Cherne, untitled autobiography, 138; George R. Leighton, "Cassandra, Inc.," 23–28; Irving Stone, "The Research Institute Biography," 90–91; Leo Cherne, Oral History, 370.

17. "Our Favorite Looker-Ahead, the Leo Cherne, Starts Off our 1943," *News Bulletin* (December 30, 1942): 1; Martha Powers to Talk of the Town, January 2, 1990.

18. George R. Leighton, "Cassandra, Inc.," 24; John Kobler, "The Rover Boys, 1941," 12–13, 98, 101, 103; *Current Biography*, 164; Irving Stone, "The Research Institute Biography," 46.

19. Leo Cherne, untitled autobiography, 56, 66, 86; Irving Stone, "The Research Institute Biography," 30, 35, 40; Leo Cherne, Oral History, 130, 352–357; Leo Cherne, photocopy of Book Outline Draft, April 19, 1990, 7; Joseph E. Persico, *The Lives and Secrets of William J. Casey: From the OSS to the CIA* (New York: Viking, 1990), 40–41; Rose Baum Kraut, telephone interview with Andrew F. Smith, February 8, 1999.

20. Irving Stone, "The Research Institute Biography," 69–70, 76; Leo Cherne, Oral History, 130, 429.

21. Leo Cherne, Oral History, 139.

22. Lawrence H. Singer, "Prophet for Profit," *Pageant* 1 (April 1945): 51. Cherne's workaholic tendencies coupled with his active participation in the International Rescue Committee and Freedom House, frequent governmental errands, and his devotion to his sculpture, placed a great strain on his family life. In 1967, after 31 years, his marriage with Julia Lopez ended in a divorce in Juarez, Mexico. The following year, he married Phyllis Brown, a former staff member of the Research Institute of America. Until her death in August 1995, Phyllis Brown accompanied Cherne on many of his trips and occasionally participated in his presentations.

23. George R. Leighton, "Cassandra, Inc.," 24.

24. Lawrence H. Singer, "Prophet for Profit," 51.

25. "Mobilization Plan, Procurement Branch," Copy No. 164 (Confidential) The War Department Mobilization Plan (1933 and 1936); Leo Cherne, untitled autobiography, 67–68; Irving Stone, "The Research Institute Biography," 48–49; Leo Cherne, "As I Recall Bill Casey," in Herbert E. Meyer, comp., *Scouting the Future: The Public Speeches of William J. Casey* (Washington, DC: Regency Gateway, Inc., 1989), 3.

26. Leo Cherne, untitled autobiography, 67–68; Irving Stone, "The Research Institute Biography," 48; Leo Cherne, notes dated July 26, 1994.

27. Leo Cherne, untitled autobiography, 68.

28. George R. Leighton, "Cassandra, Inc.," 27; John Kobler, "The Rover Boys, 1941," 12–13, 98, 101, 103; Irving Stone, "The Research Institute Biography," 49; Leo Cherne, "The Organization of the IRC and Our Relationship with Albert Einstein," paper dated January 21, 1994.

29. George R. Leighton, "Cassandra, Inc.," 28; Irving Stone, "The Research Institute Biography," 49; Leo Cherne vita, circa 1976; Leo Cherne, "As I Recall Bill Casey," 3–4.

30. Irving Stone, "The Research Institute Biography," 50; Bill Casey was sent to Washington to establish a office for the Research Institute in early 1939.

31. George R. Leighton, "Cassandra, Inc.," 27; John Kobler, "The Rover Boys, 1941," 12–13, 98, 101, 103; Leo Cherne, untitled autobiography, 78–79; Irving Stone, "The Research Institute Biography," 49; Leo Cherne, "The Organization of the IRC and Our Relationship with Albert Einstein," paper dated January 21, 1994.

32. Roosevelt Press Conference, September 26, 1939; *New York Times*, September 27, 1939; George R. Leighton, "Cassandra, Inc.," 27; Leo Cherne, untitled autobiography, 87.

33. Felix Colten, "Book Recalls Rumor of Clash in War Dept.," *Washington Post*, September 27, 1939; "New Deal Forces Divided in Clash in War Bureau," *New York World Telegram*, October 6, 1939; *Annals of the American Academy of Political and Social Science*, as cited in George R. Leighton, "Cassandra, Inc.," 27; Albert A. Blum, "The Birth and Death of the M-Day Plan," Preliminary Draft, Princeton, N.J.: Study of Civil-Military Relations, circa October 1954, 35; Leo Cherne, notes dated July 26, 1994.

34. Senator Bennett Champ Clark, *Congressional Record—Senate* 58 (October 23, 1939): 1939; George R. Leighton, "Cassandra, Inc.," 27; John Kobler, "The Rover Boys, 1941," 12–13, 98. 101, 103; Leo Cherne, untitled autobiography, 88; Irving Stone, "The Research Institute Biography," 49, 52–53; Albert A. Blum, "The Birth and Death of the M-Day Plan," 36.

35. Leo Cherne, "State of the Nation," August 22, 1967 (Washington, DC: Industrial College of the Armed Forces, 1967), 5.

36. Leo Cherne, untitled autobiography, 85.

37. *Current Biography*, 165.

38. Leo Cherne, "M-Day and the Business Man," *Harper's Magazine* 181 (July 1940): 113–124; Springfield Republican, as cited in *Current Biography*, 164–165.

39. *Current Biography*, 164–165.

40. Leo Cherne, untitled autobiography, 86.

41. George R. Leighton, "Cassandra, Inc.," 28; Irving Stone, "The Research Institute Biography," 49; Leo Cherne vita, circa 1976.

42. Leo Cherne, untitled autobiography, 80–83, 92, 134.

43. Irving Stone, "The Research Institute Biography," 72–73.

44. *Vital Speeches* 6 (September 1, 1940): 680–683; Ferdinand Lundberg, "News-Letters: A Revolution in Business," *Harper's Magazine* 180 (April 1940): 469–473; George R. Leighton, "Cassandra, Inc.," 23; *Current Biography*, 164–165; John Kobler, "The Rover Boys, 1941," 12–13, 98,101, 103; Leo Cherne, untitled autobiography, 108–109.

45. Leo Cherne, untitled autobiography, 86.

46. *Business & Legislative Report* (January 1940); *Business & Legislative Report* (April 1941); *Business & Legislative Report* (December 6, 1941): 1.

47. Leo Cherne, untitled autobiography, 91, 97; Irving Stone, "The Research Institute Biography," 74; Leo Cherne vita, circa 1976; Leo Cherne, interview with Dale Van Atta, Rochester, N.Y., December 12, 1984, 1–2.

48. Leo Cherne vita, circa 1976; Leo Cherne interview with Dale Van Atta, 1984, 1–2.

49. Irving Stone, "The Research Institute Biography," 74; Leo Cherne vita, circa 1976; Leo Cherne interview with Dale Van Atta, 1984, p. 1–2.

50. Leo Cherne, untitled autobiography, 116.

51. Leo Cherne, untitled autobiography, 123, 131, 139, 145; Joseph E. Persico, *The Lives and Secrets of William J. Casey: From the OSS to the CIA* (New York: Viking, 1990), 51.

52. Leo Cherne, untitled autobiography, 123, 131, 139, 145; Joseph E. Persico, *The Lives and Secrets of William J. Casey*, 51.

53. Leo Cherne, untitled autobiography, 35; Leo Cherne, Oral History, 482, 501; Leo Cherne, interview with Dale Van Atta, 1984. When Stone left New York, he gave Cherne all of Clarence Darrow's files, which he had collected when he wrote his biography of Darrow. Cherne kept them for decades before he gave them to the Library of Congress. See Leo Cherne to Sam Katz, April 10, 1987.

54. Pic (November 1945); Irving Stone, "The Research Institute Biography," 95.

55. Leo M. Cherne, "America's Black Market," *Saturday Evening Post* (July 25, 1942): 22, 49; Leo Cherne, "When Fathers Go to War," *Liberty* (May 15, 1943): 20–21; Leo Cherne, "Letter to the President," *Atlantic* (October 1944): 39–41; Leo Cherne, "The Army Changes Men," *Collier's* (May 27, 1944): 23, 69.

56. Joseph Wood Krutch to Leo Cherne, May 5, 1943; Hollister Noble to Leo Cherne, May 5, 1943; Hollister Noble to Leo Cherne, May 24, 1943; Hollister Noble to Leo Cherne, June 5, 1943; Hollister Noble to Leo Cherne, July 10, 1943; Hollister Noble to Leo Cherne, July 15, 1943; Leo Cherne to Hollister Noble, July 23, 1943; Hollister Noble to Leo Cherne, August 10, 1943; Hollister Noble to Leo Cherne, August 24, 1943; Hollister Noble to Leo Cherne, September 10, 1943; Robert H. Berkov to Leo Cherne, December 21, 1943; Clifton Fadiman to Leo Cherne, January 18, 1944; Anne Adams to Leo Cherne, December 13, 1944; Anne Adams to Leo Cherne, March 6, 1945; Leo Cherne, photocopy of Book Outline Draft, April 19, 1990, 13.

57. Henry Denker and Marc Daniels, "Living History of the Critical Years: 1935–1960," (New York: Research Institute of America, April 27, 1960), 21–23, 41.

58. Leo Cherne, comments at the annual board meeting of the International Rescue Committee, as recorded by Dale van Atta, New York, November 27, 1984.

Chapter 3. Rescuing the Postwar World

1. Leo Cherne, *Bretton Woods, a Cornerstone of Lasting Peace* (New York: Americans United for World Organization, 1944); Leo Cherne, Oral History, 82. Cherne remained a member of the new group and occasionally spoke at their conventions; he became inactive during the 1950s. United World Federalists file, Box 6, Cherne Archive, Special Collections and Archives of Boston University's Mugar Memorial Library.

2. "Big Names of Radio Speak from San Francisco," *The Black Cat Press Club of San Francisco*, April 25, 1945, 4; Leo Cherne typescript of Diary, dated April 29, 1945 and May 1, 1945; Leo Cherne, "Failure at Frisco," *Common Sense* (July 1945): 7–9; Leo Cherne, "Introduction," in Emery Reves, *The Anatomy of Peace* (New York: Viking Press, 1963), xvii–xviii; Leo Cherne, Oral History, 485.

3. Henry Morgenthau Diaries, March 19, 1945, Book 828-2, p. 233; March 20, 1945, Book 830, p. 24, as cited in Anthony Kubek, "The Morgenthau Plan and the Problem of Policy Perversion," *The Journal of Historical Review* 9 (Fall 1989).

4. Leo Cherne, Oral History, 383, 573–576; Aaron Levenstein in collaboration with William Agar, *Freedom's Advocate: A Twenty-five Year Chronicle* (New York: The Viking Chronicle, 1965), 7; Leo Cherne, "Talk with Helle Jensen on Japan and Germany," undated transcript, 15.

5. Jacob Landau to Leo Cherne, September 7, 1945; undated and unsigned notes on Henderson's stationary in Cherne's handwriting in preparation for the trip.

6. Leo Cherne, typescript of private diary, October 30, 1945, November 2, 1945, November 4, 1945, November 5, 1945, November 8, 1945, November 10, 1945, November 13, 1945, November 14, 1945, November 16, 1945, November 18, 1945, November 19, 1945, November 21, 1945, November 23, 1945, December 1, 1945.

7. Leo Cherne, untitled autobiography dated September 1, 1943, 143.

8. Julian Street, Jr. to Leo Cherne, December 15, 1945.

9. Leo Cherne, private diary, dates November 1–December 1, 1945; Leo Cherne, "Talk with Helle Jensen on Japan and Germany," undated transcript, 16, 19.

10. Leo Cherne, private diary, dates November 1–December 1, 1945; Leo Cherne, "Talk with Helle Jensen," 16, 19.

11. "Memo to Editors," January 23, 1946, Overseas News Agency, New York.

12. Leo Cherne, interview with Dale van Atta, Rochester, N.Y., December 12, 1984.

13. Carbon copies of: "Report on Germany," 21, "Report on France," "Summarizing Britain's Economic and Social Developments," and "Report on Europe," dated December 10, 1945, 27.

14. O. P. Echols to Cherne, dated April 1, 1946; Leo Cherne, Oral History, 560.

15. Leo Cherne, Oral History, 561; Cherne vita, circa 1976.

16. "MacArthur Asks Cherne to Draft Japan Tax Plan," unidentified newspaper clipping in Cherne's archive; "To Prepare Jap Tax," *Washington Iowa Journal,* April 16, 1946.

17. Leo Cherne, Oral History, 560.

18. Leo Cherne, private diary, April 10, 1946; Leo Cherne, Oral History, 496.

19. Leo Cherne, private diary, April 13, 1946, April 15, 1946; Leo Cherne, Oral History, 561.

20. Leo Cherne vita, circa 1976.

21. Transcription of tape of Cherne's speech on Vietnam to staff of the Research Institute of America, June 22, 1971.

22. Leo Cherne, interview with Dale van Atta, 1984.

23. Leo Cherne, typescript of Diary, April 16, 1946, April 25, 1946; Leo Cherne to David K. Niles, May 2, 1946.

24. Leo Cherne, interview with Dale van Atta, 1984.

25. Transcription of tape of Cherne's speech on Vietnam to staff of the Research Institute of America, June 22, 1971.

26. Leo Cherne, private diary, April 16, 1946; Cherne interview with Andrew F. Smith, New York, July 10, 1998.

27. Leo Cherne, private diary, "Tuesday"; Burton Crane, "Japanese Tax Law Aimed at Wealthy," *New York Times,* May 22, 1946; *New York New Leader,* May 25, 1946; "Drastic Jap Tax Plan Proposed to MacArthur," *Washington Post,* May 22, 1946; "MacArthur Considers Tax Program for Japan," *Baltimore Sun,* May 22, 1946; "U.S. Designs New Jap Taxes to Spread the Wealth," *Chicago Tribune,* May 22, 1946; *New York Journal of Commerce,* May 22, 1946; "M'Arthur Firm, Bars Purged Japs in Office," *New York Post,* May 21, 1946; Leo Cherne interview with Andrew F. Smith, New York, July 10, 1998.

28. Leo Cherne to Henry Shavell, September 4, 1946.

29. Leo Cherne, Record of Speeches and Radio and Television Appearances, 1944–1970; Harold Jaediker Taub, *Waldorf in the Catskills; The Grossinger Legend* (New York: Sterling Publishing Co., Inc.,1952), 217; Leo Cherne interview with Andrew F. Smith, New York, May 27, 1998.

30. Joseph E. Persico, *The Lives and Secrets of William J. Casey: From the OSS to the CIA* (New York: Viking, 1990), 87–89.

31. *New York Times,* July 24, 1933, L11.

32. Leo Cherne, "The Organization of the IRC and Our Relationship with Albert Einstein," paper dated January 25, 1994; Aaron Levenstein, *Escape to Freedom:*

The Story of the International Rescue Committee (Westport, Connecticut: Greenwood Press, 1983), 8–10.

33. Peter F. Drucker, telephone interview with Andrew F. Smith, December 27, 1999.

34. Leo Cherne, Oral History, 429.

35. Henry and Elizabeth Urrows, "Varian Fry, The Civilian as War Hero," *Harvard Magazine* (March–April 1990): 43–46; Mark Dawson, *Flight; Refugees and the Quest for Freedom; The History of the International Rescue Committee* (New York: International Rescue Committee, 1993), 15–19.

36. Bruce Lambert, "Joseph A. Buttinger, Nazi Fighter and Vietnam Scholar, Dies at 85," *New York Times*, March 8, 1992.

37. Stephanie Mansfield, "Muriel Gardiner, Echoes of 'Julia,'" *Washington Post*, July 6, 1983, B1.

38. Jimmy Ernst, *A Not so Still Life* (New York: St. Martin's Marek, 1984), 195–196.

39. Leo Cherne, Oral History, 428–432.

40. Undated memos from Cherne to Hovgard circa 1948.

41. Winston Churchill, speech at Fulton, Missouri, March 5, 1946.

42. Statement of IRC for Senate Sub-Committee on Refugees and Escapees, July 12, 1961, IRC Carribean file Box 24, Cherne Archive, Special Collections and Archives of Boston University's Mugar Memorial Library.

43. Aaron Levenstein, *Escape to Freedom*, 8–10.

44. Leo Cherne, Radiogram "From the Edge of the Iron Curtain," September 2, 1953; Aaron Levenstein, *Escape to Freedom*, 8–10.

45. Leo Cherne, Radiogram "From the Edge of the Iron Curtain," September 2, 1953; Aaron Levenstein, *Escape to Freedom*, 8–10.

46. Leo Cherne vita, circa 1976.

47. Leo Cherne, Oral History, 271; Leo Cherne, Radiogram "From the Edge of the Iron Curtain," September 2, 1953.

48. Leo Cherne, Oral History, 443–444.

49. Leo Cherne, Radiogram "From the Edge of the Iron Curtain," September 2, 1953.

50. Richard Salzmann, telephone interview with Dale van Atta, January 31, 1985.

51. Senator Daniel Patrick Moynihan, *Congressional Record*, May 15, 1980, pp. 11368–11369; Senator Daniel Patrick Moynihan, Memorial Service for Leo Cherne, February 3, 1999; Moynihan interview with Andrew F. Smith, Washington, DC, September 23, 1999.

52. Leo Cherne, Oral History, 265.

53. Leo Cherne, Oral History, 256.

54. Leo Cherne vita, circa 1976.

55. Harrison Salisburg, "Secret Khrushchev Talk on Stalin 'Phobia' Related," *New York Times*, March 16, 1956, 1.

56. Leo Cherne, interview with Andrew F. Smith, New York, June 10, 1998; Cherne interview with Andrew F. Smith, New York, July 10, 1998.

57. Leo Cherne, interview with Dale van Atta, New York, December 14, 1984.

58. Memo Berlin Wall, Box 4, Cherne Archive, Special Collections and Archives of Boston University's Mugar Memorial Library.

59. Carl Hovgard, "Man of the Month, Leo Cherne," *Research Review* 5 (November 13, 1958): 2–3.

60. Hervé Alphand to Leo Cherne, May 14, 1959.

Chapter 4. Combusting Spontaneously

1. Leo Cherne, "They Changed Your Life," *This Week Magazine* (November 1956) 6–7.

2. "Tale of Tragedy: Soviet Cynicism," *New York Times*, November 5, 1956.

3. Leo Cherne, interview with Dale van Atta, Rochester, N.Y., December 12, 1984.

4. "Draft Memorandum" to Leo Cherne from Dickey Chapelle regarding "The authorization for my services to the Committee" dated March 9, 1957.

5. Leo Cherne, "They Changed Your Life," 6.

6. Marcel Faust, interview with Andrew F. Smith, August 1, 1999.

7. Leo Cherne, Oral History, 464.

8. *Hungary's Fight for Freedom: A Special Report by the editors of Life* (New York: Time, Inc., 1956), 19.

9. Inez Robb, "Rebels Get Backing," clipping in Cherne's file.

10. Leo Cherne, Record of Speeches and Radio and Television Appearances, 1944–1970, information for 1956.

11. James A. Michener, *The Bridge at Andau* (New York: Fawcett Crest, 1957 [1983]); *Saving Freedom's Seed Corn; The First 25 Years of the International Rescue Committee* (New York: International Rescue Committee, 1958).

12. Leo Cherne to Elizabeth Deakman, February 4, 1977; Roberta Ostroff, *Fire in the Wind: The Life of Dickey Chapelle* (New York: Ballantine Books, 1992), 198–220; Leo Cherne to James A. Michener, January 10, 1992.

13. Leo Cherne, "From Inside Hungary, Thirty Days that Shook the World: An Editorial," *Saturday Review* 39 (December 22, 1956): 22–23, 31.

14. A. A. Berle Jr., Leo Cherne, and Clare Boothe Luce, eds., *American Friends of the Captive Nations. Hungary under Soviet Rule II: a Survey of Developments for September 1957 to August 1958* (New York: The American Friends of the Captive Nations and the Assembly of Captive European Nations in association with the Hungarian Committee, 1958), 11.

15. Leo Cherne's Record of Speeches and Radio and Television Appearances, 1944–1970, information for 1956.

16. Leo Cherne, "From Inside Hungary, Thirty Days that Shook the World: An Editorial," 22–23, 31.

17. Inez Robb, "Rebels Get Backing," clipping in Leo Cherne's file.

18. Senator Claiborne Pell, *Congressional Record*, May 19, 1980, p. 11679.

19. Henry Denker, Memorial Service for Leo Cherne, February 3, 1999; Valerie Lanyi, telephone interview with Andrew F. Smith, November 24, 1999.

Chapter 5. Uncovering Communists

1. Roger Louis Benson and Michael Warner, eds., *VENONA: Soviet Espionage and the American Response 1939–1957* (Fort George Meade, MD: National Security Agency, 1996).

2. Leo Cherne, Photocopy of Book Outline Draft, April 19, 1990, pt. 2, p. 9–13; Christopher Andrew, *For the President's Eyes Only; Secret Intelligence and the American Presidency from Washington to Bush* (New York: HarperPerennial, 1996), 181.

3. Aaron Levenstein in collaboration with William Agar, *Freedom's Advocate: A Twenty-five Year Chronicle* (New York: The Viking Chronicle, 1965), 191.

4. Leo Cherne, Oral History, 90–91.

5. Leo Cherne, Oral History, 92.

6. *The Communist in Labor Relations Today* (New York: Research Institute of America, 1946); Leo Cherne, Book Outline, 1990, pt. 2, p. 9–13.

7. Clare Boothe Luce to Cherne, April 5, 1946, Box 5, Cherne Archive, Special Collections and Archives of Boston University's Mugar Memorial Library; *Time*, April 1946.

8. Ulric Bell to Leon Henderson, April 16, 1946, Box 5, Cherne Archive, Special Collections and Archives of Boston University's Mugar Memorial Library.

9. Leo Cherne, typescript of diary, June 1, 1946; Leo Cherne, Book Outline, 1990, 14.

10. Western Union telegram to Cherne from John C. Lee, June 18, 1946, Box 5, Cherne Archive, Mugar Memorial Library.

11. Leo Cherne, "How to Spot a Communist," *Look* (March 4, 1947): 21.

12. Leo Cherne, "How to Spot a Communist," 22.

13. Leo Cherne, "How to Spot a Communist," 23.

14. Leo Cherne, interview with Dale van Atta Rochester, N.Y., December 12, 1984.

15. Wendell L. Willkie, *One World* (New York: The Limited Editions Club, 1944); Aaron Levenstein and William Agar, *Freedom's Advocate*, 12–13.

16. Memo untitled, undated beginning "This is a random sampling . . ." in RIA History file Box 5, Cherne Archive, Mugar Memorial Library; Leo Cherne, Book Outline, April 19, 1990, 11–12.

17. Cherne to George Field, October 27, 1944; George Field to Leo Cherne, November 11, 1946, Freedom House Series 1, Box 13, Seeley G. Mudd Manuscript Library, Princeton University; Leo Cherne, Diary, April 29, 1945.

18. William Agar to Cherne, January 18, 1946, Freedom House Series 1, Box 13, Seeley G. Mudd Manuscript Library, Princeton University.

19. Aaron Levenstein and William Agar, *Freedom's Advocate*, 135–136; Cherne interview with Dale van Atta, Rochester, N.Y., December 12, 1984.

20. Leo Cherne, Oral History, 232; Aaron Levenstein and William Agar, *Freedom's Advocate*, 193; Leo Cherne, Book Outline, 1990, 20.

21. Leo Cherne, Oral History, 232–233; Jack Anderson and Ronald W. May, *McCarthy: the Man, the Senator, the "Ism"* (Boston: Beacon Press, 1952), 79–103.

22. Leo Cherne, Oral History, 231.

23. "America's Town Meeting of the Air," *Herald Tribune*, April 4, 1947.

24. "America's Town Meeting of the Air"; Leo Cherne, draft "Should Communist Party be Outlawed?" Freedom House Series 1, Box 13, Seeley G. Mudd Manuscript Library.

25. "America's Town Meeting of the Air."

26. "America's Town Meeting of the Air."

27. Richard H. Rovere, *Senator Joe McCarthy* (Cleveland: World Publishing Company, 1959), 122–123.

28. Joseph R. McCarthy, *The Story of General George C. Marshall* ([n.l.] [n.p.] 1952).

29. Joseph R. McCarthy, *America's Retreat from Victory* (New York: Devin-Adair, 1951).

30. Typescript of "Author Meets the Press," WABD television broadcast, March 20, 1952.

31. Typescript of "Author Meets the Press"; Leo Cherne, Book Outline, 1990, pt. 2, 9–13.

32. Aaron Levenstein and William Agar, *Freedom's Advocate*, 195.

33. "TV Panel Makes More Noise than Sense," *Life* (April 14, 1952): 101–102, 105, 107–108, 110.

34. Leo Cherne, transcript of interview with Barry Gray, May 3, 1952.

35. Leo Cherne interview with Andrew F. Smith, New York, May 8, 1998.

36. George Field to Cherne, December 13, 1951, and Cherne to George Field, December 29, 1951, Cherne file, Freedom House, Series 2, Box 31, Seeley G. Mudd Manuscript Library.

37. Aaron Levenstein and William Agar, *Freedom's Advocate*, 195.

38. Draft memo by Cherne submitted to Henry Luce in 1952, Cherne file, Freedom House, Series 2, Box 31, Seeley G. Mudd Manuscript Library; Aaron Levenstein and William Agar, *Freedom's Advocate*, 196.

39. Leonard Sussman memo to Andrew F. Smith, November 1, 1999.

40. Natalie Robins, "Inside the FBI," *National Review*, May 11, 1992, 44.

41. Leo Cherne, "Statement by Leo Cherne before Select Committee on Intelligence, U.S. House of Representatives, December 11, 1975.

42. William F. Buckley, *The Redhunter: a Novel Based on the Life of Senator Joe McCarthy* (Boston: Little, Brown, 1999); Arthur Herman, *Joseph McCarthy: Reexamining the Life and Legacy of America's Most Hated Senator* (New York: Free Press, 2000).

Chapter 6. Lobbying for Indochina

1. Leo Cherne, "The Cold War is Hot in Vietnam," undated mimeographed paper, circa March 1961.

2. Notes for Buttinger, September 20, 1954, Vietnam Reports by Cherne file, Box 32, Cherne Archive, Special Collections and Archives of Boston University's Mugar Memorial Library.

3. Vietnam Reports by Cherne file, Box 32, Cherne Archive, Mugar Memorial Library; Joseph Buttinger, *Vietnam: A Political History* (New York: Frederick A. Praeger, 1968), 384–387.

4. William J. Lederer and Eugene Burdick, *The Ugly American* (New York: Norton, 1958); Graham Greene, *The Quiet American* (London: Heinemann, 1956).

5. Memorandum from IRC's executive director to executive committee in preparation for the June 28, 1954 executive committee meeting, IRC trip September 1954, Box 31, Cherne Archive, Mugar Memorial Library.

6. Leo Cherne, Oral History, 446. This issue of whether the IRC should have programs outside of Europe had been raised previously. Harold Oram, for instance, had once recommended that the IRC assist intellectual refugees in Hong Kong who had escaped from China. Board member Lessing Rosenwald opposed the suggestion simply because IRC's strength was in Europe. To solve this problem, a separate organization, Aid to Refugee Chinese Intellectuals, was created.

7. Leo Cherne, Oral History, 144, 450–455; Leo Cherne interview with Dale Van Atta, New York, December 14, 1984; IRC Trip September 1954, Box 31, Cherne Archive, Mugar Memorial Library. In fact, Cherne had not convinced Watson of the importance of the IRC engaging in programs outside of Europe. He resigned from the IRC Board in protest as did another Board member. Watson later became the U.S. ambassador to France.

8. Cherne, Oral History, 564; Cherne, interview with Andrew F. Smith, New York, June 10, 1998.

9. Harnett to Cherne, February 9, 1955, IRC Viet Nam 1954–1957 file, Cherne, at dinner honoring President Ngo Dinh Diem, New York, May 13, 1957, Box 32, Cherne Archive, Mugar Memorial Library.

10. *Newsweek*, November 22, 1954.

11. Leo Cherne, "Cable to Members Research Institute," September 13, 1954; IRC Trip September 1954, Box 31, Cherne Archive, Mugar Memorial Library.

12. IRC Trip September 1954, Box 31, Cherne Archive, Mugar Memorial Library; *Manilla Chronicle*, September 15, 1954; James T. Fisher, *Dr. America: The Lives of Thomas A. Dooley, 1927–1961* (Amherst: University of Massachusetts Press, 1997), 101–102.

13. "Warns U.S. of Crisis if Reds Take Over South Viet Nam," *New York Herald*, September 21, 1954.

14. Leo Cherne to William J. Donovan, Box 32, Cherne Archive, Mugar Memorial Library.

15. Donald R. Heath to Leo Cherne, November 5, 1954.

16. Joseph Buttinger, "Field Report to Freedom Fund," December 1, 1954.

17. Ibid.

18. Cherne to Dorothy D. Houghton, October 20, 1954, Box 32, Cherne Archive, Mugar Memorial Library.

19. Final Report of the International Rescue Committee, Saigon, Vietnam, IRC Viet Nam 1954–1957 file, October 23, 1957, Box 32; Leo Cherne, at dinner honoring President Ngo Dinh Diem, New York, May 13, 1957, Box 32; Summary of Reports from Vietnam October 15, [1955], Vietnam—IRC Business file, Box 31, Cherne Archive, Mugar Memorial Library.

20. Leo Cherne, "To Win in Indochina We Must Win these People," *Look*, January 25, 1955): 61–64.

21. [unidentified author] Interview with Diem, December 4 [1956], Joseph Buttinger file, Box 30, Cherne Archive, Mugar Memorial Library.

22. Cherne, Oral History, 564; Paul L. Montgomery, "Wolf Ladejinsky, Land Reformer Dies; Helped Break Feudal System in Japan," *New York Times*, July 4, 1975, 26, Ladejinsky file, Box 6, Mugar Memorial Library; Leo Cherne, "Leo Cherne's Autobiography Birth to 1938," mimeographed undated paper, 20; Cherne, interview with Andrew F. Smith, New York, June 10, 1998.

23. Memo untitled, undated, beginning "This is a random sampling . . ." in RIA History file Box 5, Cherne Archive, Mugar Memorial Library; Joseph G. Morgan, *The Vietnam Lobby; The American Friends of Vietnam* (Chapel Hill: University of North Carolina Press, 1997), 15–46.

24. Leo Cherne to Gene Gregory, October 24, 1955, Box 31, Cherne Archive; Cherne to Diem, January 25, 1956, Box 31, Cherne Archive; James T. Fisher, *Dr. America: The Lives of Thomas A. Dooley, 1927–1961* (Amherst: University of Massachusetts Press, 1997), 135.

25. IRC Press Release, March 9, 1955, IRC Press Release, March 10, 1955, Leo Cherne to Henry Luce, March 26, 1955, Leo Cherne to G. Frederick Reinhardt, April 15, 1955, IRC Viet Nam 1954–1957 file, Box 32, IRC Press Release, May 2, 1955, Leo Cherne to Carlos P. Romulo, June 8, 1955, Henry Luce to Leo Cherne, July 15, 1955, Gene Gregory to Leo Cherne, September 19, 1955, Operation Brotherhood file, Box 31, Cherne Archive, Mugar Memorial Library.

26. Roland T. Tibbetts to Leo Cherne, July 19, 1956, IRC Viet Nam 1954–1957 file, Box 32, Cherne Archive, Mugar Memorial Library.

27. James T. Fisher, *Dr. America: The Lives of Thomas A. Dooley*, 49.

28. Copy of letter from William Lederer to Verne, February 14, 1992.

29. James T. Fisher, *Dr. America: The Lives of Thomas A. Dooley, 59–60*.

30. William Lederer to Verne, February 14, 1992.

31. Thomas A. Dooley, *Deliver Us from Evil; the Story of Viet Nam's Flight to Freedom* (New York: Farrar, Straus and Cudahy, 1956).

32. Jane Miller, interview with Leo Cherne and Richard Salzmann, Box I, Cherne Papers; *Honolulu Star-Bulletin*, November 22, 1955, as cited in James T. Fisher, *Dr. America: The Lives of Thomas A. Dooley*, 98.

33. James T. Fisher, *Dr. America: The Lives of Thomas A. Dooley*, 98.

34. Edward Lansdale, *Congressional Research Service*, as cited in James T. Fisher, *Dr. America: The Lives of Thomas A. Dooley*, 101–102.

35. Leo Cherne, "Leo Cherne's Autobiography Birth to 1938," 32.

36. A. L. Singleton, "Our Healing Ambassador," *Sunday Star Magazine* (October 26, 1958): 28–29; Leo Cherne interview with Dale Van Atta, New York, December 14, 1984.

37. A. L. Singleton, "Our Healing Ambassador," 28–29; Leo Cherne, "Leo Cherne's Autobiography Birth to 1938," 25, 28.

38. Leo Cherne, "Leo Cherne's Autobiography Birth to 1938," 32, 38.

39. Memorandum from Peter D. Comanduras to CARE re Cooperation between MEDICO and CARE, July 24, 1959, Medico file, Box 24, Cherne Archive, Mugar Memorial Library.

40. Leo Cherne, "The Cold War is Hot in Vietnam," undated mimeographed paper, after January but before April 9, 1961.

41. *Saving Freedom's Seed Corn: The First 25 Years of the International Rescue Committee* (New York: International Rescue Committee, 1958); Tran Van Chuong to Cherne, September 21, 1958; James T. Fisher, *Dr. America: The Lives of Thomas A. Dooley*, 157.

42. [unidentified author] Interview with Diem, December 4 [1956], Joseph Buttinger file, Box 30, Cherne Archive, Mugar Memorial Library.

43. Leo Cherne, "The Problem and Possibilities in Vietnam," 1955, and Leo Cherne telegram to Diem, September 12, 1957, IRC Viet Nam 1954–1957 file, Box 32, Cherne Archive, Mugar Memorial Library.

44. Doris Parks to Leo Cherne, December 10, 1956–January 1957, Hilaire du Berrier to Leo Cherne, January 31, 1957–April 27, 1957, IRC Viet Nam 1954–1957 file, October 23, 1957, Box 32, Cherne Archive, Mugar Memorial Library.

45. Leo Cherne, "The Cold War is Hot in Vietnam."

46. Cherne vita, circa 1976.

47. Leo Cherne, interview with Dale Van Atta, New York, December 12, 1984.

48. Leo Cherne, Oral History, 421.

49. Leo Cherne, Oral History, 208.

50. Roberta Ostroff, *Fire in the Wind: The Life of Dickey Chapelle* (New York: Ballantine Books, 1992), 299–325; Dickey Chapelle, "Helicopters in South Viet Nam," *National Geographic* 122 (November 1962): 722–754.

51. Cherne vita, circa 1976.

52. Richard Salzmann, telephone interview with Dale Van Atta, January 31, 1985.

53. Leo Cherne, "Talk to RIA Staff on Vietnam Trip," June 21, 1965; Typescript of Barry Gray Show, debate between William vanden Heuvel on Vietnam, February 7, 1968; Leonard Sussman memo to Andrew F. Smith, November 1, 1999.

54. Robert Scheer and Warren Hinckle, "The Vietnam Lobby," *Ramparts* (July 1965): 16–23.

55. Leo Cherne, Oral History, 208.

56. Robert Scheer, "Leo Cherne, Our Man with the CIA: The Ruling Class," *New Times* (April 30, 1976): 16.

57. Joseph Buttinger to the editor of the *New Times*, undated.

58. Leonard Sussman memo to Andrew F. Smith, November 1, 1999.

59. Bruce Lambert, "Joseph A. Buttinger, Nazi Fighter and Vietnam Scholar, Dies at 85," *New York Times*, March 8, 1992.

60. Thomas A. Dooley, *The Edge of Tomorrow* (New York: Farrar, Straus and Cudahy, 1958); Thomas A. Dooley, *The Night They Burned the Mountain* (New York: Farrar, Straus and Cudahy, 1960); James T. Fisher, *Dr. America: The Lives of Thomas A. Dooley*, 114.

61. Leo Cherne, Oral History, 586.

Chapter 7. Confronting Genocide

1. John Barron and Anthony Paul, *Murder of a Gentle Land: The Untold Story of Communist Genocide in Cambodia* (New York: Reader's Digest Press, 1977), 50–51.

2. Leo Cherne, "Cambodia—Auschwitz of Asia," *World View* (July/August 1978): 21.

3. Sidney Schanberg, "The Death and Life of Dith Pran: A Story of Cambodia," *New York Times Magazine*, January 20, 1980, 20.

4. Leo Cherne, "Into a Dark, Bottomless Hole, an Appeal to the Board of Directors of Freedom House," June 17, 1975, mimeographed paper; Leo Cherne, "Cambodia—Auschwitz of Asia," 21.

5. Cherne to McGovern, draft letter, dated August 31, 1978; Leo Cherne, "McGovern Shows Where Allegiances Lies," *New America* (October 1978): 6.

6. Lionel Olmer, e-mail to Andrew F. Smith, January 11, 2000.

7. "Pressure Groups," *The Wall Street Journal*, April 26, 1978.

8. Shepard C. Lowman, interview by Andrew F. Smith, Washington, DC, May 18, 1999.

9. Albert Shanker, "Where We Stand," *New York Times*, January 12, 1997.

10. Thelma Richardson, telephone interview with Andrew F. Smith, December 5, 1999.

11. Leo Cherne, *A Personal Recollection* (New York: International Rescue Committee, 1978), 8.

12. Aaron Levenstein, *Report of the Citizens Commission on Indochinese Refugees*, January 1985, mimeographed paper developed by the International Rescue Committee, 22–23; Henry Kamm, "Rights Group Cancels Malaysia Visit," *New York Times*, February 14, 1978.

13. Aaron Levenstein, *Report of the Citizens Commission on Indochinese Refugees*, 25–26.

14. Aaron Levenstein, *Escape to Freedom: The Story of the International Rescue Committee* (Westport, CT: Greenwood Press, 1983), 265–266.

15. Aaron Levenstein, *Report of the Citizens Commission on Indochinese Refugees*, 119.

16. "Statement of Bayard Rustin to the Senate Judiciary Committee, March 14, 1979; Aaron Levenstein, *Escape to Freedom*, 266; Shepard Lowman, interview with Andrew F. Smith, Washington, DC, May 18, 1999.

17. Leo Cherne, "Lane Kirkland," 1981 Freedom Award Dinner, New York, April 9, 1981, 3; "Pressure Groups," *The Wall Street Journal*, April 26, 1978.

18. Leo Cherne, "Cambodia–Auschwitz of Asia," 21–25.

19. Robert P. DeVecchi, Memorandum on "Bayard Rustin" dated January 28, 1997.

20. "Pressure Groups," *The Wall Street Journal*, April 26, 1978.

21. Leo Cherne, "Hell Isle"; Aaron Levenstein, *Escape to Freedom*, 230–231.

22. "IRC and the Cambodian Refugee Emergency," IRC Press Release, December 5, 1979.

23. Aaron Levenstein, *Escape to Freedom*, 256–257.

24. Denis D. Gray, "Marchers become blood donors," *Bangkok Post*, February 6, 1980, 1.

25. "The International Rescue Committee in 1979 (A Summary of IRC activities on Five Continents)" no date; *New York Times*, December 18, 1979.

26. "Stage Folk Give $192,841 for Cambodian Relief," *New York Times*, December 6, 1979.

27. Liv Ullmann, interview with Andrew F. Smith, November 10, 1998.

28. Graham Hovey, "Relief Group Says Cambodians Lag With Food Aid," *New York Times*, December 19, 1979, A13.

29. *Time*, February 18, 1980, 47.

30. Don Graff, Commentary, clipping in the Cherne press book dated 1980.

31. "Get this show off the road," *Bangkok Post*, January 31, 1980; Bernard-Henri Lévy, "March on Death," *New Republic* (January 26, 1980): 11–12.

32. "A Stony Silence Greets Survival Marchers; Sit-In on Border Bridge," *Bangkok Post*, February 7, 1980, 1, 3.

33. "Vigil on Border," *New America*, April 1980, 12; "Joan Baez Leads the March into Bangkok," *The Nation* (Bangkok), February 2, 1980.

34. "Get this show off the road," *Bangkok Post*, January 31, 1980.

35. "'Survival March' Starts Next Week," *Bangkok Post*, January 23, 1980.

36. Joan Baez, "Open Letter to the Socialist Republic of Vietnam," *New York Times*, May 30, 1979; Robert Lindsay, "Peace Activists Attack Vietnam on Rights," *New York Times*, June 1, 1979; "Soviet Assails Joan Baez for Anti-Vietnam Letter," *New York Times*, August 15, 1979; Georges T. Paruvanani, "Music Alone Is Not Enough," documentary video about Joan Baez's concern with human rights and the March for Survival in February 1980.

37. Robert DeVecchi, telephone interview with Andrew F. Smith, December 5, 1999.

38. "Joan Baez Wings in for Border March," *Bangkok Post*, February 2, 1980; "Joan Baez Leads the March into Bangkok," *The Nation* (Bangkok), February 2, 1980; Georges T. Paruvanani, "Music Alone Is Not Enough."

39. Denis D. Gray, "Marchers Become Blood Donors," *Bangkok Post*, February 6, 1980, 1; *Bangkok World*, February 6, 1980.

40. "A Stony Silence Greets Survival Marchers, 1, 3; Grant Peck, "Marchers' Pleas Fall on Deaf Ears," *The Nation* (Bangkok), February 7, 1980, 1, 8.

41. Transcription of press conference, Bangkok, February 4, 1980; John Burgess, "Cambodians Ignore Border March," *Washington Post*, February 7, 1980, A32; Robert DeVecchi telephone interview with Andrew F. Smith, December 5, 1999.

42. "A Stony Silence Greets Survival Marchers," 1, 3; Grant Peck, "Marchers' Pleas Fall on Deaf Ears," 1, 8; Henry Kamm, "Marchers With Food Aid Get No Cambodian Response," *New York Times*, February 7, 1980, A3; John Burgess, "Cambodians Ignore Border March," *Washington Post*, February 7, 1980, A32.

43. "A Stony Silence Greets Survival Marchers," 1, 3; Grant Peck, "Marchers' Pleas Fall on Deaf Ears," 1, 8.

44. Henry Kamm, "Marchers With Food Aid Get No Cambodian Response," A3; *Time*, February 18, 1980, 47.

45. "A Stony Silence Greets Survival Marchers," 1, 3.

46. *Bangkok World*, February 7, 1980, 3.

47. "Get this Show Off the Road"; Kim Gooi, "The Vietnamese 'Land People,'" *The Nation*, February 8, 1980, 1, 8.

48. "A Stony Silence Greets Survival Marchers," 1, 3.

49. "A Stony Silence Greets Survival Marchers," 1, 3; John Burgess, "Cambodians Ignore Border March," A32.

50. Joan Baez, "Letter to the Editor," *New York Times*, March 4, 1980.

51. Unidentified clipping, Cherne Publicity Book dated 1980.

52. "The International Rescue Committee in 1979 (A Summary of IRC Activities on Five Continents)," no date.

53. "The Cambodian Refugee Crisis; Recommendations," issued March 12, 1982.

54. *Bangkok Post*, September 16, 1982.

55. Leo Cherne, "Closing the Doors to People in Danger," *Washington Post*, October 24, 1982.

56. Aaron Levenstein, *Report of the Citizens Commission on Indochinese Refugees*, January 1985, mimeographed paper developed by the International Rescue Committee, 116.

57. Cherne vita, circa 1976.

58. Cherne vita, circa 1976.

59. Aaron Levenstein, *Escape to Freedom*, 269.

60. "The International Rescue Committee in 1979."

61. Leo Cherne, A Personal Recollection, 28.

62. Aaron Levenstein, *Report of the Citizens Commission on Indochinese Refugees*, 119.

63. Sydney Shranberg, "The Death and Life of Dith Pran: A Story of Cambodia," 16; Cherne, annual board meeting of the International Rescue Committee, New York, November 27, 1984.

64. Helle Bering-Jensen "Profile: Leo Cherne, The Best-Kept Secret of American Foreign Policy," *Insight* (July 15, 1991): 38.

65. Liv Ullmann, telephone interview with Dale Van Atta, December 20, 1984.

66. Stacy Weiner, "The Remarkable Leo Cherne," *The Jewish Monthly* (April 1994): 35.

Chapter 8. Sculpting the World

1. Leo Cherne, Oral History, 58–59; Leo Cherne, interview with Dale Van Atta, New York, December 14, 1984.

2. Leo Cherne, Oral History, 58–59; Leo Cherne, interview with Dale Van Atta, New York, December 14, 1984.

3. Henry Denker, Memorial Service for Leo Cherne, February 3, 1999.

4. Irving Stone, "The Research Institute Biography," carbon copy undated, 68.

5. *Current Biography* (New York: H. W. Wilson Co., 1940), 166; Leo Cherne, interview with Dale Van Atta, New York, December 14, 1984.

6. George R. Leighton, "Cassandra, Inc.," *The New Yorker* 16 (October 5, 1940): 23; Leo Cherne interview with Dale Van Atta, New York, December 14, 1984.

7. Lawrence H. Singer, "Prophet for Profit," *Pageant* 1 (April 1945): 52; Leo Cherne, interview with Dale Van Atta, New York, December 14, 1984.

8. Leo Cherne, photocopy of Book Outline Draft, April 19, 1990, p. 10.

9. Leo Cherne, interview with Dale Van Atta, New York, December 14, 1984.

10. Leo Cherne, untitled autobiography dated September 1, 1943, 137–138; Lawrence H. Singer, "Prophet for Profit," *Pageant* 1 (April 1945): 51.

11. Leo Cherne, interview with Dale Van Atta, New York, December 14, 1984; Leo Cherne, "Leo Cherne's Autobiography Birth to 1938," mimeographed undated paper, 28, 30.

12. Undated memo from Cherne to Hovgard circa 1948.

13. Leo Cherne, interview with Dale Van Atta, New York, December 14, 1984; Leo Cherne, "Leo Cherne's Autobiography Birth to 1938," 27.

14. Leo Cherne, interview with Dale Van Atta, New York, December 14, 1984.

15. Leo Cherne, interview by Andrew F. Smith, New York, May 8, 1998.

16. Irving Stone, "The Research Institute Biography," carbon copy undated, p. 68.

17. Leo Cherne, untitled autobiography 1943, 137.

18. Leo Cherne, untitled autobiography 1943, 137–138; Lawrence H. Singer, "Prophet for Profit," 51; Leo Cherne, interview with Dale Van Atta, New York, December 14, 1984; Leo Cherne, "Leo Cherne's Autobiography Birth to 1938," 27.

19. Leo Cherne, interview with Dale Van Atta, New York, December 14, 1984.

20. Rochelle Girson, "Schweitzer in Alvastone," *Saturday Review* (December 17, 1955): 13; Leo Cherne, "Leo Cherne's Autobiography Birth to 1938," 28–29.

21. "Certificate Registration of a Claim to Copyright in a Work of Art or a Model or Design for a Work of Art," dated September 1, 1955; Rochelle Girson, "Schweitzer in Alvastone," *Saturday Review* (December 17, 1955): 13; Leo Cherne, "What Led Me to Sculpture," *Society of Medalists News-Bulletin* (November 1959): np; Leo Cherne, "Leo Cherne's Autobiography Birth to 1938," 30; Leo Cherne, interview with Andrew F. Smith, New York, May 8, 1998.

22. Albert Schweitzer to Leo Cherne, January 17, 1956; Leo Cherne to William Greene, July 7, 1964.

23. Leo Cherne, "Leo Cherne's Autobiography Birth to 1938," 33; Leo Cherne, "What Led Me to Sculpture," np.

24. "Leo Cherne: Sculpture's Surprise Success," *Look* (December 23, 1958): 106.

25. Stefan Lorant, *Lincoln, a Picture Story of His Life* (New York: Harper, 1957), 248; Leo Cherne, "The Face of Lincoln; a Palimpsest of Human Paradox," *Saturday Review* (February 16, 1957): 14; Leo Cherne, "Head of Abraham Lincoln" (New York: Alva Museum Replicas, Inc., nd), np; Leo Cherne, interview with Dale Van Atta, New York, December 14, 1984; Leo Cherne, "Leo Cherne's Autobiography Birth to 1938," 35–36.

26. Dwight Eisenhower to Leo Cherne, April 2, 1957; Leo Cherne's Sculpture File; Marguerite Higgins, "President Takes Museum's Lincoln Head for Nehru,

Artist will Replace It," *New York Herald Tribune*, December 8, 1959; "Gifts from Ike," *U.S. News and World Report* (December 21, 1959): 4; Leo Cherne to William Greene, July 7, 1964; Leo Cherne, "Leo Cherne's Autobiography Birth to 1938," 35–36; Leo Cherne, interview with Andrew F. Smith, New York, May 8, 1998.

27. Leo Cherne to William Greene, July 7, 1964.

28. Leo Cherne to William Greene, July 7, 1964.

29. "Leo Cherne: Sculpture's Surprise Success," 106.

30. Leo Cherne, interview with Dale Van Atta, New York, December 14, 1984.

31. "Certificate Registration of a Claim to Copyright in a Work of Art or a Model or Design for a Work of Art," dated August 17, 1959; Boris Pasternak to Leo Cherne, September 23, 1959; "Pasternak in Bronze," unidentified clipping circa 1959, 99; Leo Cherne, interview with Dale Van Atta, New York, December 14, 1984; Leo Cherne, "Leo Cherne's Autobiography Birth to 1938," 37.

32. Bill vanden Heuvel to Marie Gomez, October 12, 1999.

33. Christopher Barnes to Leo Cherne, August 13, 1980; Christopher Barnes, *Boris Pasternak: a Literary Biography* (New York: Cambridge University Press, 1989–1998).

34. "Certificate Registration of a Claim to Copyright in a Work of Art or a Model or Design for a Work of Art," dated March 19, 1958; Leo Cherne, "What Led Me to Sculpture," np; Leo Cherne, "Sigmund Freud" (New York: Alva Museum Replicas, Inc., nd), np.

35. "Certificate Registration of a Claim to Copyright in a Work of Art or a Model or Design for a Work of Art," dated February 16, 1960; Leo Cherne, "What Led Me to Sculpture," np.

36. "Certificate Registration of a Claim to Copyright in a Work of Art or a Model or Design for a Work of Art," dated February 29, 1960; Leo Cherne, "What Led Me to Sculpture," np.

37. "Certificate Registration of a Claim to Copyright in a Work of Art or a Model or Design for a Work of Art," dated February 29, 1960; Leo Cherne, "What Led Me to Sculpture," np.

38. "Notes dictated by Leo Cherne—March 12, 1998;" Marie Gomez, e-mail to Andrew F. Smith, December 19, 1999; Karen Salzmann, telephone interview with Andrew F. Smith, December 20, 1999.

39. Winston Churchill to Leo Cherne, February 14, 1963; "Certificate Registration of a Claim to Copyright in a Work of Art or a Model or Design for a Work of Art," dated May 10, 1963; Leo Cherne, interview with Andrew F. Smith, New York, May 8, 1998.

40. Robert F. Kennedy to Leo Cherne, September 6, 1963; Leo Cherne to William Greene, July 7, 1964.

41. Leo Cherne to William Greene, July 7, 1964; "Certificate Registration of a Claim to Copyright in a Work of Art or a Model or Design for a Work of Art," dated November 12, 1964; "JFK Remembered in West Berlin," *New York Sunday*

News, November 15, 1964; Walter Carlson, "Bronze Likenesses of Kennedy Placed on View at U.S. Pavilion," *New York Times*, July 10, 1964; Leo Cherne, "Head of John F. Kennedy," undated mimeographed two page paper.

42. "Jack Frost and Another Frost Inspire Wintry Verse," *New York Times*, January 16, 1964; Leo Cherne interview with Dale Van Atta, New York, December 14, 1984; Jerry Steibel, Memorial Service for Leo Cherne, February 3, 1999.

43. Leo Cherne, interview with Dale Van Atta, New York, February 8, 1985.

44. Leo Cherne, "Leo Cherne's Autobiography Birth to 1938," 39.

45. Ibid.

46. Ibid.

47. Leo Cherne, interview with Dale Van Atta, New York, December 14, 1984; Leo Cherne, "Leo Cherne's Autobiography Birth to 1938," 40.

48. Leo Cherne, "Why We Can't Withdraw," *Saturday Review* (December 18, 1965):17–21; Leo Cherne interview with Dale Van Atta, New York, December 14, 1984; Leo Cherne, "Leo Cherne's Autobiography Birth to 1938," 40–41.

49. "Certificate Registration of a Claim to Copyright in a Work of Art or a Model or Design for a Work of Art," December 1965; Leo Cherne, interview with Dale Van Atta, New York, December 14, 1984; Leo Cherne, "Leo Cherne's Autobiography Birth to 1938," mimeographed undated paper, 41–42.

50. Leo Cherne, "Portrait of a President," Freedom House Award Dinner, February 23, 1966, 2; Leo Cherne, interview with Dale Van Atta, New York, December 14, 1984; Leo Cherne, "Leo Cherne's Autobiography Birth to 1938," 42.

51. Leo Cherne, "Leo Cherne's Autobiography Birth to 1938," 42.

52. John P. Roche to Leo Cherne, March 6, 1967; Lyndon Johnson to Leo Cherne, October 3, 1967.

53. Leo Cherne's Sculpture File.

54. Leo Cherne, "The Face of Freud," *The Saturday Review* (September 27, 1958): 23; Leo Cherne's Sculpture File.

55. Leo Cherne, interview with Dale Van Atta, New York, December 14, 1984.

Chapter 9. Ransoming Prisoners

1. Anthony Drexel Duke, as cited in Aaron Levenstein, *Escape to Freedom: The Story of the International Rescue Committee* (Westport, CT: Greenwood Press, 1983), 113–114.

2. Leo Cherne, Oral History, 47–48, 54.

3. Leo Cherne, Oral History, 54–55.

4. Leo Cherne, Oral History, 530.

5. Leo Cherne, Oral History, 49.

6. Leo Cherne, Oral History, 528–532.

7. Leo Cherne, Oral History, 426; Roberta Ostroff, *Fire in the Wind: The Life of Dickey Chapelle* (New York: Ballantine Books, 1992), 245–267.

8. Leo Cherne, Oral History, 533–535.

9. Leo Cherne, Oral History, 540–545.

10. Leo Cherne, Oral History, 537; Aaron Levenstein, *Escape to Freedom*, 101.

11. Leo Cherne, Oral History, 540–545.

12. Leo Cherne, Oral History, 552–554.

13. Leo Cherne, Oral History, 552–554, 559.

14. Leo Cherne, Oral History, 552–558; Hugh Thomas, *Cuba or the Pursuit of Freedom*, updated edition (New York: Da Capo, 1998), 1297.

15. Bob Brock, "Cuba will Get to Answer Charges It's Going Red," *Dallas Times Herald*, May 15, 1959, p. 22C; "Communist Trend in Cuba is Denied," *New York Times*, May 18, 1959; "Cuba Replies to CBS," *Times of Havana*, May 18, 1959.

16. *New York Times*, July 13, 1960; *Daily News*, July 13, 1960; *Herald Tribune*, July 13, 1960; IRC press release, July 12, 1960, Cuban Tractor file, Box 24, Cherne Archive, Special Collections and Archives of Boston University's Mugar Memorial Library.

17. Memo to Arthur M. Schlesinger, Jr., from William vanden Heuvel, April 17, 1962, IRC—Cuba 1960–1971 file, Box 30, Cherne Archive, Special Collections and Archives of Boston University's Mugar Memorial Library.

18. *Reader's Digest*, August 1960, IRC Carribean file, Box 24; Charles Sternberg to Leo Cherne and Armando A. Pedroso, July 31, 1961, Cuban Tractor file, Box 24, Cherne Archive, Mugar Memorial Library.

19. "IRC Cuban Refugee Appeal," October 26, 1960, Armando A. Pedroso to Nicholas Biddle, November 28, 1960, "Caribbean Crisis: A Danger and an Opportunity; Program for Federal Action to Help Solve the Caribbean Refugee Problem; Subcommittee of Caribbean Refugee Problem, IRC," January 30, 1961, and Claiborne Pell to Dean Rusk, March 23, 1961, IRC Carribean file, Box 24, and Memo to Arthur M. Schlesinger, Jr., from William vanden Heuval, April 17, 1962, IRC—Cuba 1960–1971 file, Box 30, Cherne Archive, Mugar Memorial Library.

20. "Verbatim Record of the Nine Hundred and Twenty-first Meeting" of the United Nations Security Council, January 4, 1961, p. 61.

21. IRC press release, January 5, 1961, IRC Carribean file Box 24, Cherne Archive, Mugar Memorial Library.

22. Hugh Thomas, *Cuba or the Pursuit of Freedom*, 1363–1369.

23. Leo Cherne, "Operation Rescue Interim Report to Sponsors," undated mimeographed report; Leo Cherne, "The Tractor-Cuban Prisoner Exchange," undated mimeographed report.

24. Memo from Executive Director (Chester S. Williams) to Executive Committee (vanden Heuval; Biddle; Cherne; Emmet; Salzmann; Kermit Roosevelt), June 30, 1961; Cherne to Milton Eisenhower, July 1961; minutes of IRC Executive Committee meeting held June 21, 1961, IRC Carribean file, Box 24, Cherne Archive, Mugar Memorial Library.

25. Cherne to Milton Eisenhower, July 1961, Memo from R. Salzmann, May 25, 1961, IRC Carribean file, Box 24, Cherne Archive, Mugar Memorial

Library; Leo Cherne's Record of Speeches and Radio and Television Appearances, 1944–1970, information for 1961, np; Barry Gray Show, "Cuban Tractors," May 24, 1961; Leon Dennen, "Castro Offer Poses a Moral Dilemma," *Iowa City Press-Citizen*, May 31, 1961; Leo Cherne, "Operation Rescue Interim Report to Sponsors"; Leo Cherne, "The Tractor-Cuban Prisoner Exchange"; Leo Cherne interview with Dale Van Atta, New York, December 14, 1984; Leo Cherne, "Talk with Helle Jensen on Japan and Germany," undated transcript, p. 20; Hugh Thomas, *Cuba or the Pursuit of Freedom*, 1371.

26. Aaron Levenstein, *Escape to Freedom*, 100.

27. Leo Cherne, "Castro's Cuba: Should the U.S. Re-Evaluate Its Policy," Court of Reason, Chanel 13, May 27, 1964, 2.

28. Gil Loescher and John A. Scanlan, *Calculated Kindness: Refugees and America's Half-Open Door*, 1945 to the Present (New York: Free Press,1986), 66.

29. Memo to Arthur M. Schlesinger, Jr., from William vanden Heuval, April 17, 1962, IRC—Cuba 1960–1971 file, Box 30, Cherne Archive, Mugar Memorial Library; *Annual Report for the Year Ended December 31, 1961* (New York: International Rescue Committee, 1962), 1, 3–6; *Annual Report for the Year Ended December 31, 1962* (New York: International Rescue Committee, 1963), 2–8; *30th Anniversary Year, Annual Report for the Year Ended December 31, 1963* (New York: International Rescue Committee, 1964) *Annual Report for the Year Ended December 31, 1964* (New York: International Rescue Committee, 1965), 3–5; *Annual Report for the Year Ended December 31, 1965* (New York: International Rescue Committee, 1966), 2–5; Aaron Levenstein, *Escape to Freedom*, 104.

30. Harry Conn, "Refugees—The World's Forgotten People," *ALF-CIO American Federationist* (September 1966).

31. *Annual Report for the Year ended December 31, 1965* (New York: International Rescue Committee, 1966), 2–5; Harry Conn, "Refugees—The World's Forgotten People"; Andreas Castellano, telephone interview with Andrew F. Smith, December 23, 1999.

32. Aaron Levenstein, *Escape to Freedom*, 112.

33. James Carter to Leo Cherne, June 18, 1980, as cited in Aaron Levenstein, *Escape to Freedom*, 121–122.

Chapter 10. Guiding Intelligence

1. Leo Cherne, interview with Andrew F. Smith, New York, June 4, 1998.

2. Leo Cherne to Richard Nixon, October 28, 1965, Cherne file, Freedom House, Series 1, Box 13, Seeley G. Mudd Manuscript Library, Princeton University.

3. Leo Cherne, interview with Andrew F. Smith, New York, June 4, 1998.

4. Richard Nixon to Leo Cherne, December 15, 1971.

5. Leo Cherne, interview with Andrew F. Smith, New York, June 4, 1998.

6. Leo Cherne, "Leo Cherne's Autobiography Birth to 1938," mimeographed undated paper, 36.

7. Lionel Olmer, fax to Andrew F. Smith, December 27, 1999.

8. Joseph E. Persico, *The Lives and Secrets of William J. Casey: From the OSS to the CIA* (New York: Viking, 1990), 53–57, 68.

9. Ibid., 87–89.

10. Ibid., 91–92.

11. Ibid., 128.

12. Ibid., 89–91.

13. William Casey, interview with Dale Van Atta, December 19, 1984; Leo Cherne, "As I Recall Bill Casey," in Herbert E. Meyer, comp., *Scouting the Future: The Public Speeches of William J. Casey* (Washington, DC: Regency Gateway, 1989), 5–6; Joseph E. Persico, *The Lives and Secrets of William J. Casey*, 127–129.

14. Senate Select Committee to Study Governmental Operations with Respect to Intelligence Activities, final report, "Foreign and Military Intelligence," 94th Congress, 2nd Session 1976, 63; Anne Hessing Cahn, *Killing Detente: The Right Attacks the CIA* (University Park: Pennsylvania State University Press, 1998), 100–101.

15. Christopher Andrew, *For the President's Eyes Only; Secret Intelligence and the American Presidency from Washington to Bush* (New York: HarperPerennial, 1996), 272.

16. Anne Hessing Cahn, *Killing Detente*, 100–101.

17. Lionel Olmer, interview with Dale Van Atta, Washington, DC, January 1, 1985.

18. A. A. Berle Jr., Leo Cherne, and Clare Boothe Luce, eds., *American Friends of the Captive Nations. Hungary under Soviet Rule II: a Survey of Developments for September 1957 to August 1958* (New York: American Friends of the Captive Nations and the Assembly of Captive European Nations in association with the Hungarian Committee, 1958); Announcement of "William J. Donovan Memorial Award," November 17, 1959; Leo Cherne, interview with Dale Van Atta, New York, December 14, 1984.

19. Lionel Olmer, e-mail to Andrew F. Smith, December 15, 1999.

20. Ibid.

21. Richard Pipes, "Team B: The Reality behind the Myth," *Commentary* 82 (October 1986): 30–31; Leo Cherne, draft letter to the editor, *Playboy Magazine*, December 17, 1982; Arnold Beichman, "Beyond Langley's Corridors," *Washington Times*, January 30, 1989; Lionel Olmer, e-mail to Andrew F. Smith, January 11, 2000.

22. The Rockefeller Commission's findings were made public in *Commission on CIA Activities within the United States* (Washington, DC: Government Printing Office, June 10, 1975). For the official proceedings see U.S. Congress, House, Select Committee on Intelligence, U.S. Intelligence Agencies and Activities Volume 1–4, 94th Congress, 1st Session, July–December 1975. Christopher Andrew, *For the President's Eyes Only*, 400–404.

23. "Intelligence Panel Expanded by Ford," *Washington Post*, March 12, 1976, 6; Leo Cherne to James Baker III, September 14, 1988.

24. Leo Cherne interview with Dale Van Atta, New York, December 14, 1984; Christopher Andrew, *For the President's Eyes Only*, 413.

25. Leo Cherne, Time Log, July 12, 1976, Box 2, Leo Cherne Papers, Gerald R. Ford Library, Ann Arbor, Michigan, as cited in Anne Hessing Cahn, *Killing Detente*, 103.

26. Lionel Olmer, interview with Dale Van Atta, Washington, DC, January 1, 1985.

27. Leo Cherne, interview with Dale Van Atta, New York, December 14, 1984.

28. Arnold Beichman, "Beyond Langley's Corridors," *Washington Times*, January 30, 1989.

29. George Bush to Leo Cherne, January 17, 1977.

30. Judith Miller, "Intelligence Advisory and Oversight Units Named," *New York Times*, October 21, 1981; Leo Cherne, interview with Dale Van Atta, New York, December 14, 1984.

31. Leo Cherne, "Statement in Support of the Nomination of William J. Casey to be Director of Central Intelligence," January 12, 1981.

32. Martin Anderson, *Revolution* (San Diego: Harcourt Brace Jovanovich, 1988), 354–363.

33. Clare Booth Luce telephone interview with Dale Van Atta, January 31, 1985.

34. George Bush to Leo Cherne, July 16, 1990.

35. John M. Crewdson, "Group Led by C.I.A. Board Nominee Reportedly Got $15,000 from Agency," *New York Times*, February 20, 1976; Leo Cherne's notes from an IRC Executive Committee meeting; John M. Crewdson, "Cherne Unit Not Tied to C.I.A. Fund," *New York Times*, February 21, 1976; George Bush to Charles Sternberg, April 14, 1976.

36. A. O. Sulzberger, Jr., "U.S. Overseas Radio Dispute Again," *New York Times*, May 15, 1980; Senators Daniel Patrick Moynihan and Jacob Javits, *Congressional Record*, May 15, 1980, pp. 11368–11370; Senator Claiborne Pell, *Congressional Record*, May 19, 1980, p. 11679; Senator Claiborne Pell, *Congressional Record*, May 22, 1980, pp. 12149–12150.

37. Robert Scheer, "With Enough Shovels," *Playboy Magazine* (December 1982): 312; Leo Cherne, draft letter to the editor, *Playboy Magazine*, December 17, 1982.

38. Eric Thomas Chester, *Covert Network: Progressives, the International Rescue Committee, and the CIA* (Armonk, New York: M.E. Sharpe, 1995).

39. Shepard C. Lowman, interview with Andrew F. Smith, Washington, DC, May 18, 1999.

40. David Cohen, telephone interview with Andrew F. Smith, December 22, 1999.

Chapter 11. The Falling Curtain

1. Leo Cherne, "Memorandum," June 21, 1989.

2. Ibid.

3. JFB (Joseph Buttinger) to Lucius D. Clay, May 26, 1960.

4. Ronald Reagan, "Text of Film by President Ronald Reagan," October 31, 1983, 6; Fred Demech, interview with Andrew F. Smith, Arlington, Virginia, June 17, 1999.

5. Ronald Reagan, "Text of Film by President Ronald Reagan," 6; Fred Demech, interview with Andrew F. Smith, Arlington, Virginia, June 17, 1999.

6. Harry R. White to Edward B. Flanagan, July 29, 1992; Thomas J. Watson, Jr., and Peter Petre, *Father, Son & Co.: My Life at IBM and Beyond* (New York: Bantam Books,1990); Harry R. White, "The Building of a Profession," 13–20, 90, unidentified clipping. In fact this was not Cherne's fiftieth annual speech. Cherne's first speech had been in January 1940. Someone miscounted; it was actually his fifty-first speech. See the Sales Executive Club's "Our Favorite Looker-Ahead, the Leo Cherne, Starts Off Our 1943," *News Bulletin* (December 30, 1942): 1.

7. Harry R. White, "The Building of a Profession," 13–20, 90.

8. Brochure for event, January 12, 1990; video of event.

9. Henry A. Kissinger, as cited in Leo Cherne, *Millennium* (New York: Oppenheimer Funds, 1990), np.

10. "Leo Cherne Retires as Chairman of the International Rescue Committee," press release, International Rescue Committee, August 31, 1991.

11. *Leo Cherne Refugee Emergency Fund* (New York: International Rescue Committee, Inc., 1983); Lionel Olmer, e-mail to Andrew F. Smith, August 19, 1999.

12. Lionel Olmer, e-mail to Andrew F. Smith, August 19, 1999.

13. Ibid.

14. *Leo Cherne Refugee Emergency Fund* (New York: International Rescue Committee, Inc., 1983).

15. Peter Drucker file, Box 5, Cherne Archive, Special Collections and Archives of Boston University's Mugar Memorial Library.

16. Lionel Olmer, e-mail to Andrew F. Smith, August 19, 1999; Peter F. Drucker, telephone interview with Andrew F. Smith, December 27, 1999.

17. Henry Denker, Memorial Service for Leo Cherne, February 3, 1999; Lionel Olmer, e-mail to Andrew F. Smith, December 21, 1999.

18. Henry Denker, Memorial Service for Leo Cherne.

19. Lionel Olmer, e-mail December 21, 1999.

20. Marie Gomez, e-mail to Andrew F. Smith, December 20, 1999; Lionel Olmer, e-mail to Andrew F. Smith, December 21, 1999.

21. John Richardson, e-mail to Andrew F. Smith, December 18, 1999.

22. Lionel Olmer, e-mail to Andrew F. Smith, December 21, 1999.

23. Quotes taken from Memorial Service for Leo Cherne.

Selected Bibliography

A. Books by Leo Cherne

Cherne, Leo. *M Day and What It Means to You*. New York: Simon and Schuster, 1940.

———. *Your Business Goes to War*. Boston: Houghton Mifflin Company, 1942.

———. *The Rest of Your Life*. Garden City, NY: Doubleday, Doran and Co., 1944.

B. Selected Professional Publications with Leo Cherne as Author or Co-Author

Berle, A. A., Jr., Leo Cherne and Clare Boothe Luce, eds. *American Friends of the Captive Nations. Hungary under Soviet Rule Volumes 1–5*. New York: American Friends of the Captive Nations and the Assembly of Captive European Nations in Association with the Hungarian Committee, 1957–1961.

Cherne, Leo. *Social Security Coordinator*. New York: Tax Research Institute of America, 1937.

———. *War Coordinator*. New York: Research Institute of America, 1939.

———. *Adjusting Your Business to War*. Foreword to the First Edition, by the Hon. Louis Johnson. 2nd ed. New York: Research Institute of America, 1940.

———. *Federal Tax Coordinator*. New York: Research Institute of America, 1940.

———. *Guide to Tax Economy*. New York: Research Institute of America, 1940.

———. *Business and Defense Coordinator*. New York: Research Institute of America, 1941.

———. *Guide to Tax Economy*. New York: Research Institute of America, 1941.

———. *Materials for a Course in Government Contract Problems, Taken from the Business and Defense Coordinator of the Research Institute of America*. New York: Research Institute of America, 1941.

———. *Social Security Coordinator*. New York: Research Institute of America, 1941.

———. *Guide to Tax Economy*. New York: Research Institute of America, 1942.

———. *Price Control.* New York: Research Institute of America, 1942.

———. *How Material and Production Controls Work.* New York: Research Institute of America, 1943.

———. *Manpower: Solving the Problems of Labor Shortage.* New York: Research Institute of America, 1943.

———. *Pay Increases under Wage and Salary Stabilization.* New York: Research Institute of America, 1943.

———. *Your Business after the War.* New York: Research Institute of America, 1943.

———. *Management Coordinator.* New York: Research Institute of America, 1944.

———. *Bretton Woods, a Cornerstone of Lasting Peace.* New York: Americans United for World Organization, 1945.

———. *Payroll Coordinator.* New York: Research Institute of America, 1945.

———. *Tax Coordinator.* New York: The Research Institute of America, Inc, 1946.

———. *Payroll Tax Coordinator.* New York: Research Institute of America, 1957.

Cherne, Leo, and William J. Casey. *Adjusting Your Business to the New Legislation.* New York: Research Institute of America, 1941.

———. *Materials for a Course in Industrial Procurement.* New York: Research Institute of America, 1941.

———. *Government Contract Problems.* New York: Research Institute of America, 1942.

———. *Price Control.* New York: Research Institute of America, 1942.

———. *Wage and Salary Stabilization.* New York: Research Institute of America, 1942.

Cherne, Leo M., William J. Casey, and Victor Stanislaus Karabass. *Wartime Purchasing Procedures.* New York: Research Institute of America, 1942.

Cherne, Leo M., Herman Howard Cohen, Ola C. Col, and Rose Baum. *Guide to Tax Economy.* Stamford: New England Law Press, 1937.

Cherne, Leo, and Harold Beryl White. *Adjusting Your Business to the New Legislation.* Stamford: R. S. Taylor, New England Law Press, 1939.

Cherne, Leo, Harold B. White, Joseph Lewis Simon *et al. Adjusting Your Business to War.* Foreword by Hon. Louis Johnson. New York: Tax Research Institute of America, 1939.

Cherne, Leo, et al. *Handbook of Production Controls; How to Operate under CMP, Scheduling and Priorities.* New York: Research Institute of America, 1943.

———. *Contract Termination: Guide for Prime and Subcontractors.* New York: Research Institute of America, 1944.

Gompers, Louis, Leo Cherne, and Abraham Singer. *Proceedings Supplementary to Judgment and Execution.* 4th ed. New York: Stratford Law Publishing Company, 1944.

Gompers, Louis, Leo Cherne, et al. *Proceedings Supplementary to Judgment and Execution, Annotated.* New York: Publication Sales Corporation, 1936.

———. *Proceedings Supplementary to Judgment and Execution, Annotated.* 2nd ed. New York: Publication Sales Corporation, 1937.

———. *Proceedings Supplementary to Judgment and Execution, Annotated.* 3rd ed. New York: Publication Sales Corporation, 1938.

Rogers, Hugo Edward, and Leo M. Cherne. *Payroll Tax Saving Service.* New York: Whitgard Services, 1936.

Rogers, Hugo Edward, Herman Howard Cohen, Leo M. Cherne, and Harold Beryl White. *Legal Tax Saving Methods.* New York: Tax Research Institute of America, Tax Saving Association, 1936.

C. Selected Articles, Chapters, and Reports by Leo Cherne

Cherne, Leo M. "What American Business Thinks of Profit Sharing." *Congressional Digest* 18 (January 1939): 11–13.

———. "M-Day and Distribution." *Twelfth Conference on Distribution* (Boston: Retail Trade Board; Boston Chamber of Commerce, 1940): 27–30.

———. "M-Day and the Business Man." *Harper's Magazine* (July 1940): 113–124.

———. "M-Day and the Druggists." *American Druggist* 102 (September 1940): 34–35, 88, 90, 92.

———. "When They Start to Bark Orders for Industry to March What Will the Druggists Hear on M-Day." *American Druggist* 102 (October 1940): 46–47.

———. "America's Black Market." *Saturday Evening Post* (July 25, 1942): 22, 49, 53–54.

———. "When Fathers Go to War." *Liberty* (May 15, 1943): 20–21, 71.

———. "Letter to the President." *The Atlantic* (October 1944): 39–41.

———. "Failure at Frisco." *Common Sense* (July 1945): 7–9.

———. "How to Spot a Communist." *Look* (March 4, 1947): 21–23.

———. "The Bronx Revisited." *Tomorrow* (September 1950): 18–23.

———. "Does Business Want War?" *Nation's Business* 40 (January 1952): 37–40.

———. "The Writer & the Entrepreneur." *Saturday Review* (January 19, 1952): 10–11.

———. "Canada: Boom Unlimited." *Saturday Review* (June 7, 1952): 13–14, 45–46.

———. "Rum, Sugar, Tourists & Dollars." *Saturday Review* (October 18, 1952): 48, 50, 52–53.

———. "The World & U.S. Business." *Saturday Review* (January 24, 1953): 13–14, 41–43.

———. "Wanted: a Market for a $275,000,000 Product." *Printers' Ink* 244 (July 17, 1953): 33–35.

———. "Face the Fireball or Run for Cove." *Federalist Annual* (New York: Writers Board for World Government, 1954), 20–21.

———. "Harry A. Bullis: Portrait of 'New Businessman." *Saturday Review* (January 23, 1954): 24–25, 57–58.

———. "Recession? Depression? Or Whatnot?" *New York Times Magazine* (March 28, 1954): 14.

———. "What Should be Televised?" *New York Times Magazine* (August 22, 1954): 7, 25, 27, 29–30, 32.

———. "Peace Alone is not Our Object." *Saturday Review* (October 29, 1955): 7–8.

———. "Prosperity is No Panacea." *Saturday Review* (January 21, 1956): 26–27, 54.

———. "Step into the Future." *Family Weekly* (March 18, 1956): 6–7.

———. "Is the New Russia a Myth?" *New York Times Magazine* (June 17, 1956): 10, 50, 54.

———. "Calcutta: Metropolis of Misery." *Look* (July 10, 1956): 58–59.

———. "They Changed Your Life." *This Week Magazine* (November 1956): 6–7.

———. "Your Life 10 Years from Today." *Wisdom* 1 (November 1956): 54–57.

———. "I Spoke with Cardinal Mindszenty." *America; National Catholic Weekly Review* 96 (November 17, 1956): 187.

———. "Thirty Days that Shook the World: An Editorial." *Saturday Review* (December 22, 1956): 22–23, 31.

———. "How We'll Live in '77; a Look Ahead 20 Years." *Together* (January 1957): 20–23.

———. "The World's Biggest Problem: Population Explosion!" *This Week Magazine* (January 6, 1957): 10–11.

———. "The Face of Lincoln; a Palimpsest of Human Paradox." *Saturday Review* (February 16, 1957): 14.

———. "The Face of Freud." *Saturday Review* (September 27, 1958): 23.

———. "What Led Me to Sculpture." *Society of Medalists News–Bulletin* (November 1959): np.

———. "Deepening Red Shadow over Vietnam." *New York Times Magazine*, April 9, 1961.

———. "Introduction." In Emery Reves, *The Anatomy of Peace*. New York: Viking Press, 1963, xvii–xviii.

———. "Why We Can't Withdraw." *Saturday Review* (December 18, 1965): 17–21.

———. "The Realist and Reality, Response to Hans J. Morgenthau's 'The House that Cherne Built.'" *The New Leader* (February 13, 1967).

———. "A Time of Profound Change." *The Credit World* 55 (September 1967): 18–19.

————. *A Personal Recollection.* New York: International Rescue Committee, 1978.

————. *A Personal Recollection: Citizens Commission on Indochinese Refugees.* New York: International Rescue Committee, February–March 1978.

————. "Cambodia—Auschwitz of Asia." *World View* (July/August 1978): 21.

————. "Hell Isle." *New York Times*, February 3, 1979.

————. "As I Recall Bill Casey." In Herbert E. Meyer, comp., *Scouting the Future: The Public Speeches of William J. Casey.* Washington, D.C.: Regency Gateway, 1989, 3.

D. Selected Unpublished Manuscripts by Leo Cherne

Cherne, Leo. Untitled carbon copy of his autobiography dated September 1, 1943.

————. "Report on Germany," p. 21, "Report on France," "Summarizing Britain's Economic and Social Developments," and "Report on Europe." Dated December 10, 1945.

————. Oral History, 1960–1961.

————. "The Cold War is Hot in Vietnam." Undated mimeographed paper, circa March 1961.

————. "Record of Speeches and Radio and Television Appearances, 1944–1970."

Cherne, Leo, and Aaron Levenstein. "Through the Gates of Fear." Book proposal, undated.

E. Selected Articles about Leo Cherne

Anon. "Only 28, But 19,000 Depend Upon Him for Business Opinions." *Future—The Magazine for Young Men* 3 (November 1940): 7.

————. "TV Panel Makes More Noise than Sense." *Life* (April 14, 1952): 101–102, 105, 107–108, 110.

————. "Profile of the Week: Leo Cherne, Renaissance Man, Made in USA." Translation of article from *Die Weltwoche*, Zurich, September 13, 1957.

————. "Leo Cherne: Sculpture's Surprise Success." *Look* (December 23, 1958): 106.

Bering-Jensen, Helle. "Profile: Leo Cherne, The Best-Kept Secret of American Foreign Policy." *Insight* (July 15, 1991): 36–39.

"Cherne, Leo M." *Current Biography.* New York: H. W. Wilson, 1940, 226–228.

Hovgard, Carl. "Man of the Month, Leo Cherne." *Research Review* 5 (November 13, 1958): 2–3.

Kobler, John. "The Rover Boys, 1941." *Saturday Evening Post* (October 11, 1941): 12–13, 98.

Leighton, George R. "Cassandra, Inc." *New Yorker* 16 (October 5, 1940): 23–28.

Singer, Lawrence H. "Prophet for Profit." *Pageant* 1 (April 1945): 51.

Van Atta, Dale. "Leo Cherne's Magnificent Obsession." *Reader's Digest* (May 1986): 119–122.

Weiner, Stacy. "The Remarkable Leo Cherne." *Jewish Monthly* (April 1994): 35–38.

F. Selected Speeches by Leo Cherne

——. Cherne, Leo M. "M-Day." *Vital Speeches* 6 (September 1, 1940): 680–683.

——. "Defense and Economic Dislocation." Conference of Mayors, Morrison Hotel, Chicago, Ill., September 12, 1941.

——. "Twentieth Century Authoritarianism; a Religion for those who Have Lost Religion But Not Their Religions Needs." *Vital Speeches* 15 (August 15, 1949): 648–650.

——. "Operation Breakthrough; American Complacency Destroyed." *Vital Speeches* 24 (December 24, 1957): 139–143.

——. "A Masterpiece of Confusion: the Letter from the 'Little Vietnamese Girl.'" *Vital Speeches* 24 (April 1, 1958): 361–364.

——. "Countering the Soviet Challenge." Industrial College of the Armed Forces, Washington, DC, May 15, 1959.

——. "Rehabilitation: The World's Central Problem." *Vital Speeches* 27 (October 15, 1960): 18–23.

——. "Remarks of Leo Cherne at Commemoration of June 17, 1953 East German Revolt." New York, June 15, 1961.

——. "A Re-Appraisal of Containment." Industrial College of the Armed Forces, Washington, DC, November 27, 1962.

——. "Statement on U.S. Psychological Warfare." House Committee on Foreign Affairs, May 1, 1963.

——. "30 Years in the Struggle against Tyranny." Overseas Press Club, New York, May 14, 1963.

——. Transcript of Leo Cherne on Barry Gray Show, re Kennedy Assassination. November 24, 1963.

——. "The Year of New Governments." Sales Executives Club of New York, January 1964.

——. "Revolution in Our Time, the Tragedy of its Betrayal." Kellogg Center, Michigan State University, February 28, 1964.

——. "Opportunities for Progress." Third General Session, 52nd Annual Meeting, Chamber of Commerce of the United States, Washington, DC, April 26–29, 1964.

——. "Tribute to Hon. Angier Biddle Duke." George Washington Awards Dinner, Hotel Waldorf-Astoria, April 29, 1964.

———. "Castro's Cuba: Should the U.S. Re-Evaluate Its Policy?" Court of Reason, Chanel 13, May 27, 1964.

———. "Mobilization—The New Revolution." European Travel Conference, New York, October 1, 1964.

———. "A 25-Year Look Back." *Vital Speeches of the Day* 31 (March 15, 1965): 349–352. [25th Anniversary Address, Sales Executive Club, Hotel Roosevelt, January 5, 1965.]

———. "Remarks." Financial Executives Institute, Rochester Chapter, March 29, 1965.

———. "Talk to RIA Staff on Vietnam Trip." June 21, 1965.

———. "Statement for Congressman Ryan Hearings." August 12–13, 1965.

———. "Development Program for Southeast Asia: A Summary." Wingspread Symposium on Southeast Asia, September 17–19, 1965.

———. "Address before the Sales Executive Club of New York, January 4, 1966.

———. "Portrait of a President." Freedom House Award Dinner, February 23, 1966.

———. "Address to National Association of Insurance Agents." New York, September 19, 1966.

———. "Television and the Public Interest." TVAR, February 17, 1967.

———. "State of the Nation." Washington, DC: Industrial College of the Armed Forces, August 22, 1967.

———. "Annual Address." Sales Executives Club of New York, January 11, 1968.

———. "Remarks." RIA Membership Sales Meeting, Saddle Brook, New Jersey, February 6, 1968.

———. "Discover America Meeting." Brussels, June 27, 1968.

———. "1969: Nixon and the Year of Confrontation." January 7, 1969, Sales Executive Club, New York.

———. "ICAF Alumni Association Luncheon Lecture." February 25, 1969.

———. "Good God, The Seventies." *Talk of the Month*, 34th International Marketing Congress, Cleveland, Ohio, May 10–14, 1969.

———. "Ladies' Home Journal Symposium of the '70s." Ponte Vedra, September 10, 1969.

———. "The State of the Nation." *Perspectives in Defense Management* (December 1969): 1–10.

——— "Statement by Leo Cherne before Select Committee on Intelligence." U.S. House of Representatives, December 11, 1975.

———. "Acceptance Address, John Dewey Award." United Federation of Teachers, May 20, 1978.

————. "International Aspects of Refugee Resettlement in the U.S." Keynote address, RRP/Houston Midway Information Exchange Workshop, February 4–6, 1981, Houston, Texas.

————. "Lane Kirkland." 1981 Freedom Award Dinner. New York, April 9, 1981.

————. "Commemoration of the 25th Anniversary of the Hungarian Revolution." Washington, DC; October 23, 1981.

————. *Millennium* (New York: Oppenheimer Funds, 1990), np.

Index

DATE DUE
